D1248187

IN THE BEGINNING, LOVE

Mark Van Doren
and
Maurice Samuel

IN THE BEGINNING, LOVE

Dialogues on the Bible

EDITED AND ANNOTATED BY
Edith Samuel

The John Day Company
An Intext Publisher New York

Acknowledgments

The Jewish Publication Society of America, Philadelphia, Pennsylvania: Quotations used throughout the book unless otherwise stated are from the 1917 English translation of the Holy Scriptures, c. 1917 and 1955. All rights reserved. Little, Brown & Co.: Copyright 1914, 1942 by Martha Dickinson Bianchi from *The Complete Poems of Emily Dickinson*, edited by Thomas H. Johnson, by permission of Little, Brown and Co. Schocken Books Inc. Copyright © 1946, 1961 by Schocken Books Inc. Reprinted by permission of Schocken Books Inc., from *A Jewish Reader*, edited by Nahum N. Glatzer. The University of Chicago Press Copyright © 1959. From the *Apocrypha: An American Translation* by Edgar J. Goodspeed, by permission of The University of Chicago Press, publisher. Alfred A. Knopf, Inc. Copyright © 1934, 1935, 1938, 1944, 1948. Reprinted from *Joseph and His Brothers* by Thomas Mann. Reprinted by permission of Hill and Wang, a division of Farrar, Straus & Giroux, Inc., from *Collected and New Poems: 1924-1963* by Mark Van Doren. Copyright © 1963 by Mark Van Doren. Mentor Books, New American Library, "The Chosen People" by W. N. Ewer and "A Reply" by Cecil Browne appearing in *The Silver Treasury of Light Verse*, ed. Oscar Williams, 1957. *The Potting Shed* by Graham Greene. Viking 1956, 1959. Random House Leo Tolstoy, *War and Peace.* Constance Garnett trans. Quotations from pp. 901-5. Livy. B. O. Foster translation. London: William Heinemann, 1926, 1948. Loeb Classical Library edition entitled *Livy. IV*. Harvard University Press, for quotations from E. A. Speiser, "The Wife-Sister Motif in the Patriarchal Narratives," in *Biblical and Other Studies*, ed. Alexander Altmann. 1963.

Library of Congress Cataloging in Publication Data

Van Doren, Mark, 1894-1972.
In the beginning, love; dialogues on the Bible.

Fifteen conversations as presented between 1953 and 1972 on the radio program The words we live by.
1. Bible. O.T.—Criticism, interpretation, etc. I. Samuel, Maurice, 1895-1972. II. Samuel, Edith, ed. III. Title.
BS1171.2.V35 1973 221.6'6 72-12076
ISBN 0-381-98236-X

The John Day Company, 257 Park Avenue South, New York, N.Y. 10010

Published on the same day in Canada by Longman Canada Limited.

Printed in the United States of America
Designed by The Etheredges

THE BEGINNING OF *In the Beginning, Love* A NOTE FROM THE EDITOR

1.

Nearly two years after our marriage, my husband, Maurice Samuel, gave me what he called a wedding gift: words in air. "They're out there somewhere," he said, flinging up his arms to suggest the vastness of space. "If you want to find them, and set them down, and start making books, let it be your project." With a wide grin he added, "Don't thank me. Wait a few years, a decade. See what comes of it. Maybe you won't want to thank me."

I do want to thank him, and with all my heart. But it is at once too early and too late—too early because the decade does not fall due until November, 1973, too late because my husband died on May 4, 1972.

2.

The "words in air" were conversations on the Bible—more formally, "literary dialogues"—between the poet, teacher and critic Mark Van Doren and Maurice Samuel, author, lecturer and translator. They were featured on the National Broadcasting Company radio network under the title "The Words We Live By," the summer series of "The Eternal Light" program, produced under the auspices of The Jewish Theological Seminary of America. The conversations between "two of America's foremost men of letters"—as the announcer introduced them—began as a weekly summer program in 1953. As late as October 1972, I could still tune in each Sunday to hear some of their final recorded talks.

In his Epitaph for my husband at the end of this book, Mark Van Doren movingly recalls their first meeting. The Seminary's choice of these two men was inspired. At the time, Mark Van Doren had already won the Pulitzer Prize for his poetry and was in his thirty-second year of teaching English at Columbia University. Maurice Samuel had already written his prize-winning book, *The World of Sholom Aleichem*, and a dozen more besides; he was, in addition, the country's leading lecturer on Jewish themes. Both men were passionate readers and expounders of the Bible, ready, willing and abundantly able to talk together about their favorite book, *the* Book, "forever."

Thus were the conversations launched, and from the audience response in the two decades that followed, evidently a good many people felt that they could eavesdrop forever, too. The topics changed every summer, ranging from "Joseph and His Brothers" (1953) to "The Making of a People" (1970). Among their themes over the years were "Moral Dilemmas of the Bible," "The Psalms as Human Documents," "The Poetry of the Bible," "Dreams and Visions in the Bible," and "Democracy and the Bible."

3.

The conversations were always spontaneous, unrehearsed, and completely without text. Both men, experienced teachers and talkers, dismissed the idea of scripts; it was not their style. Separately and together, they mulled over topics that interested them. Once they made their choice, they blocked out the main points they wanted to cover, and separated, each to think, read and jot down notes. Studio time was reserved for recording all of a season's talks, usually a week during the spring. They met again in the NBC studios, compared their notes, and then were ready to sit down and talk before live microphones. At a signal from the producer, the dialogue flowed freely—and sometimes in several directions at once. Notes were pushed aside, outlines disappeared. Mark would recall a line from Shakespeare, Maurice would quote a rabbinical aphorism, or a phrase from Proust, or a verse of a popular song. Mark might cite Robert Frost, prompting Maurice to remember a passage in Marcus Aurelius or Chaim Nachman Bialik or Voltaire, Maimonides or Joyce. The dialogues were never Socratic, as both men were aware. They happily ranged from manners to morals, Isaiah to Martin Luther King, Jr., the atomic bomb to the rearing of children, psychoanalysis to picket lines, but always they came back to the Bible.

The reader of these conversations is, of course, deprived of the sound of their voices: Mark Van Doren's gentle midwestern drawl, alternately smiling and serious, punctuated by warm chuckles and eager affirmations; and Maurice Samuel's precise, stern and occasionally staccato Lancashire-accented English, with rolling *r*'s, sibilant *s*'s, quick chortles and sudden bursts of laughter. Nevertheless, I believe that any admirer of good conversation, poetry or literature, or any reader of the Bible will find much in these printed exchanges to delight the mind and spirit.

I fell under the spell of these conversations very early, several years before I met my husband or Mark. One hot July Sunday in 1953, I chanced to tune in and lingered to hear the rare good talk. I thought I knew the story of Joseph, which was their theme, but suddenly I became aware of how little I understood it. I was hooked. I immediately went back to reread the Book of Genesis; the next day I bought a copy of Thomas Mann's *Joseph* trilogy and plunged into the heady experience of learning under the guidance of these two exhilarating, unstuffy, unpedantic and disembodied voices. It was then that I formed the conviction that these colloquies were just too *good* to remain lost in space. After our marriage, I tried to persuade Maurice to take up the task of retrieval. He was always too busy on some new book, and Mark, too, was preoccupied with other commitments. My husband's gift to me of his words in air—offered with Mark Van Doren's prior consent and cheerful blessing—was the beginning of this book.

4.

What strikes the ear agreeably may—or may not—find favor with the eye. Accordingly, in preparing these conversations for the printed page, I have filled out incomplete or interrupted sentences, deleted orphaned phrases, repetitions and the like. The conversations here are thus not always exactly "as broadcast." Apart from such inevitable revisions, they are as close to their originals as publication allowed; even the digressions, where they add information or insight or a grace note, or lead the talk into new channels, have been retained.

Fifteen conversations about love, human and Divine, do not, of course, exhaust this enormous and important theme, nor are they presented here with any such claim. They are *conversations*: evocative, often controversial probings; exchanges of knowledge, experience, and opinion. As he follows these dialogues, the reader is invited —alone or in company; silently, aloud, or in marginal jottings—to challenge the participants, pose his own questions, supply new points, and extend the conversations far beyond the covers of this book.

It will help if he has at his elbow a copy of the Bible; and to spare him the chore of locating each passage, I have supplied copious references. Unless otherwise indicated, the Biblical quotations throughout are taken from the 1917 English translation of The Holy Scriptures published by The Jewish Publication Society of America. This translation follows the style and much of the language of the magnificent King James Version.

For those of inquiring mind, I have added some informal notes at the end of this book. I offer them without any pretense of having special expertise, simply for what they are: nuggets of information I have culled from authoritative sources to satisfy my own curiosity. I pass them along, as from one avid Bible reader to another.

5.

Some words of thanks are due and overdue. The Jewish Theological Seminary of America and the National Broadcasting Company have graciously waived their rights in this undertaking and have, in addition, lent every cooperation in hunting down master tapes in archives and attics. Their help is acknowledged with sincere appreciation. I am deeply grateful to Dr. Ben Zion Bokser, spiritual leader of the Forest Hills Jewish Center and program editor of "The Eternal Light," who kindly consented to review the text of the conversations before publication—a task my husband had anticipated performing himself. I owe thanks to Rabbi Alexander M. Schindler, president-elect of the Union of American Hebrew Congregations, who has been cheering on this project for the last six years. A very special expression of gratitude is reserved for my friend and former colleague, Mr. Milton E. Krents, executive producer of radio and TV for the Seminary, who has been unfailingly kind to me, as he always was to his friends, Maurice and Mark. It was Milton who performed the great *mitzvah*, the good deed, of bringing the two men together.

Mark Van Doren, that golden soul, died suddenly last December 10 while this book was in its final stages. He was immensely pleased—as Maurice would have been, too—that these conversations were about to see the light of print; and I in turn was pleased to be able to gladden his heart. To me, Mark always seemed to be luminous with goodness; the beauty, simplicity and clarity of the man actually seemed to shine through and from him. Whenever we used to speak of Mark at home, and it was often, Maurice and I invariably came back to the biblical Hebrew word, *hesed.* He was for us the personification of the idea of loving-kindness.

Maurice and now Mark—so Dorothy Van Doren and I like to think—are "out there somewhere" in the vastness of space. This book retrieves some of their words and, I hope, something of their living spirit.

EDITH SAMUEL

January 14, 1973
New York

CONTENTS

THE BEGINNING OF *In The Beginning, Love:*
A NOTE FROM THE EDITOR v

I GOD'S LOVE FOR MAN 1

A book "drenched with love" · The nature of the "choice" · Why Abraham? · The lover's quarrel between God and His people · God's love for all mankind · Some attributes of God · Clearing up an old misunderstanding · The Creation as an act of love · The omnipresence of God · Man's fits of goodness · The true cynic · Belief in love

II MAN'S LOVE FOR GOD 16

The command to love God: A counsel of perfection? · The pagan vs. the biblical attitude · The Epicurean view · Lucretius on the gods · Plato and Socrates on love · Knowledge of God and love of God · "Liking" God and loving Him · The father image and the psychoanalysts · Arguing with God · Withdrawing from the world to love God: Is it a true form of love?

III MAN'S LOVE OF MAN 31

More thoughts on withdrawing from the world · Love of God expresed through love of man · Exploring "Thou shalt love thy neighbor as thyself" · Who is a "neighbor"? · What is true love of self? · Loving mankind and loving every man · Karl Marx and Jonathan Swift · Varieties of anti-Semites · Platon Karataev in WAR AND PEACE *· The mystery of loving · Is true love blind? · Correcting a friend · Why are men afraid of God? · David's relation to God*

IV LOVE IN THE BEGINNING 47

Antinomianism defined · Can you trust love? · The person who cannot love · The love of husband for wife · Who is wicked? · Jezebel and Lady Macbeth · Love of power as a denial of love · Rebuking a loved one · Did Adam love Eve? · Milton's vision of perfect love · Platonic love · The first appearance of love in the Bible: Abraham and Sarah · The complaining wife · The misunderstood Patriarchs · Sarah and Hagar, "the other woman" · Perfect love in Paradise · The diminution of love

V GOSSIPING ABOUT FATHER ABRAHAM AND HIS FAMILY 61

The human side of the personalities in the Bible · Why don't moderns read the Bible? · The Bible as a "must" in modern education · Gossiping about the people in the Bible · Bygone American customs · College students and the Bible · The universal, everlasting problems in the lives of the Patriarchs · Abraham and Isaac · "Everybody is a psychologist!" · The AKEDAH, *the binding · The sacrifice by Abraham · How a Roman sacrificed his son: a story from Livy · Virtue turned to vice · The difference between morality and morale · Sarah and Isaac · The stupid angel · The love between Abraham and Sarah · Ishmael as a juvenile delinquent · The strain between "the true wife" and the maidservant · Esau, Simeon and Levi as juvenile delinquents in the "first family"*

VI ISAAC, THE SUFFERING, SILENT SERVANT 76

The narrative style of the Bible—Isaac's pregnant silence · Isaac as the suffering servant · The birth of Isaac · Isaac's unfitting name · Isaac's silent acquiescence · Isaac meets Rebekah · The blindness of Isaac · Esau and Jacob · Was the blessing really given to the wrong son? · Sending for a wife from the old country · Esau as a primitive · From the simple to the complex · Rebekah, decisive bride, decisive mother · Biblical names in American families · Merry old Uncle Isaac

VII THE CONFLICTING LOVES OF JACOB 92

Jacob, a prisoner of love · The first to fall in love · · Preferential love · The coarseness of Laban · The deception on the wedding night · A failure of love · · Parental favoritism · Acting "as if" · Who is a civilized man? · A master teacher talks about teaching · The principle of equality · Jacob, the emotional Patriarch · Are all men gentlemen? · The imperfections of the people in the Bible · Struggle in the Bible · Some reflections on Joseph and Judah · Does love make the world go round?

VIII THE TRAGIC LOVERS: DINAH AND SHECHEM 107

The sin of Jacob's son · Was Dinah a "gadabout"? · Violence, then love · The wooing of Dinah by Shechem · The guile of the brothers · The tragedy of their arrogance and pride · Travelers abroad · Jacob's deathbed curse · Did Dinah love Shechem? · Dinah and Job · Dinah, the family darling · Of legends, history, and fairy stories

IX THE FRIENDSHIPS OF MEN: SAUL, DAVID, AND JONATHAN 122

David and Saul, a tormented love · How the people got their first king · The displeasure of Samuel the prophet · How Saul was picked · Saul's vacillation and inauspicious beginning · Saul's tenderness and jealousy toward David · David's love for Saul · Two opportunities abandoned · Saul's bitterness toward Jonathan · Love at first sight between David and Jonathan · Aristotle on friendship · David's lament · The sweetness of Jonathan · Jonathan as a medieval knight · Roland and Oliver · On dying young

X DAVID, THE UNIVERSAL MAN OF THE BIBLE 137

David as the *lover in* the *Bible · David, the* uomo universale · *David vs. Solomon as lover · The Queen of Sheba's minuet · David's great loves · Michal, the imperious princess · How Michal killed David's love · Poor Paltiel · The beauty and nobility of Abigail · Nabal the churl · David's great hates: Joab and Shimei · The adulterous love for Bathsheba · David's sin, punishment, and repentance · The denunciation by the prophet Nathan · David as a listener · David and Absalom · The love of fathers for sons in the Bible*

XI FOUR DISASTERS—AND ONE COMEDY 152

"Old, unhappy far-off things" · Samson and his two Philistine wives · Samson as a primitive · A pawn of God · "Dittology" in the Samson story · Meaning in history · Ahab and Jezebel · Jezebel as the symbol of human alter-egotism · Parents who show off children · Execution by defenestration · Amnon and Tamar · The embitterment of Absalom · Judah and Tamar · Providence in human history · Ahasuerus's love for Esther · 254 beauty contestants · The fool king, Ahasuerus · The Book of Esther

XII THE LOVELIEST OF THE LOVE STORIES 169

The Book of Ruth · Which of the two love stories is the more significant? · The crossroads · Two daughters-in-law · Ruth's speech in Hebrew · How to write a short story · The setting of the book · The Moabites and the Israelites · Daily life in the midst of turmoil · Hollywood and the Bible · Ruth and Naomi come to Bethlehem · Enter Boaz · Naomi as manager · The lovableness of people in love stories · The grandeur and intimacy of Ruth · The ending as a note of triumph

XIII AN IDYLL OF DOMESTICITY 185

The Book of Tobit · Tobias's faithful dog · Rembrandt and Tobit · Tobit the exile · Hannah, and her bickering · Sarah and the seven unlucky bridegrooms · Raphael, archangel and traveling companion · The journey of Tobias, Raphael, and the dog · The magical fish in the Tigris · Tobias falls in love with Sarah of Ecbatana · Sholom Aleichem's Tevye and Tobit · The "little people" · The books "exiled" from the Bible · Tobit and his ever-ready shovel · GALGENHUMOR *in Tobit · The end of the adventure · Prearranged marriages and freedom of choice · The angel reveals himself · The happy ending and the splendid funeral*

XIV THE SONG OF SONGS: LOVE LYRIC AND/OR ALLEGORY? 202

How was the book intended? · The incomparability of the love lyrics · The beauty of language · Selections from the book · The Shulammite maiden, her lover, and King Solomon · The book as allegory · Some rabbinical interpretations · The interpretations refuted · An epithalamium? · Deeper meanings beneath the surface · Love transcending two lovers · Why do lovers swear by the stars?

XV THE LANGUAGE OF THE BIBLE 218

The Song of Songs as lyrical drama · Solomon loses the girl · The intensity of the lyrical language · What lovers ever talked like Romeo and Juliet, or Antony and Cleopatra? · The meaning of great poetry · "Terrible as an army with banners" explored · How to murder meaning · Living with the Bible · Reading the Bible as a "piety" · A translation for our day · The genius of the King James Version · Should the Bible "sound old"? · Where is magnificent thinking, magnificent language? · Rendering the Bible in "social-center English" · Is the time out of joint? · What are man's "ego needs"? · Skinner's rats and the human heart · Did man die in the twentieth century? · The Bible and the future of the human species

EPITAPH FOR MAURICE SAMUEL
BY MARK VAN DOREN 233

NOTES 237

ABOUT MARK VAN DOREN AND
MAURICE SAMUEL 259

INDEX 261

I

GOD'S LOVE FOR MAN

VAN DOREN: Maurice, we have a topic of the greatest richness and depth for me, and I'm sure for you: Love: human and divine. The source and fountain of all the examples that we shall treat in connection with this topic shall always be the Bible—the Hebrew Bible, or as many refer to it, the Old Testament. One reason why our subject interests me so much is that we shall be able—I hope—to correct an erroneous notion about the Hebrew Bible. In the minds of many people today (and in the past, as well), the Old Testament is characterized largely by bitterness, gloom, wrath, and vengeance—as if it were not a *loving book.* Whereas for me, it is a book drenched with love. During the course of our conversations, we are going to have many, many opportunities to prove that this is true, and nothing will give me greater pleasure than to do so.

SAMUEL: I agree with your observation. This erroneous notion, as you call it, does exist, and it has persisted for many centuries. Very likely some of it is traceable to a misunderstanding of what people have called God's "arbitrariness" in "choosing" the Jewish people. You know that jingle, "How odd/Of God/To choose/the Jews" —to which a Jew replied, "Oh no, it's not!/God knows what's what."[1] That's putting it on a rather jocular level, but it does indicate the source of a misunderstanding as to God's intentions toward man.

VAN DOREN: I'm not sure, Maurice, that the impression is created just there. God's choosing of the Jews could seem to be the story of a choice which was followed on His part always by indulgence, if not flattery, of the chosen. Whereas, of course, it is true that He is frequently angry with His people, judges them, and punishes them; and He is often said to be, quite properly, a God of jealousy, and a God of wrath, even though He is also called a God of mercy and a God of loving-kindness. My point would be that a great many readers (but they are not really readers; I don't think they read the Bible, or they wouldn't say what they say) remember only the judgment and the wrath, and do not remember the mercy and the loving-kindness.

SAMUEL: Yes, but they also don't remember that what was called "the choice" was, if I may put it in this way, a sort of *natural* development, because the very first

man whom He chose, as it were, was a man who "kept GEN. 26:5
My charge, My commandments, My statutes, and My laws."
Now, notice: Abraham was not the *discoverer* of monotheism. We read in Genesis that generations before Abraham, in the time of Enosh, the grandson of Adam and Eve,
"then began men to call upon the name of the Lord." It GEN. 4:26
wasn't that Abraham first glimpsed the idea of God, but that he *obeyed* God's commandments, statutes, and laws. In other words, Abraham was, in the religious sense, according to the tradition, the first *civilized* man; and God saw in this the possibility of the continuity through the Patriarchs. As a matter of fact, Moses tells the children of
Israel the reason for the choice in Deuteronomy: "because DEUT. 4:37
He loved thy fathers." If people will trouble to read the Hebrew Bible carefully, they won't find any basis for that "arbitrariness" which has frequently been attributed to God.

As you've suggested, there are these alternations: indulgence and punishment, indulgence and punishment; it's as though there were a long—one might call it an "affair"—between God and His people, in which they couldn't get along. Sometimes I've thought of the relationship as—if I may use the phrase—a parody in reverse; that is, one takes an idea that's lighthearted and perhaps even flippant, and turns it into something serious. Hollywood has a formula for what's supposed to be a good movie: boy meets girl, boy loses girl, boy finds girl. To reverse that, the basis of man's relationship to God as depicted in the Bible is: man finds God, man loses God, man finds God. That is the recurrent story, with installments apparently reaching on into eternity.

VAN DOREN: This notion of a lover's quarrel between God and His people is, of course, something that anyone can understand at any time, since all love relations —no matter how individual they are, how peculiar, how local, or even how eccentric they may be—probably include quarreling and misunderstanding and making up, and rediscovery. You may remember that Robert Frost said in one of his poems, "I had a lover's quarrel with the world"[2]—meaning that the world for him is alternately right and wrong, and he is alternately right and wrong with reference to it. In other words, he's always falling out of love with it, and then falling in love with it again.

This alternation comes to a climax—at any rate, as far as explicitness of statement is concerned—in the Book of Judges. The biblical account is fascinating, and I pity those people who remember only the dark half of it. We're told in Judges that for several centuries between the time the people arrived in the Promised Land and the beginning of the monarchy, God alternately blessed and
E.G., *see* JUDG. punished His people. For varying periods of time—perhaps
3:30, 8:28 forty years, perhaps eighty—the land "had rest"; the people would live at peace with Him—they loved Him, they remembered Him, and they kept His commandments. But
E.G., *see* JUDG. then they would fall away, worship idols, and do evil in
3:7, 4:1, 10:6 His sight; and then He would punish them by giving them over into the hands of their heathen neighbors—the Canaanites, the Moabites, the Midianites, the Philistines, for example. And so for seven years, or eighteen years, or forty years, they would be smitten by their enemies. From time to time, some outstanding personality, like Gideon, or Samson, or Deborah, would arise among them to be a Judge—that is to say, to be one who could remind them of their great heritage, their duty, and their love—and then back would come their rest and their peace. That alterna-

tion always suggests to my mind the image of a sea with waves that churn violently, disappear for a time, then churn again, and again subside.

SAMUEL: That's a very good image, Mark. The *Tanach*,[3] the Hebrew Bible, is a tumultuous book. It is the record of a great wrestling of a people with itself; but at the same time, this special relationship between God and the Jewish people described in the Bible is not exclusive of God's care for the rest of the world. Again and again, both in the Bible and in the biblical commentaries, we are reminded that His care and His love for other peoples are continuous. Over and over again, the Israelites are commanded to "Love the stranger," for God loves the stranger, DEUT. 10:18–19
and gives him food and clothing. He sent His prophets to rebuke other peoples, too: Jonah was directed to go to Nineveh, and Jeremiah prophesied about the surrounding JER. 48–49
peoples of Moab, Edom, Ammon, and Damascus, for instance. But it appears that there was a kind of special aptitude in the Jews for receiving this type of instruction, this alternating indulgence and punishment, as you've called it. And even with this aptitude, it took the Jews centuries to become a faithful people. I've often thought that the Jews never really believed God's threats to throw them out of their country, and the traumatic effect of being actually thrown out and sent to Babylonia shocked them into faithfulness. It's as though the people said, "Look! He went and did it after all!" Apparently the threats never sank in over that long period when God was warning them repeatedly to change their ways. They were living in their own country—frequently under oppression—and for four hundred years, five hundred years *six hundred years*, they

were still there. And all of a sudden, He did it! That first exile, I think, is what brought about the great change. One can say that the Bible is the record of the people struggling to accept the idea of the One God; after the cataclysmic horror of the Babylonian conquest in 586 B.C.E., one may say of the Jewish people as a whole that, in spite of partial defections, they continued in firmness.

Has it ever occurred to you, Mark, how terribly hard it must be for a people—it *was* terribly hard!—to get used to the notion of God's overwhelming love? It's not at all like a human love. It reminds me of a benevolent *1984*. God watches you. He's the *bokhen l'vavot*: He examines the hearts, He looks into the thoughts of man, and sees his secret heart. And man doesn't know where to escape.

VAN DOREN: Yes, and of course there's the curious fact that God knows men not only collectively, but individually. He not only loves man, or mankind (and I quite agree with you, it's proper to say that that means *all* men, everywhere), but He loves *every* man. Thus, every man carries this burden of knowledge that God loves him. The knowledge is very deep, and it could be disturbing—disturbing in the sense only that the knowledge could prompt thoughts and feelings which are extraordinary, to say the least.

SAMUEL: If one takes it literally, a man feels that he's being watched all the time, that even his dreams are subject to that intense and never-ending observation.

VAN DOREN: And of course, what impressed the Jews so much in the old days was God's constantly telling them that He himself was invisible. He said, in effect, "You have never seen Me. To be sure, I spoke with Abraham. He heard My voice. Moses was granted a fleeting glimpse of My back once, on Sinai, but no one else has seen Me, for I am invisible. You saw the fire out of which I spoke, but you have not seen Me." That invisibility is a tremendous fact. He was not an image; there could be no image of Him. He was not a thing, not a person. Of course, in some very great sense, He was a Person—He was *the* Person—but they could not *see* Him. They had to *believe* in Him. The reason it makes sense, perhaps, to say that they had to believe in Him was simply that they could not see Him. Always He remained invisible; but the pressure from Him was all the greater for that very reason. *see* EXOD. 33:23

SAMUEL: You spoke a moment ago, Mark, about the mistaken notion held by many people, that the Hebrew Bible is filled predominantly with wrath, vengeance, and sternness. A passage from the Second Commandment[4] is very often quoted to support that view:

> *. . . for I the Lord thy God am a jealous God, visiting the iniquity of the fathers upon the children unto the third and fourth generation of them that hate Me; and showing mercy unto the thousandth generation of them that love Me and keep My commandments.*

EXOD. 20:5–6
DEUT. 5:9–10

The Hebrew original reads *la-alaphim*, and literally, it means "to thousands." The English text here makes it "thousandth." Now, if one wanted to be pedantic and arithmetical, one would set off those two figures: He punishes unto the fourth generation, and shows mercy (or loving-kindness, as the word is sometimes rendered) to thousands of generations, so it's a proportion of four to a minimum of two thousand. That is the proportion of wrath to love.

VAN DOREN: And that ratio is what I lament to see is not remembered. The loving-kindness of God is thousands of times greater and more enduring than His wrath. To be sure, His wrath and His punishments are terrible; and since they are graphically described, they are bound to leave a deep impression. I regret that the many examples of His love don't leave an even deeper and longer-lasting impression.

Let me come back to your mention of Abraham. To me, God's noticing Abraham 'way off there in the distance is a tremendous event. It's as if God said to himself: "Among all the men that live and creep upon the surface of the earth, there is *one* to whom I can say certain things that I believe he will understand. Furthermore, I believe in him and in his capacity to transmit what I tell him to those about him, and to his descendants." And God never ceases to remind the people that that had happened. He has Moses tell the people that His original love was for a few men, the Patriarchs.

see DEUT. 7:7–8

SAMUEL: Yes, Moses told them, in effect: "The Lord chose you not because you are great and not because you are strong. There are many greater and stronger peoples. He chose you because of the transmission that has come through you."

VAN DOREN: I hope I'm not straining any point here, Maurice, when I say that I believe that what He saw in Abraham was, among other things, a capacity for love. Now I'm using that word in spite of the fact that "love" is not used in the Hebrew Bible of Abraham himself. But in my opinion, God saw in him the power not only to love God and His word (that is to say, thoroughly understand the word, because love and understanding are very closely connected), but also to love others—his wife, his son, his people—in the sense that he could trust them to understand. So that Abraham's calling was not only to be called, but to call—to remind others of this immense event: the speaking to him in his own ear of God's voice.

SAMUEL: The calling of Abraham, and God's "choice" of Abraham's descendants have been the source of much misunderstanding throughout history. I was reading a passage just the other day which is an interesting commentary on another misunderstanding—a very bitter one—the accusation of "racialism" which has been leveled against the *Tanach,* the Hebrew Bible, and against the Jewish outlook.[5] This is a letter by Moses Maimonides, the twelfth-century physician, philosopher, and Jewish scholar, giving advice to a proselyte to Judaism as to how he ought to pray:

> *I received the question of the wise scholar, Obadiah the proselyte. You ask as to whether you, being a proselyte, should utter the prayers: "Our God and God of* our fathers; *Who has separated* us *from the nations; Who has brought* us *out of Egypt."*

In other words, Obadiah is asking if he can use the first person there, because *his* fathers were not Jews. Maimonides now gives his answer:

> *Pronounce all prayers as they are written and do not change anything. Your prayer and blessing should be the same as that of any other Israelite, regardless of*

> *whether you pray in private or conduct the service. The explanation is as follows: Abraham, our father, taught mankind the true belief and the unity of God, repudiating idolatry; through him many of his own household and also others were guided to "keep the way of the Lord, to do righteousness and justice"* [GEN. 18:19]. *Thus he who becomes a proselyte and confesses the unity of God, as taught in the Torah, is a disciple of Abraham, our father. Such persons are of his household. Just as Abraham influenced his contemporaries through his word and teaching, so he leads to belief all future generations, through the testament he gave to his children and his household. In this sense Abraham is the father of his descendants who follow his ways, and of his disciples, and of all the proselytes.*
>
> *You should therefore pray, "Our God and God of our fathers," for Abraham is also* your *father. . . .*

Then Maimonides adds this rather touching remark:

> *Do not think little of your origin: we are descended from Abraham, Isaac, and Jacob, but your descent is from the Creator. . . .*[6]

You see, he broadens it out to include all mankind. And this is Maimonides, the rationalist.

VAN DOREN: That's very interesting, Maurice. I didn't know the passage. Maimonides's reference to the Creator as *the* source of all being reminds me of the possibility that the very first act in the Bible—the creation of the world and of man in it—was an act of love. I don't know why we shouldn't think so, or say so. There's a very old question: Why did God trouble to create the world? It was going to cause Him trouble, and we know it did. *We* cause Him trouble all the time; we disturb Him. He is afflicted by us. He grieves over us.

SAMUEL: Yes, there's that strange and beautiful passage in Isaiah: "In all their affliction He was afflicted." ISA. 63:9
In this case, He suffers with His people. But He suffers with mankind.

VAN DOREN: The act of creation was a complete act because we (meaning all mankind) were created free—free to love Him, but free also *not* to love Him for a while, free to forget Him, as we so often have. He created us in that sense. Recently I was reading a discussion—I forget where—of a lack that is in most novels. The critic in question made the statement that most novelists do not love their characters. He didn't mean by that that novelists should be sentimental about the characters or favor them always——

SAMUEL: Excuse me, Mark, I know what you mean. Sholem Asch once made the remark to me about another novelist.

VAN DOREN: What did he say?

SAMUEL: Asch said, "He doesn't describe his characters; he spies on them."

VAN DOREN: That's right. Whereas a great novelist—no matter in what language he writes, or in what age he writes, and history has nothing to do with this—a great novelist loves his characters in the sense that he leaves them free. They have powers within themselves which he respects—powers even to make errors, to be good or to be bad. But it's as if the characters themselves make this determination. When you're reading any first-rate story, isn't it your impression that the people in it are somehow free of the story-teller? They seem to make up their own minds, and to do what *they* will.

SAMUEL: They have a certain density of being that the writer cannot affect: he can turn them for you to observe, to respect, to like—but he doesn't remold them. They were there before he put them into the book, and they continue after he's finished the book. That, by the way, is one of the characteristics of biblical personalities. They're there; nobody invented them, as it were. They were put into the scene, and they act out their parts. This is a reflection of the loving Creator, of course. It reminds me of Michelangelo's famous sonnet, "The more the marble wastes,/The more the statue grows." In other words, you don't make a statue—you just cut away the marble which surrounds it, and there it is. That's the feeling you get about biblical characters. Loving them, you see them in the tangle of events; you remove all that is superfluous, and there they are.

God's love for man, for each man individually, is nowhere better exemplified for me than in that very moving passage in Exodus when God, speaking through Moses, tells the people that when they lend money to the poor, they may not exact any interest; and if they do happen to take a cloak from a poor man as a pledge, they've got to return it before nightfall. God seems to be expostulating as He makes a very poignant observation:

. . . thou shalt restore it unto him [before] the sun goeth down; for that is his only covering, it is his garment for his skin; wherein shall he sleep? and it shall come to pass, when he crieth unto Me, that I will hear; for I am gracious. EXOD. 22:25–26

Now this intimacy, this direct link between God and man, has its reverse side. Human beings can't stand so much love. Possibly they run away from it—or try to run away—because the sheer weight of care about what the human being is is more than the human being can stand. There's a complaint in Psalms:

. . . whither shall I flee from Thy presence? PSALM 139:7–10
If I ascend up into heaven, Thou art there;
If I make my bed in the netherworld, behold, Thou art there.
If I take the wings of the morning,
And dwell in the uttermost parts of the sea;
Even there would Thy hand lead me, . . .

Sometimes you want to get away from Him, and you feel that you can't.

VAN DOREN: And yet, Maurice, the knowledge that one was not loved, and never would be loved surely would be still more dreadful, wouldn't it?

SAMUEL: Of course, but human beings don't reflect that way. We are impulsive and act on short-range considerations. If we acted on serious, long-range considerations, our lives would be very different. Most of us are convinced, for example, that smoking cigarettes shortens our lives—and we go on smoking! Now just imagine: if with regard to this immediate love that we have of our bodies and our health we are neglectful of the most obvious warning, then how much remoter is the eternity that we conceive of as being our portion! And how much remoter our relationship to the universe, and to God! To me, the astonishing thing is not that human beings are so bad, but that they have these fits of goodness, which is the demonstration of God's love for man.

VAN DOREN: Yes, and those fits of goodness I would call fits of remembering, fits of being able to remember that love exists, and that love is directed to them, or to us. The person who cannot believe in love, who does not think it exists, is the true cynic. By "cynic," the Greeks meant, I feel, a man who believed that virtue is a fiction, and that people get advantage in pretending that it exists, acting as if it does—whereas it doesn't. But I would extend the notion still further, and say that a cynic is a person who believes that love does not exist. George Santayana, the philosopher, once remarked in a little essay on love that not to believe in love is "a great sign of dullness."

SAMUEL: He means a stupidity, a profound stupidity.

VAN DOREN: Yes, a stupidity; whereas, the person to whom Santayana is referring might very well think that he is very bright and sharp. "Ah-ha!" he says to himself. "I know that there's no such thing as love. People just talk about it."

SAMUEL: I know of people who take pleasure in reflecting that when a cat licks her kittens, it's purely a chemical attraction on the fur of the kitten for a chemical substance on the tongue of the cat; and then they finish up by saying, "Mother love is merely an extension of that and nothing more." That's the kind of person you're referring to.

VAN DOREN: And they talk as if they *knew* that was true! I shall always remember two little lines from Emily Dickinson[7] I saw the other day:

That love is all there is
Is all we know of love.

II

MAN'S LOVE FOR GOD

SAMUEL: Mark, we must move on and look at another aspect of our theme, man's love of God, the converse of our topic last time. To me, man's love of God has always been a deeply puzzling subject, perhaps because over and over again in the Hebrew Bible, man is *commanded* to love God.[8] The most familiar phrasing of that command occurs in Deuteronomy:

DEUT. 6:5 *And thou shalt love the Lord thy God with all thy heart, and with all thy soul, and with all thy might.*

Now I don't know how to reconcile that command with love. It's all the more puzzling to me because the command to love is a fundamental law, yet it is not included in the Ten Commandments.

VAN DOREN: We come across that law not a dozen times, but a hundred times: man's duty is to love God, man *must* love God. I'm not so sure that I'm so puzzled by this, Maurice, in view of the point we mentioned last time: the fact that God is invisible. God, of course, is a Person in the Hebrew Bible; He is a Person like no other. He is a Person who feels as well as thinks; who hopes, regrets, plans; who is dejected, and is afflicted, as Isaiah put it. He is a Person; but He is out of sight. He has appeared only as a voice, and then most rarely; so that the command to love Him would be something like the command to remember something that is very hard to remember, because the senses do not assist.

SAMUEL: The Ten Commandments are within our power to understand and to carry out. For example, the laws to honor your father and mother, not to lie, and not to murder are comprehensible to all men. But "Thou shalt love the Lord thy God"—there is a counsel of perfection, almost an impossibilism. Nevertheless, I suppose, it has to be said.

You were just speaking of the Jewish view of God, and I was struck by the difference between the pagan attitude toward the gods, and the biblical attitude of a loving God. I don't remember in what I've read of Greek and Roman literature the feeling that one is close to, or beloved by, Jupiter, say, or by Apollo. A pagan can have a god as his patron saint, as it were; but the understanding in the sense of the passage I quoted in our last talk—that God takes care of the little man and worries about him—is absent. Nor do you find the feeling of father love, which is expressed in the Hebrew Bible often in anthropomorphic terms. It's very interesting that the Jews of two thousand-odd years ago used the name "Epicurus" as an indication of atheism. The Epicureans held that there were gods, and they ought to be worshiped, but then they went further to say that the gods weren't interested in the destiny of man, and this is one of the reasons why the Jews regarded them as atheists. Nowadays, in plain Yiddish, the term, an *apikoyres*, means an unbeliever. An Epicurean wasn't an unbeliever; he merely thought that the gods didn't care about the human being.

VAN DOREN: That's right. You'll find that expressed in the great poem *On the Nature of Things*, written by Lucretius, who was trained as an Epicurean. The poem, as a matter of fact, attacks religion; to Lucretius, religion is only a superstition which afflicts men and makes them fearful and miserable. Lucretius said in his poem that of course there are gods, but they live in a niche in the universe. They live in a place where there is no rain, no hail, no snow, no cold, no hot. They enjoy themselves up there utterly cut off from men, and they do not even hear the prayers of men—they are just not interested in men.

Maurice, I think I once heard you say that you could hardly conceive of a Roman saying, "Jupiter loves me." You cannot imagine Plato saying that either. Even Plato, who in his *Symposium* and elsewhere is so singularly moving and powerful about love and about desire, even Plato or even Socrates, assumes that the object of love had better be abstract—that is, you had better not fasten your love upon perishable things like food or drink, or persons, men or women—but you must love that object which will never cease to be there; that object in which, as Dante says, the mind or the intellect can rest.

But the mind, the intellect, can rest in that object which will continue to have its own purposes, and will be somehow separate from us. It is something that we must go to and love, rather than something that comes to us and makes us love it.

SAMUEL: Pliny the Elder has a passage in which he says that to suppose that the great head of things, whatever it be, pays any regard to human affairs is downright ridiculous. The Hebrew Bible destroyed for the world this remoteness from God, and brought in this sense of intimacy with Him; and in return for doing that, as it were, men were commanded to love God.

In all great religions, of course, there are various schools of thought about man's relationship to God. You will find in the Jewish tradition two approaches to God—not exclusive, but two points of vantage: one is the knowledge of God, and the other is the love of God. You can think of the rationalists as those who cultivated the knowledge of God; and of the mystics as those who cultivated the love of God. One of the best examples of these two vantage points appears in a very wonderful story, "Between Two Cliffs," by the great Jewish writer Isaac Loeb Peretz.[9] Peretz tells about a young Jewish student who is caught between mighty spirits. One is the Rabbi of Brisk, a tremendous intellect and severe scholar; the other is the Hasidic Reb Noah (or Noachke) of Biale, who is full of tenderness, kindliness, and sees God almost exclusively under the aspect of the love of one's father. The young student, who is a follower of Reb Noachke, feels himself trapped between these two, and doesn't know which is the stronger.

There is a difference, of course, between the knowledge of God, and the love of Him. Pascal remarks, "The knowledge of God is very far from the love of Him." One can see this illustrated, I suppose, in the fact that one doesn't think of philosophers primarily as lovers of God. Spinoza, for example, was described as a "God-drunken man"; he himself praises the intellectual love of God. Yet, in spite of all of this, I can't think of him as loving God in the sense that a simple loving person does. A story is told—I no longer remember where I read it—that Voltaire once pictured Spinoza walking about in his room late one night, then looking up at heaven, and saying to God, "*Mais je crois, entre nous, que vous n'existez pas*"; "Between You and me, I don't think You exist." And he was *speaking* to Him!

VAN DOREN: Well now, Maurice, I'm not willing to let go quite so easily of the notion that the love of God is an altogether different thing from the knowledge of Him. I know you aren't either. But when you speak of certain kinds of knowledge of God, the kind that Spinoza said he had with his intellectual love of God; or when we think of Socrates's love of ideas, or of the truth, the love of all there is; or when we think of any philosopher's statement that for him to say that he loves the truth is merely to say that he asserts its existence, and is willing to accept the truth as his only——

SAMUEL: And is also willing to suffer for it.

VAN DOREN: Yes, willing to suffer for it, too. We are talking here of a very special kind of man. I agree with you that at the opposite end of the human scale, there can be the rare person of the utmost simplicity—a man or a woman, young or old, without any intellectual equipment at all, as far as we can tell; without any training in philosophy, or without any ostensible logic or metaphysic in his or her makeup—of whom we can say that he or she loves God, although there is no knowledge in the person that a philosopher would recognize. Now for me, that only is a reminder of the very deep connection there is between love and knowledge. I'm not sure that we can love anything without knowing it; or that we can know anything without loving it. Maybe the philosopher starts at the wrong end by trying to prove that God exists, by trying to acquire certain knowledge of Him so that *therefore* we might love Him; he might begin at the other end of love itself, and try to explain it. Charles Lamb, apropos of this, once made a delightful comment. He said he didn't want to meet a certain man whom he didn't like by reputation. "I don't want to meet him," Lamb said, "because I'm sure I would like him."

SAMUEL (*laughing*): You know the old story of the Irishman who said, "I don't like bananas, and I'm glad I don't like 'em, because if I liked 'em, I'd eat 'em, and I don't like 'em."

VAN DOREN: Mark Twain turned this very adroitly once when he was insisting that he was never going to cease to hate a certain person. He said, "I would like to meet that man, get thoroughly acquainted with him—and kill him." Humanly, of course, this would be almost impossible!

(*laughter*)

SAMUEL: Let me get back to something that has often troubled me, the queer attitude of people who mistake a kind of liking for God for love of Him. That saying we used to hear, "Somebody up there likes me," is offensive; it's a notion that God is a very good-natured sort of Person, easily obliging—in short, "He's all right!" The people who take this attitude are not at all aware of the passionate concern which a real love of God would imply. They remind me of that passage in the *Rubáiyát* of Omar Khayyám:

Said one—"Folks of a surly Tapster tell,
And daub his Visage with the Smoke of Hell;
They talk of some strict Testing of us—Pish!
He's a Good Fellow, and 'twill all be well."

(LXIV, FITZGERALD TRANSLATION)

That's God as a "good fellow," of whom these people say, "Oh, He'll do things for me!" It's a silly, terribly trivial attitude which is not love of God at all.

VAN DOREN: Nevertheless, Maurice, in so saying, you are admitting, it seems to me, that the God one is commanded to love and must love, if one is to be happy at all, that God is still remote; but He is remote, I think, only in this sense: we are commanded to love Him even though He may not do us favors, even though it may seem in our lives that He is not interfering in our favor. The kind of love we are commanded to have for Him, as I understand it in the Hebrew Bible, is one for which no payment is expected.

SAMUEL: Yes, it is a completely disinterested love. It's odd that Spinoza—a very chilly sort of man, I've always felt—has a penetrating remark on your own observation just now. He said, "He who loves God cannot endeavor to bring it about that God should love him in return." Among Jews there's a story about an utterly selfless man who'll give away his portion in Paradise, his life-to-come, to prove that he serves God entirely without any motive of self. Graham Greene once wrote a very fine play[10] about a Roman Catholic priest who, to save a beloved one's life, gives away his faith. He prays, "Let him live, God. Take away what I love most. Take away my faith but let him live."

VAN DOREN: Well now, that's why, Maurice, I want to keep harping—if I seem to do so—upon the obligation to love. It is difficult to love God in this way. For Spinoza, who was a pure philosopher, it was difficult to come to the point where one could love God *regardless*—that is, without expecting love in return. Even in the human sphere, isn't it true that surely we could not be said to love someone *only* because that person loved us? The loves of men for men, and men for women are most impressive when they seem to have no strings on them, and there are many, many cases where *A* loves *B* without any clear evidence that *B* returns the love, but *A* loves *B* in any case. So the love of God is difficult, and perhaps *therefore* must be commanded. Let me ask you once more if there's a difference (I know there's a great difference), a categorical difference between loving God and loving the Law. You remember, not only in Proverbs, but in Psalms and elsewhere in many of the poetical portions of the Bible, suddenly the speaker will say, "Oh, how I love PSALM 119:97
Thy law!"

SAMUEL: Yes, it's love for His Torah, there, His Law. And there's another famous passage: "How lovely are Thy tabernacles" from Psalm 84, meaning, of course, how lovely is the way of living in God, under His ways.

VAN DOREN: Now there, you see, the thing that is loved is at least abstract, because law by definition is abstract. Law is not for individuals; love is for all.

SAMUEL: The notion of loving God, even if He doesn't love me, is a very difficult one, and it's all the more complex—to me, at least—if we think of it in abstract terms. Now for me, one of the loveliest expressions of a man's feeling for God lies actually in the father image. It's fashionable nowadays to speak with *de haut en bas*, looking down one's nose, at the father image. It's been spoiled by the psychoanalysts. In fact, any kind of liking for one's father is already a sign of some kind of inward psychological corruption. I don't know what they're driving at. Coventry Patmore has a very beautiful poem, "The Toys," which is relevant. Incidentally, people don't read him any more.

VAN DOREN: That's all the more reason why we should talk of him now. I speak as a poet, you know.

SAMUEL: Yes, but you haven't reached the classic stage yet where you aren't read.

VAN DOREN: Well, maybe I have. Go ahead.

SAMUEL: Here's the poem in full:

My little Son, who look'd from thoughtful eyes
And moved and spoke in quiet grown-up wise,
Having my law the seventh time disobey'd,
I struck him, and dismiss'd
With hard words and unkiss'd,
—His Mother, who was patient, being dead.
Then, fearing lest his grief should hinder sleep,
I visited his bed,
But found him slumbering deep,
With darkened eyelids, and their lashes yet
From his late sobbing wet.
And I, with moan,
Kissing away his tears, left others of my own;
For, on a table drawn beside his head,
He had put, within his reach,
A box of counters and a red-vein'd stone,
A piece of glass abraded by the beach
And six or seven shells,
A bottle with bluebells,
And two French copper coins, ranged there with careful art,
To comfort his sad heart.
So, when that night I pray'd
To God, I wept, and said:
Ah, when at last we lie with tranced breath,
Not vexing Thee in death,
And thou rememberest of what toys
We made our joys,
How weakly understood,
Thy great commanded good,
Then, fatherly not less
Than I whom thou hast moulded from the clay,
Thou'lt leave Thy wrath, and say,
"I will be sorry for their childishness."[11]

It's a very beautiful thing, this father image, and I am averse to the attitude which doesn't permit us for—what shall I say?—for self-expression, even though we know its limitations, this kind of anthropomorphism. We say "Our Father in heaven," or as the Hebrew original says it, "*Avinu she be-shamayim,*" and it is permissible. We have no way of handling this relationship, this enormous abstract relationship, which nevertheless floods us with feeling; we have no way of handling it, just as the poet has no way of handling thoughts except through words, and the sculptor except through stone.

VAN DOREN: Far from disagreeing with you, Maurice, I would say that the unspeakable distinction of the Hebrew Bible is that it *does* make God a Person; it *is* anthropomorphic. The habit of dismissing things these days under that term, anthropomorphism, doesn't bother me at all. The reason that this God lived, and lives, is that He is a Person; and as a matter of fact, I think He is lost only when we forget that, only when we begin to think of Him as merely the Truth, even all the Truth.

SAMUEL: Returning to that distinction, Mark, between liking and loving, most human beings, it occurs to me, want God to *like* them, not to love them. I mentioned in our last talk the burden of God's love and the responsibility which it throws on us; and perhaps most people don't want to carry that burden. They would prefer just to be liked; and they'd like God to say, "Yes, you're a good chap. I'll do this and that for you." This trivialization troubles me.

VAN DOREN: That's true, I quite agree. I'm reminded, however, of something we hear every now and then: a man says of his wife, "I not only love her, I like her." Now that does add a little dimension, doesn't it?

SAMUEL: Yes, when it's put on as a nuance, as an additional tonality. But some people would like to have a kind of friendly acquaintanceship with God. The Romans had a formal relationship to their gods. It was a social relationship. We talked before about the absence of any real human passion in them toward the gods. They went to their services, and they did what was "meet." (That was a favorite expression of theirs; in his poem "Ulysses," Tennyson has his hero say, "pay meet adoration to my household gods.") The Jews don't have this distant attitude toward God, and it's revealed in some of their names for Him: *Gottenu, Tottenu*, God, Father, Little Father, Darling, Beloved One. They feel an intimacy even when they quarrel with Him. Sholom Aleichem's wonderful character Tevye the dairyman,[12] argues with God, and tells Him, "Look, You didn't do right!"—just like a child crying to his father, "Daddy, you didn't do right by me! You should have done this, or done that." Nevertheless, Tevye loves God and worships Him. And Tevye wasn't the only one to argue with God. There's a story of ten rabbis who once put God on trial.[13] The head of the court was a famous Hasidic rabbi called the Grandfather. The ten rabbis assembled; they didn't have to call in God because He's everywhere; and they tried Him on the count of having made the Jewish people suffer too much. Not only did they try Him, but they found Him *guilty!* (*laughing*) I don't know if it made any difference to their faith, or to the faith of the Jewish people, but this sort of intimacy expressed itself in close, almost flesh relations.

VAN DOREN: Your distinction between "loving" and "liking" keeps haunting me. I remember once hearing Dr. Martin Luther King, Jr., speaking to a congregation of Negroes in the chapel of Fisk University in Nashville. He said, "I think I shall never *like* Senator Eastland of Mississippi, but I must learn to *love* him." That was the central point of his powerful oration: "You must love the white man. I do not expect you ever to *like* him, but you must learn to love him."

SAMUEL: It's a very important and decisive distinction.

VAN DOREN: It may be anticipating our next talk, when we shall take up the topic of man's love for man, but it's my feeling that any true discussion of man's love of man must have as its source and background these powerful conceptions of God's love of man, and man's love of God.

SAMUEL: Mark, can you ever conceive of love of God being of such a character that it justifies a man withdrawing from the world in order to contemplate Him, be alone with Him, and shun all human company and activities, because everything else is trivial and even repulsive by comparison?

VAN DOREN: No.

SAMUEL: That streak appears in all religions, including Judaism, although it is a deviant. The Essenes withdrew from the world, essentially; and before them, the Rechabites,[14] who are already spoken of in the *Tanach*, the Hebrew Bible. In the modern world, we've had among the Hasidim rabbis who went in for what we called *hitbodidut*, solitude away from the madding throng, away from the pressure of human affairs. It's a deviation in the Jewish tradition, but it has been there, and I suppose will recur again and again. Is that a true love of God?

VAN DOREN: No, I should say not. I would call it a deviation; perhaps it is merely the carrying out to a logical conclusion of only one portion of the idea that man should love God with all his heart, his soul, and his might. But I'm sure that the original emphasis, and the emphasis that persists and should persist, is that which does not remove man, any more than it removes God. Man in the world remains in the world.

SAMUEL: We'll come back next time to this question of man's love to man, and whether that is really not a form of man's love for God.

VAN DOREN: The great trouble, Maurice, with the man who leaves the world in order to love God without interruption and without contamination is that he may begin to love an image of his own mind. He may begin to love hallucinations and illusions, or symbols that, with a kind of intellectual and spiritual pride, he fabricates out of his own fancy purely. Don't you think that that might be the trouble?

SAMUEL: Yes. He mirrors himself in God all the time, and may become fanatical and self-centered. A great medieval Jewish moralist who lived in Spain, Bahya ibn Pakuda[15] wrote about "those who love God." He describes them like this:

> *In communing with Him, they are at home; in the business of the world, they are silent. Their hearts are filled with the love of God, but not with desire for the doing of men, and not with pleasure in their talk.*

He doesn't go on to recommend withdrawal from the world, but he does recognize a certain turning away from the world, which perplexes me. When we begin to talk about man's love of man, we shall have to consider to what extent these two concepts, love of God and love of man, intermingle, and are necessary to each other.

III

MAN'S LOVE OF MAN

VAN DOREN: Maurice, I'm a little troubled by one point we made in our last talk. When we said that those who withdrew from the world in order to love God perfectly, hermits or people of any sort who make a profession of loving God in seclusion, perhaps we agreed prematurely that those persons, *in all cases*, at any rate, had substituted a means for an end, and had lost sight of their original purpose. I think it was not difficult for us to understand each other when we said that perhaps the noblest form of that kind of love would be love conducted *in* the world, even though a kind of solitude was found in the soul wherein the exercise could be carried on. I've been thinking since of those people who retire from the world for purposes connected with religious duties and orders; they have every right to say, as they often do, that they have not *literally* retired; they are thinking about the world with an intensity not found in most people who think about the world when they're in it.

SAMUEL: Yes, there are many of them who believe that great concentration on prayer serves the world. That's true, I think, in all religions, or certainly in many.

VAN DOREN: That's right. They are constantly praying for the world, and therefore are in it, in a true sense. But it's also true, isn't it, that one can find extreme examples of withdrawal among secular men. A scholar, say, retires to write a book. It may take him five years to finish it, and he seems to be doing nothing else except that in the five years. He may be very well justified in doing it, but he also can become fanatical about his work, and blind to what his book should mean to the public. We know that such a case can happen, and we have books of pedantry that are the result of this kind of concentrated and withdrawn research. I merely wanted to point out that we perhaps have not recognized the shade of truth that exists in withdrawal.

SAMUEL: The question of withdrawal from the world, and of serving the world, and the interrelation between the two—these are enormous subjects. Certainly one may withdraw for a time, just in order to think things over, or to discipline oneself, or to get a perspective. No, what I had in mind when I spoke about it was the extreme type, and there are such types everywhere. I'm thinking of those who say, "Farewell, proud world, I'm going home," not when they're dying, but simply when they want to forsake all their problems and responsibilities. What they are saying, really, is, "I'm through with the world!" I think *that* is contrary to the spirit of true religion—every religion, everywhere. It has been carried to extremes among certain Buddhists, for example, who, at the age of sixty or sixty-five, say, "Well, I'm through. I take my beggar's bowl, I have no concern with the world"—although they *have*, apparently, because they go out into the world with their bowl. Among Jews, there has been the type of temporary withdrawal that's called "taking the Exile upon oneself." (In Yiddish, the phrase used is *oprikhtn goles.* It refers to the practice of performing the penance of exile, especially in old age.) A man leaves his home, goes out into the world at large, with nothing at all except what people will give him, and learns what it is to eat the bread of charity. How was it that Dante put it? "How salt the savor is of other's bread;/ How hard the passage to descend and climb/By other's stairs."

Now of course, to be able to do that without rancor against anybody, not to feel yourself humiliated, to accept that position with grace is, in itself, a considerable achievement. And if it's done for a time, as a discipline and in order to bring one closer to the world actually, rather than to make oneself remoter from it, then it's a creative act.

VAN DOREN: Yes, Maurice, and in order to bring back to the world—when one returns to it—something priceless, something that perhaps could not have been produced, shaped, and perfected in busy hours.

SAMUEL: That, however, should be the occupation and preoccupation of extraordinary men. The wonderful little Jewish book called *Ethics of the Fathers*[16] contains a saying, "Do not separate thyself from the community."[17] It isn't meant as a specific warning against the kind of withdrawal we're talking about; the sense is that a man should participate in the joys and the sorrows of the community and be part of it. But for the large mass of human beings, such withdrawal is probably unnatural. It may be the result of a temporary upset, and not a thing to be encouraged, or perhaps sometimes, not even to be condoned. "Go and mingle with your fellow men" is the healthy attitude.

VAN DOREN: Well now, Maurice, having made that reservation, we are free to proceed. We have the topic before us of man's love of man, a very famous topic, one that can be discussed superficially or profoundly. There are sentimental aspects of it that I daresay we shall have very little sympathy with. I raised the question in our last talk whether ultimately, man's love of man is a real and true thing unless somehow it has the shadow upon it of God's love of man, and man's love of God. Do you agree that there's a real relation?

SAMUEL: That there's an interplay? Yes, one might even go so far as to say—as some have done—that love of God is expressed almost exclusively through love of man. You remember Coleridge's line in "The Rime of the Ancient Mariner": "He prayeth best, who loveth best/ All things both great and small." But going back to that perplexity of mine that I brought up in our last talk, we are commanded repeatedly, "Thou shalt love the Lord thy God." We are also commanded:

Thou shalt love thy neighbor as thyself. LEV. 19:18

This has been a stumbling-block to me in my attempts to visualize its actual application. "Thy neighbor as thyself" means *all other human beings.* We must love them as we love ourselves, without discrimination, so that it's a sin to dislike anybody.

VAN DOREN: You're not assuming, then, that the word "neighbor" really means the man next door?

SAMUEL: No. *Rea* is the Hebrew word. It means friend, fellowman, companion, the person outside of you.

VAN DOREN: Any person outside of you, wherever he may be. I can conceive of two reasons why this is difficult to understand. To "love thy neighbor as thyself" needs to mean no more than this: you put the same value upon anyone else that you put upon yourself. You insist upon paying to anyone else the same respect that you pay to yourself. You do not dismiss anyone else as somehow "outside."

SAMUEL: Yes, but suppose a man loves himself egotistically, exhibitionistically, and selfishly, so that the love he transfers to another is to make that person also egotistical, exhibitionistic, and selfish? I don't suppose they meant by "as thyself" that you must love him with all of the egotisms that you have for yourself.

VAN DOREN: No, but love of self does not necessarily mean to me that kind of love.

SAMUEL: Not necessarily.

VAN DOREN: Well, I think that it doesn't.

SAMUEL: There are such loves.

VAN DOREN: Oh, of course there are, just as there can be perversions of anything. But true love of self, it seems to me, is merely a kind of willingness to accept oneself as the true beginning, beyond which you can go on to other love. A person who just cannot love himself cannot love others.

SAMUEL: That's a pregnant remark. If a man dislikes himself, it's no good telling him he must love other people.

VAN DOREN: That's right. He doesn't know how! The second reason I can think of to explain the difficulty behind the command is this: It is hard to understand the difference between loving *all* men (as, say reformers love all men, or people who want to save the world love all men) and loving one man (the way one man can love another). It has often been pointed out that lovers of mankind are cold and hard. In other words, they don't love any individual man, but they love Man.

SAMUEL: Let's take an extreme instance, say Karl Marx. Now Karl Marx, I presume, acted out of love of mankind. One presumes that—give him the benefit of the doubt—but he was in his personal relations a very nasty person. He was brutal in his statements about various people—for example, about Bakunin, who was on the extreme left; about capitalists, and about the Jews, by the way.[18] He wrote with such venom, and with an enjoyment of his venom, that you ask yourself, "Can a man who is predominantly hateful, that is, full of hate, toward individuals be actually motivated by the love of the species?" And of course, it's not so easy to answer.

VAN DOREN: You may remember that Jonathan Swift, the author of *Gulliver's Travels*—a very curious kind of man, to be sure, but a genius—once said: "I hate and detest that animal called man; although I heartily love John, Peter, Thomas, and so forth." In other words, he could love any individual whom he knew, but he could not love Man. The professional lover of mankind seems to confine his love to the species, as you say, to man in general; whereas oftentimes, in his relations to individuals, we find him singularly cool and remote, without feeling. But the great thing would be to be able to do both.

SAMUEL: There's a charming passage somewhere in Sholom Aleichem about anti-Semites and so-called anti-Semites. You'll find some anti-Semites who hate the Jewish people. But when you go to one of them and ask, "Do you hate that fellow Yankel?" he'll reply, "Oh no, Yankel's a nice fellow. He's all right!" "Do you hate Shmuel over there?" "No, he's a very decent fellow, that Shmuel." Anti-Semites of this kind have it in their mind that they hate the Jewish people, but actually, they don't dislike anybody.

But then there are other types who *love* the Jewish people; when you ask one of them, "What about so-and-so?" you may get an explosion: "THAT fellow, that no-goodnik! He's not worth the ground he walks on!" There are these curious inversions.

VAN DOREN: By the way, the first type of man is the preferable type.

SAMUEL: Oh yes, because with him, it's a fault, certainly; there's a quirk in his mind, but actually, there isn't in him the poison, the hatred that's in the other. But this is a complex subject, and let me get back to that deep problem we're both wondering about: the commandment to love everybody indiscriminantly, or if we personalize it, it's a person, actually, who loves everybody he meets.

While I was thinking over the material for these conversations, I suddenly remembered the character Platon Karataev in *War and Peace.* He appears quite incidentally but in a marvelous vignette in which Tolstoy showed that he was a great moral genius, as well as a great artist. He gives us the picture of the kind of man who loves everybody he meets. I want to quote some passages that occur toward the latter part of the book, when Pierre Bezuhov, an aristocrat who is one of the principal characters in *War and Peace,* meets Platon for the first time. Pierre has been arrested by some of Napoleon's soldiers on suspicion of having taken part in setting fire to Moscow. He's thrown into a barracks with other Russian prisoners of war—mostly simple, poor people—where they are all maltreated by the French. Pierre is sitting in the filthy straw and darkness, and suddenly he is conscious of a presence near him. This is how Tolstoy describes it:[19]

Close by him a little man was sitting bent up, of whose presence Pierre was first aware from the strong smell of sweat that rose at every movement he made. . . . Peering intently at him in the dark, Pierre made out that the man was undoing his foot-gear. And the way he was doing it began to interest Pierre. . . . Pierre was conscious of something pleasant, soothing, and rounded off in [his] deft movements, and even in the very smell of the man, and he did not take his eyes off him.

"And have you seen a lot of trouble, sir? Eh?" said the little man suddenly. And there was a tone of such friendliness and simplicity in the sing-song voice that Pierre wanted to answer, but his jaw quivered, and he felt the tears rising. At the same second, leaving no time for Pierre's embarrassment to appear, the little man said in the same pleasant voice:

"Ay, darling, don't grieve," he said, in that tender caressing sing-song in which old Russian peasant women talk. "Don't grieve, dearie; trouble lasts an hour, but life lasts for ever! Ay, ay, my dear. And we get on here finely, thank God; nothing to vex us. They're men, too, and bad and good among them."

. . . Platon Karataev remained for ever in [Pierre's] mind the strongest and most precious memory, and the personification of everything Russian, kindly, and round. When next day at dawn Pierre saw his neighbor, his impression of something round was fully confirmed; Platon's whole figure . . . was roundish, his head was perfectly round, his back, his chest, his shoulders, even his arms, which he always held as though he were about to embrace something, were round in their lines; his friendly smile and big, soft, brown eyes, too, were round. . . .

Attachments, friendships, love, as Pierre understood them, Karataev had none; but he loved and lived on affectionate terms with every creature with whom he was thrown in life, and especially so with

> *man—not with any particular man, but with the men who happened to be before his eyes. He loved his dog, loved his comrades, loved the French, loved Pierre, who was his neighbor. But Pierre felt that in spite of Karataev's affectionate tenderness to him . . . he would not suffer a moment's grief at parting from him. And Pierre began to have the same feeling towards Karataev.*

Now it is a marvelous thing, yet how many human beings are capable of forgoing a desire for some discrimination, that desire: "I want to be liked a little more by you. You can like everybody, but like *me* a little bit more." That's the human attitude.

VAN DOREN: Here you are using the word "like."

SAMUEL: Well, even love.

VAN DOREN: Yes, I know, but you remember we spoke last time of "liking" and "loving," and inevitably we slip back and forth between those terms. Now, about this little man, Platon (or at least Pierre thought of him as a little man), who loved Pierre only because he, Pierre, happened to be there at that moment—the next fellow who took Pierre's place would be loved just the same. I quite agree with you that there is no escape from the conclusion that ultimately, we love individuals whom we prefer. There are certain individuals whom we *like* better than we like other men. While we don't love them, perhaps, any more than we love other men, still, we like to be with them, we like the way they talk, or the way they look. As a matter of fact, we don't know why we like them so much because surely, one of the great mysteries in life is why *A* likes *B*. We shall never discover why.

SAMUEL: No, people try to look at it psychoanalytically and psychologically, and whatnot, but I suppose the answer is beyond reach—and I suppose that it's best it should remain so. You remember Elizabeth Barrett Browning's poem; she didn't want to be loved for any particular gift, or for a look, or a trick; she wanted to be loved just for the sake of love.[20]

VAN DOREN: I can understand that. Can't you, very well indeed?

SAMUEL: Yes, they call that in Hebrew *ahavah she lo t'luyah ba-davar*, love that is not dependent on anything whatsoever; it simply comes as itself, and manifests itself without any reason. It is supposed to be, of course, the most enduring kind of love.

VAN DOREN: This reminds me, Maurice, of something that you and I have sometimes disagreed about, namely, that good friends—let us say men who love one another, and it could apply to men and women, too—can afford to be frank to one another in naming one another's faults. Now I have some reservations about that, even though I know that the Book of Proverbs says many times that a man should be frank in censuring his friends. Just the other day I happened to chance upon a marvelous couplet in Proverbs:

PROV. 27:17 *Iron sharpeneth iron;*
So a man sharpeneth the countenance of his friend.

SAMUEL: Yes, and in Proverbs, too, you have:

PROV. 27:5 *Better is open rebuke*
Than love that is hidden.

The most famous counsel of all on this particular subject, of course, is that passage in Leviticus:

LEV. 19:17 *Thou shalt not hate thy brother in thy heart; thou shalt surely rebuke thy neighbor, and not bear sin because of him.*

VAN DOREN: But you know this is complicated, and it isn't easy to live out. My observation is (and I am being very personal) that whenever a friend of mine has pointed out a fault that seemed to be a fundamental one, I was hurt.

SAMUEL: You were *hurt*? Well, there's nothing wrong in that!

VAN DOREN: Yes, but it made a very serious difference.

SAMUEL: It would change your attitude toward him? For a time?

VAN DOREN: For a time. You see, I'm quite willing to agree that we should have our faults pointed out to us. And yet, perhaps we don't *really* think that we have any —any fundamental ones, at any rate. The trouble comes when you start asking: What fault is more fundamental than what *other* fault? Now, when a friend comments on a fault, we might very well reply that it seems quite trivial; but yet our vanity makes our minds race ahead and abstract that little fault, and it doesn't take long before that little fault seems to be magnified into a huge one.

SAMUEL: There's a passage in Proverbs bearing on this which puzzles me: ". . . love covereth all transgressions." Does it mean that if you love a person, you cover all his sins, and you don't observe them? Or does it mean that you do observe them, and do speak of them? Is it perhaps that we don't know how to tell somebody his faults? Is it perhaps that every one of us rejoices a little to be able to correct someone else? What makes our hackles rise when we're being corrected—is it our knowledge of the other fellow's feeling of triumph or superiority?

PROV. 10:12

VAN DOREN: Yes, but maybe true love, or true friendship, is based upon a blindness to faults in the object of love. Maybe what we mean when we say, "So-and-so loves so-and-so" is that he does not see the other's faults. Everyone else can see them: the policeman, the census-taker, anyone who is indifferent to him can see his faults, but *A* does not see the faults of *B*. Now, to be sure, from time to time, *A* may josh his friend *B*, just in a kidding way, and say, "You're crazy!" or "You don't understand this!" but that must be said in a certain way, or it pulls the rug out from under the other.

SAMUEL: Well, again that very wise book, Proverbs, has a pertinent comment:

PROV. 27:6 *Faithful are the wounds of a friend;*
But the kisses of an enemy are importunate.

That word "wounds" would seem to mean that you're supposed to be hurt by the friend's correction. Your *amour propre* is outraged, and you think to yourself, perhaps: "He would see that in me, wouldn't he!" and "He *has* to remark on it!"

VAN DOREN: Perhaps, Maurice, all I'm trying to say is that you had better be careful!

(*laughter*)

SAMUEL: It needs several lifetimes of study to try and puzzle out the meaning of various passages in the Bible—not that they all have to be in harmony with each other, either. You can sometimes find opposite advice, too. Proverbs has two consecutive verses which contradict each other:[21]

PROV. 26:4 *Answer not a fool according to his folly,*
Lest thou also be like unto him.

PROV. 26:5 *Answer a fool according to his folly,*
Lest he be wise in his own eyes.

So there you have it: answer a fool, and don't answer him.

VAN DOREN: Yes. I find an inconsistency between the proverb about "open rebuke" which you just a moment
PROV. 17:9 ago mentioned, and the proverb which goes: "He that covereth a transgression seeketh love." "Covereth," there, means, I think, ignores, pulls away, or appeases.

SAMUEL: Yes, yes, or says nothing about it.

VAN DOREN: And "seeketh" there would mean "promotes." The remainder of that verse reads: "But he that harpeth on a matter estrangeth a familiar friend." Now that might refer to things we might say about what others have done. But a lover tends to ignore and to refrain from talking about the faults in the person he loves.

SAMUEL: The phrase "harpeth on" is used in the sense of "nags." Other English translations use "repeats." But to go back to covering or ignoring a fault: is it *commended*? It's almost a form of flattery, isn't it? You might even go so far as to call it "toadying," I think. If you ignore the transgression, you are *aware* of it. It's not what you implied before, that you don't *see* the fault in the person. You do see it, and ignore it, and perhaps it's not to the advantage of your friend that you should do so. You should be worrying about it. This is what God's love is, by the way. God is always worrying about the faults in people. He wants to correct them, and that is why we're afraid of Him. And that is also why His love is oppressive. He won't let us get away with nonsense, and with saying, "Oh, now, You're a nice God. Why don't You forget all about this? Why do You keep nagging me about behaving? Be a good fellow!"

VAN DOREN: Yes, and yet, Maurice, there is a very wonderful relation between David and God described in the Books of Samuel. David does many things of which God disapproves, and for some of which He punishes David. And yet God is certain all the time of David's love for Him, and is able to forgive and to understand him. The knowledge that David loves *Him* somehow makes all the difference. Yes, of course there is an acute observation of David's flaws, and even of his sins.

SAMUEL: Now Mark, we've got onto a subject which might absorb the rest of our talks, and I suppose we'll have to leave this and move on. I'd like to begin our next talk with the question of love being the *only* guiding principle in life. This view has often been advocated, as you know, as the only valid principle; people who disagree with it, who do not recognize its validity, call the principle "antinomianism." We'll start with that in our next conversation.

IV

LOVE IN THE BEGINNING

VAN DOREN: Maurice, what did you mean by that term "antinomianism"?

SAMUEL: It's a term which comes up frequently in religious discussions, and it means, in brief, that no law is needed once you love. In other words, love is its own guide, and it is the *only* guide in life. Wordsworth was expressing the idea in his "Ode to Duty":

Happy will our nature be
When love is an unerring light,
And joy its own security.

Statements have been made in various religions to the effect that love is enough. The difficulty with that point of view is, of course, can you trust love? If you're supposed to love your neighbor as yourself, then certainly this would mean that a man must love all human beings as himself. But one doesn't expect a man to love all *women* in the same way, and there are infinite interpretations to be given of this biblical commandment. When the command is misinterpreted or misunderstood, the possibility of running into the dangers of antinomianism is very great.

VAN DOREN: I'm afraid, Maurice, that the chief difficulty here would be that of trying to understand the meaning of love unless one is, in some sense, a lover. Love has never been defined, surely, and there isn't any quick way of saying what love is. If some person (I daresay he would be a monster!) were to come along and ask, "What on earth do you mean by this word?" it would be awfully hard to tell him, unless he had experienced it. He might say, "It's just a thing, a word. You say it's important, but how can you prove that love is what runs the world and what keeps it good?" You and I, Maurice, might very well understand that love is what keeps the world good. It's the only thing that makes sense out of the world at all, so that I daresay, it's only through love that the world becomes intelligible. But I agree with you: there are tough problems involved.

SAMUEL: Even the problem of man-and-woman love isn't simply resolved when you say, "If a man loves a woman, then everything is solved." It's not at all correct. As I read, and no doubt as you read the Bible, Mark, you see how the presentation of the problem there is partly complicated by changing customs. The Bible covers a long stretch of time, and you will find different shadings, different approaches. I always find it rather difficult to understand the frequent, and one might say passionate, admonition about love for one's wife in the Bible, especially when I come across statements such as those in Proverbs:

And have joy of the wife of thy youth. PROV. 5:18–19
A lovely hind and a graceful doe, . . .
With her love be thou ravished always.

This is given in Proverbs in a time when there was polygamy! I suppose all of us who have been brought up in the Western tradition of monogamy have trouble in understanding how that could be said in an age when having several wives—well, it wasn't the norm, because people couldn't afford it, but if I may so put it, all the best people had a number of wives, all except Adam, of course!

VAN DOREN: I take that phrase "the wife of thy youth" to refer to the wife with whom we fell in love first, and therefore, perhaps, in some sense, the most completely. But I'm interested in your remark that love for one's wife, or love for anybody, might not be enough. I would say that it might very well be enough if it were genuinely present. When love does not seem to be enough, it's because there isn't enough love.

SAMUEL: Well, then, you would have to add that a wicked person cannot love.

VAN DOREN: By the way, I would define a wicked person as a person who cannot love.

SAMUEL: Would you say that Jezebel loved her husband, Ahab? Would you say that she was ready to lay down her life for him? That she thought always of his comfort, his advancement, his state of mind? You'd say those things, but she was a wicked person: she led him toward his ruin. Was that love?

VAN DOREN: As I read that portion of I Kings which treats of Ahab and Jezebel—both of them quite terrible people, although Jezebel was worse—I think of Macbeth and Lady Macbeth. The question might be whether Lady Macbeth loved Macbeth. I think it's perfectly easy to see that there's something that Jezebel, like Lady Macbeth, loves more than her husband. She loves power. Jezebel happened to be a queen, and there was an ambition in her nature which was very strong and bitter. Her character is very sharply drawn in the episode of Na-
I KINGS 21 both's vineyard. You'll remember that King Ahab coveted that plot of ground, and when Naboth flatly refuses his offer to buy it, or exchange it for another piece of property, the king is not strong enough even to make a rejoinder to Naboth. He comes home, "sullen and displeased," lies down on his bed, turns his face to the wall, and refuses to eat. Jezebel comes to him and asks, "What's the matter with you?" And when he tells her, she says, "We can take care of him. Now you rouse up, and we'll fix him." But, if you please, there she is supporting her husband. She is bringing back the iron into his soul, but it's the iron that she loves rather than the soul itself. Therefore, I think you would have to say that Jezebel's chief love was of power.

SAMUEL: Then you would say that Jezebel did not love Ahab. Love of power is not love in our sense, is it?

VAN DOREN: No, I think not.

SAMUEL: When we use the phrase "love of power" we mean a certain corruption in a person which drives him to want increasing dominion over others. It's an expression of mastery which we couldn't call "love." But we haven't got another word for it.

VAN DOREN: We spoke in our last talk about the meaning of various passages in Proverbs relating to the willingness of the true lover, or true friend, to reprove the object of his love. I daresay there is truth in those passages. Nevertheless, I still believe that love is endangered by reproof and criticism because, as I said last time, any fault that is found might turn out to seem to be—in the person in whom it is found—a fundamental fault; and no fundamental fault, surely, must be reproved. That is going into the soul—the very center of the soul—and denying it. If I love *X*, I love *X*, period. There are no reservations, no questions about it. I don't know why I do. I couldn't defend it; I couldn't explain it to anyone who didn't see why. I simply do. Love, for me, is as simple as as that. It's something like the love that the people of God had to have for Him. You remember, He kept commanding them to love Him, and you raised the question of what it means to be *commanded* to love.

SAMUEL: Let me interrupt, Mark. You're raising so many questions, I don't know where to begin. On the rebuking of a friend: there is an element, perhaps—as I mentioned last time—of unconscious superiority in the man who does the rebuking, the attitude, "I'm good enough to correct you!" or it's so taken by the one who is rebuked; and there is nothing more bitter than a quarrel between friends. You remember the lines in Coleridge's poem "Christabel": "And to be wroth with one we love/ Doth work like madness in the brain." The element of love in such a situation is so outraged, apparently, that love becomes the basis of a greater hostility than indifference would have been.

VAN DOREN: William Blake's famous poem, "A Poison Tree," tells us something pertinent. It begins:

I was angry with my friend:
I told my wrath, my wrath did end.
I was angry with my foe:
I told it not, my wrath did grow.

The poem goes on to describe how the wrath grew into a tree which bore, incidentally, a poisoned apple—something, I daresay, which is going to be relevant to our discussion later. But there, to be sure, is the suggestion that if wrath *does* rise in the heart of a friend, he had better at least express it, and get it out of his system, as we say. If he is forgiven, well and good.

SAMUEL: You've brought us to our subject for today, Mark: love as it is presented in the Hebrew Bible, and as it develops through the ages during which the Bible was written. Let's go back to the beginning. Do you see any element of love appearing in the biblical account of the relationship of Adam and Eve? I've always looked upon them not as real persons (the only ones in the Bible, by the way, who to me are not personalities), but as symbols. Sometimes I consider them as the eponym, if you like, of the time when human beings ceased to be animal, became "human," and recognized the distinction between themselves and the animal world. Whenever I try to figure them as human beings, I'm appalled by the problems that suggest themselves. Adam and Eve had no childhood, they never went to school. They never had any complexes, either, because we all collect our complexes in childhood, and it's with our complexes that we love. They are symbols: Adam, Man, and Eve, Woman. *Adam* is the Hebrew word for "man," and *Chavvah*, which is translated into "Eve" or "Eva," is "life"—"mother life." I don't see these two with any family problems, I don't see them grieving over the death of Abel, I don't see them having a relationship. The *midrashim*—the Jewish legends, folktales, and commentaries—do try to inject a "human interest" touch, if you can call it that. They speak of God as having arranged the wedding ceremony, acting as the cantor, and as having invited all the angels to come and celebrate the nuptials. It's not very real to me.

VAN DOREN: It's real, Maurice, only if a happy marriage is real. It's relatively difficult, I'd say, to understand what goes on in a perfectly happy marriage—if one exists. I imagine there's no marriage which is absolutely happy every second of its career.

SAMUEL: No human being is happy every second—and shouldn't be, I suppose.

VAN DOREN: No, but virtually all love stories have to be about love which is, in some sense, truncated or frustrated. The lovers are separated by accident, or by misunderstanding, or by misdeeds on their part for a time. As a matter of fact, every now and then I reflect upon the fact that such a great love story as that in Hawthorne's *The Scarlet Letter* is so touching to us, partly because the lovers, Arthur Dimmesdale and Hester Prynne, are almost never together. Their whole lives, insofar as they are lovers, are spent apart, and so separation is the prevailing theme of love. Or, if the lovers are together, as in the case of Antony and Cleopatra, then there is difficulty. We don't know how to imagine a perfectly simple love, but the love of Adam and Eve presumably was that.

I would say, by the way, that we shouldn't take any particular pride in our incapacity to imagine perfection. I think it's too bad that we can't. Milton tried in *Paradise Lost*—not too successfully, I grant—to imagine the happiness of Adam and Eve. It was an uneventful happiness. Every day was the same. The landscape was beautiful beyond words, the weather was perfect, fruit was always available to Adam and Eve, who merely had to reach out their hands—it was almost put into their hands. They were children of God without any problems of the sort that we recognize as human, although they were going to have a terrible problem—which they failed to solve. Milton endeavored once in his *Paradise Lost* to imagine them talking to each other. There's a long passage in which Eve is telling Adam how much she loves him:

With thee conversing I forget all time,
All seasons, and their change; all please alike.
Sweet is the breath of morn, her rising sweet,
With charm of earliest birds; pleasant the sun
When first on this delightful land he spreads

His orient beams on herb, tree, fruit, and flower,
Glist'ring with dew; . . .

(PARADISE LOST, BOOK IV, 1. 639)

Eve goes on to make a kind of catalogue of all the things she loves, and then she says she wouldn't love them unless Adam were there, too. He is a partner in her love of these other things. That takes us back to the platonic conception of love. True platonic lovers are those, by definition, who love the same things, enjoy the same things. In Plato's case, it was an intellectual operation: two platonic lovers both love the truth. Most love some idea.

SAMUEL: Milton's passage is certainly beautiful, but it leads me to two almost negative reflections. Have you ever read Robert Graves's *Wife to Mr. Milton?*

VAN DOREN: No, I've never read that.

SAMUEL: It's a very powerful, and a very depressing book. If Graves is accurate in his portrayal, one wonders whether Milton himself was ever capable of any kind of love at all. That's one reflection. The other is this: it has always struck me as almost fitting that love does not appear in the Bible at all until we come to Abraham and Sarah, and there love is not mentioned at all, but is implied by a single remark. It occurs when Abram takes Sarai (their names had not yet been changed at the time of this episode) down to Egypt, and he says to her, "I know that GEN. 12:11
thou art a fair woman to look upon" Just in this one remark you can see that there is a love relationship between the man and the woman. One begins to ask whether this isn't a genuine reflection of reality. Do men and women

savages "love" in our sense? Is there this capacity for deeper companionship? My feeling is, no—or at any rate, it is in such an embryonic stage that we wouldn't call it love. And there's a certain fittingness that what we recognize as love does not appear in the Bible until we come to the founder of religion, to the man who knew God.

VAN DOREN: The legends, Maurice, endeavor to make some contribution to an understanding of this in the case of Adam and Eve. The Jewish legends mention that Adam had a wife before Eve—Lilith[22]—who, like Adam, had been created out of the dust. But the relations between Adam and Lilith were not at all like that between Adam and Eve, and that's what Milton was talking about in the passage I cited. My point with regard to that passage is that Eve loved all the things in her world because she saw them and felt them with Adam—and that remains true with us today. I think the normally happy husband loves to tell his wife what he enjoys: he comes home bursting to tell her what happened today. He wants her to share his experience, and she likewise wants to tell him what she experiences, and that's why they like to go places together, take trips together, see things together. But I don't want to make too much of this. I grant that it is quite impossible for the human imagination to do any real work with Adam and Eve because they existed before the imagination has the stuff that it now deals with, namely, error and difficulty.

SAMUEL: The legends try very hard to humanize Adam and Eve with all sorts of pretty stories of their relationship, but for me the attempt hasn't worked. It's only when we get to the Patriarchs that we find a tremendous forward step taken in man-and-woman relations. And even then, it isn't at all like what we nowadays conceive of as love. The mooning, the longing, the romantic element don't appear. There is a deep and I might almost call it (if you won't misunderstand me) a *businesslike* love, that is, a straightforward recognition without any of the lyrical outbursts that we shall discuss later, when we come to The Song of Songs. The patriarchal loves are deep and abiding, and tremendously significant, but they are connected with the business of living, and what is more, with the business of an important destiny which has been allocated to these first-rate figures.

VAN DOREN: Maurice, you make me think of something, as you always do. Quite possibly, the wife in our day—or in any other day—who says to her husband, "You don't tell me often enough that you love me. You don't make speeches. You don't become lyrical with expressions of your love for me!"—such a wife is probably making a fundamental mistake. It seems to me that she ought to be willing to understand that since her husband is giving his entire life to her, spending all of it, actually, with her in mind, that is sufficient expression. If this woman exists—and I'm afraid that she does, because we hear of women who do this—then she'd be wiser if she stopped telling her husband, "You don't say you love me!"

SAMUEL: A lot of advertising is based on that. You know, "Send her flowers every so often to show her that you love her." The florist is tremendously interested in your family life, we take it!

VAN DOREN: Yes, but one good reason why a husband may not remember to say "I love you" every hour of every day is that, in his opinion, he doesn't need to. It's evident that the "business of living," as you called it (and that's not a bad term to use in connection with the Patriarchs) is being conducted by him with her in mind. Everything he does is for her, and he assumes that everything she does is for him. Well, this isn't exciting, and this isn't anything you can tell great love stories about, but it is what actually keeps the world together. It is what happens in almost all portions of the world all the time.

SAMUEL: The family life of the Patriarchs bursts upon the biblical narrative with a fullness of problems that encompasses almost all the kinds of problems that we encounter. For example, here are the three Patriarchs, Abraham, Isaac, and Jacob, in all of whom there was a deep attachment to their wives. Two of them, Abraham

see GEN. 29:28

and Jacob, were polygamous, nevertheless. Jacob married two women almost simultaneously—the two marriages were only a week apart.

VAN DOREN: But he married only one willingly.

SAMUEL: And the fact that he discriminated against Leah has been considered a very serious defect in his character, and is often commented on in the *midrashim.*

Getting back to "love in the beginning"—and for me the real beginning was with the Patriarchs, not with Adam and Eve—look at the universal, everlasting problems which they posed. Here were three men on whom an immense destiny rested. Their wives were not quite

privy to the greatness of this destiny. God never spoke to Sarah to tell *her* of her role in His plan; but He told Abraham: "I will bless her, and she shall be a mother of GEN. 17:16
nations; kings of people shall be of her." These three men —let's call them geniuses—were married to very fine women, but the women did not know what it was that drove the men; so that as we read the biblical account, we get the impression that the women are often—I won't say at loggerheads, but at cross-purposes with their husbands. For example, in her attitude toward Hagar, the secondary wife of Abraham, Sarah shows a spirit which is unbecoming to somebody who ought to know that she's married to a man of destiny, and that all the things happening fall in with the Great Plan, or the Great Unfolding. It's very clear from the biblical text that Abraham cared GEN. 21:8–20
a great deal for Hagar, and that he was distressed at having to send her and their son, Ishmael, away. He cared greatly GEN. 17:18–20
for the boy, Ishmael, and before he had a son by what they called "the true wife," he had implored God to see that Ishmael should have some important destiny, and God had promised it to him. But Sarah insisted that Hagar and Ishmael be cast out without any regard for Abraham's feelings.[23] Isn't the fact that Sarah couldn't share her husband's greater outlook a diminution of her love for him?

VAN DOREN: Of course it was a diminution of love, and that's what I've been trying to say: the love of Adam and Eve had no diminution. You would say, perhaps, that it never even began, so that there was nothing to diminish. I would say that we're asked to understand that there was *everything* to diminish about it, and that much happened, in the way of diminution, when the fruit of the tree was eaten. But the life of those two persons together during all the days when the sun rose and the trees and the flowers were so beautiful for each because of the other—that was the perfect love.

SAMUEL: Let's not forget: it was love in Paradise, and therefore it was not love in our sense of the word.

VAN DOREN: We'll come back to Adam and Eve, and Abraham and Sarah, Hagar and Ishmael, and to some other fascinating personalities next time, Maurice.

V

GOSSIPING ABOUT FATHER ABRAHAM AND HIS FAMILY

VAN DOREN: Maurice, when we talked last time about the beginning of love in the Hebrew Bible, the very beginning, which is the story of Adam and Eve, you had some difficulty in understanding their relationship as a love story. You may remember that I made every effort to suggest that theirs was possibly *the* perfect love story, and since it was perfect, difficult these days to comprehend. Our incomprehension can be traced to that very story: Adam and Eve were expelled from Eden, and as a result, all of us are out of Paradise. We have lost the power to imagine what was in Paradise. It's so much easier for the human imagination to deal with imperfection than with perfection. Nevertheless, I am now quite willing to grant with you that we are about to talk of the true beginning of love as men now understand the term: love as it began to appear not in those abstract, symbolic, mythical figures of Adam and Eve, but in the figures—utterly human—of Abraham and Sarah. We tend to think of them as old, although, of course, they weren't always old. We have that picture of them, early in Genesis, when Sarah is young and very beautiful, and Abraham is afraid, indeed because of her beauty, that she will be taken from him. But I suppose that insofar as anyone thinks of them these days, Abraham and Sarah are old.

SAMUEL: Some side thoughts just occurred to me, Mark, as you were speaking. Why is it that interest has drifted away from figures like the Patriarchs, from figures in the Bible generally, when they appear to us as being the greatest presentation of the human picture? Why are we—you and I and thousands of others—still in a minority as we contemplate these figures and find in them archetypes of human relations, and human aspirations, and suffering? You and I, and others like us, think of these biblical personalities as enormously interesting human beings independently, let us say, of religious belief or acceptance of the record as being literal and historical. I wouldn't expect the majority of people to be greatly concerned about such matters; but even so, the number of those of us who *are* concerned seems to be dwindling. What is it that's happened?

VAN DOREN: That question troubles me very deeply these days. I would extend it. I would say: What has happened to every other region which I think the minds of man used to know in common? Now, to be sure, when I say "used to know," I'm referring to a time when fewer persons were involved in the possession of a common knowledge. With universal education these days, there are so many to inform, and so many to educate that the problem of making any knowledge common at all—that is to say, universal—is said to be all but insuperable. I'm not at all sure that it is. I think we have given up trying to discover what it is that all children, for instance, should know. I sometimes think that the professional educators of our day are on the wrong track. They are studying the psychology of learning; they are trying to find out how any child learns anything, and when he ought to be taught it. I like to think that educators should be troubled with the question of what all children should know. If their conferences were devoted to that problem; if they came out with a body of knowledge—knowledge of events, of persons, of sayings, of great lines or paragraphs of verse or prose, of mathematical figures and formulae, and certainly knowledge of the Bible—if they came out with this body of knowledge and said, "All children[24] in our culture should know these things as soon as possible," I think it might make all the difference in the world.

SAMUEL: Or you could put it another way: persons who are not deeply acquainted with, and as it were, involved in the biblical literature, are simply ignorant of the fundamental folklore of the Western world; the Bible has to be considered one of the "musts" in modern education. I remember your once telling me, Mark, that when you were a child—and it was true for me, too—the stories and the figures of the Bible were a reality. One *gossiped* about the Bible every day. As a matter of fact, what you and I do to a large extent in these conversations on the Bible is, I think, gossiping about those people in the Bible!

VAN DOREN: Yes, like the generation of my grandparents in the American Middle West. That generation knew no other history nearly so well as it knew the history of Abraham and Sarah, and Jacob and Joseph.

SAMUEL: To me, it isn't a precious or specific kind of knowledge which should be left to the experts. One should not have to say of a person who knows the Bible, "Oh, yes, that man is interested in the Bible," with the kind of tone we reserve for the specialist, "Oh, yes, that man is interested in Goethe, or Chaucer." The Bible is the foundation of the thinking of the Western world. These personalities in the Bible are *ourselves* as we first appeared in history. I don't know if there is a "way"—but a good contribution to the restoration of interest in the Bible would be to stop going to see movies about the Bible. That would be very helpful, I think. Do you?

VAN DOREN: Yes, because they leave anyone who knows the true stories so disappointed. The wrong things are blown up!

SAMUEL: Mark, you've been a teacher for forty years. What's been your experience with students? Specifically, with Jewish students? Have you found among them an acceptable degree of knowledge about these Bible figures? Do they know who Abraham was? Isaac? Jacob?

VAN DOREN: No. There was a period of ten years or so when, in a certain course of mine at Columbia College, I asked the students to read with me a very considerable portion of the Hebrew Bible. I was interested in the persons of that book, and their stories, and so we read the narrative portions, in particular. I discovered that all the students who read with me were profoundly moved—and this was just as true of the Jewish students as the non-Jewish students. *They* hadn't read these portions, either; it was a novelty for them. . . .

SAMUEL: A discovery!

VAN DOREN: Yes, a discovery . . . to be really intimate with Abraham, for instance, or Jacob. It was an experience they hadn't had. Those names, of course, might have been more familiar to them than to the non-Jewish students; but still, they had somehow missed the experience of the imagination; and now that they had it, they were very grateful to the Book which had given that experience to them.

SAMUEL: Bringing this back to the subject of love in the Hebrew Bible, think of the problems—enormous, universal, and everlasting—that occur in the lives of the Patriarchs! Look at the implications, the possible researches into human motivation in our day that are suggested by these men! Consider the relationship, for example, of Abraham to his son Isaac; narrow that down to just one incident—the famous sacrifice. It's incredible to me that people should not know that such an incident took place; but beyond that, I am overwhelmed when I think how much there is to be meditated about that single episode, which is told in exactly three paragraphs of chapter 22 of Genesis. The chapter opens:

GEN. 22:1–2

> *And it came to pass . . . that God did prove Abraham, and said unto him: "Abraham"; and he said: "Here am I." And He said: "Take now thy son, thine only son, whom thou lovest, even Isaac, and get thee into the land of Moriah; and offer him there for a burnt-offering upon one of the mountains which I will tell thee of."*

Isaac wasn't the "only son" of Abraham, of course; but he was the only son by the true wife. The text tells us that he loved his son, yet he takes him, binds him to the altar, and is ready to offer him as a sacrifice.[25] What went on in the mind of that father? The boy was *willing* to be sacrificed—how was that conceived?

VAN DOREN: Very painfully, I should say. The interesting thing about Genesis at that point is that it says nothing whatever about what went on in Abraham's mind when this command was given. All we read in the text is that instruction by God to take Isaac and sacrifice him. The very next sentence reads:

GEN. 22:3

> *And Abraham rose early in the morning, and saddled his ass, and took two of his young men . . . and Isaac . . . and went unto the place of which God had told him.*

There's no attempt even to fathom the depths of the man's doubts, which had to be overcome perhaps; or to fathom the depths of his faith, which didn't, of course, have to be overcome. Now, one of the great merits of these stories of the Bible is that they have no psychology in them, no discussion of motivation.

SAMUEL: Oh, I wish we had less psychology in our modern books!

VAN DOREN: We have almost nothing else!

SAMUEL: That word has become an affliction to me. Everybody is a psychologist!

VAN DOREN: Look at this extraordinary passage: in so few words, we get this dreadful command, and then the utterly simple obedience to it. Now, as you think about it, you can understand the simplicity of that obedience, because not only was it Abraham's *nature* to obey, but it was his *destiny* to obey—the two things coincide. There is no thought, no impulse, even, on his part—I dare say—to refuse his destiny at this point. That is very exciting. All of the stories have that wonderfully carved quality. The events and impressions are made out of some durable stuff that is made to last, chiefly, I believe, because they are not misted over with speculation as to what these persons thought.

SAMUEL: No, the Bible gives you the material—do with it what your imagination permits you.

VAN DOREN: In this sense, we have been doing just that; and I quite agree with you that it's a pity that so many people these days do not have the infinite pleasure of speculating concerning things which the Bible itself does not state.

SAMUEL: The sacrifice of Abraham plays a very large part in Jewish thinking. There's a special word for this incident, the *Akedah*, in Hebrew, which means "the binding," specifically, the binding of Isaac to the altar. I've thought more than once—and surely it must have occurred to you, too—of the interesting parallel between the *Akedah* and the story of Titus Manlius, the Roman consul and war hero who took the name Torquatus, and his son. Livy tells how the son, a brave young man, goes out to engage in single-handed combat with an enemy leader, disobeying the command of his father. Although he kills his opponent, the father condemns him to death in order to demonstrate that discipline is discipline. Livy puts these words into the mouth of the father:[26]

> *"For my part, I admit to a natural affection of a father, and I also acknowledge the bravery that you, my son, have shown. But since the authority of a consul's order must either be established by your death, or be annulled forever, I expect you, if you have a drop of my blood in you, to assert our discipline by submitting to your punishment. Go, lictor, bind him to the stake."*

The boy is executed, to the horror of the whole Roman army which has been assembled to witness the execution. Livy adds: "The brutality of the punishment, however, rendered the soldiers more obedient to their commander. . . . The stern act did much good."

That's a fascinating contrast. Both fathers are in a similar position. Abraham is told he must sacrifice his son; God orders him to do so, and he dares not disobey. The consul acts out of loyalty to his own conception of what is best for the discipline of the army, and the welfare of Rome. In the *Akedah,* the imagination dwells on the love of God which existed in Abraham and Isaac; Livy's story, on the other hand, is brutally cruel. These Romans were warriors, and in order to maintain the discipline of the army, and keep it in good condition as a fighting machine, they regarded this horrifying action as a "salutary" lesson! To me, there's a world of difference between the two episodes.

VAN DOREN: Of course there is! The only point of resemblance between the two is that both acted for a reason out of sight, as it were—beyond the present moment. I suppose the three most interesting words in Livy's passage were "I expect you." It's not "I order you," or "I insist," but "I *expect* you."

SAMUEL: For me, that incident illustrates the debasement of the good when it is placed at the service of evil. There was no element in it of God, morality, or love, but rather, what was contemplated was the conquistadorial career of Rome. A virtue carried to its opposite extreme may carry many of the characteristics of virtue, and can be mistaken for it—whereas actually, it has become a vice.

VAN DOREN: Now of course, nothing like that happens in the narrative of the sacrifice in Genesis. Once He has given His command, God does not say to Abraham: "I *expect* you to follow it!" Perhaps God did not expect it, because He made His people free, and Abraham was free to disobey this command. It's as if God waited to see if Abraham would do it, and as we know, Abraham did do it. The silence in which he obeyed is to us tremendously eloquent. There was no appeal—as in the case of Torquatus—to a code or to a discipline.

SAMUEL: It's the difference between morality and morale. Morale can be placed at the service of anything, but morality is—for us, in the biblical sense—placed at the service of God *only.*

VAN DOREN: Maurice, we hear very little in the Bible about how Isaac, the dearly beloved son of Abraham and Sarah, born to them in their old age, is brought up. Nothing is said, either, about what Sarah might have thought about the sacrifice.

SAMUEL: No, nothing is said about Sarah's reaction in the biblical text.

VAN DOREN: As I remember, there are legends to the effect that Sarah knew her husband was taking Isaac somewhere; and when she asked him where, Abraham made up a story about what he and the boy were going to do on their trip away from home. But that's exactly where the legends, fascinating as they are, are less powerful than the book which they decorate. Wouldn't you agree?

SAMUEL: Well, the Jews haven't written a second Bible, that's quite evident!

VAN DOREN: No, and never will, chiefly because they don't have any need to. However, there is Sarah herself, whom we see 'way back there in time, so beautiful a young woman that her husband on at least two occasions when they go among strangers, is beset with fear that she will be taken away from him, and he passes her off as his sister.[27] But here she is now, a very old woman with a single son, whose life is in danger.

SAMUEL: Long ago I heard a legend—I don't remember where, now—as to how this episode affected Sarah. An angel, a rather stupid angel, apparently——

VAN DOREN: Now wait a minute! Can there be a *stupid* angel?

SAMUEL: Well, let's judge from what I'll tell you. An angel was sent to tell her about what had happened. He was supposed to say, "Your boy nearly died." But instead he said, "Your boy died, nearly." And before he got out the word "nearly," Sarah died of shock. The legend illustrates her love for the boy. You can imagine this happening to modern parents. Say, a father has to send his son off to war to defend the country, and for one reason or another, has to keep this news away from the mother. I don't think it is difficult to imagine that Abraham simply dreaded having to tell Sarah what he was going to do. It's as if at the back of his mind he was saying to himself: "This will turn out in some way that won't be so horrible for both of us."

VAN DOREN: I think the reason we find Abraham's moment of speechlessness so moving is that we know for a certainty that the command was difficult for him. Abraham says not a word after getting that command; he just goes about fulfilling it, in simple obedience. If he had said to God, "I obey You automatically; it's nothing at all to carry out Your orders," we shouldn't find the story so interesting, would we?

SAMUEL: Well, then his action wouldn't be human; it would be that of an automaton. In fact, then the

Akedah would begin to resemble the story of Torquatus, who behaved as an automaton. As you correctly pointed out, God doesn't say to Abraham, "I *expect* you"; nor is there any suggestion of a choice on Abraham's part. Livy *praises* Torquatus; it was "good" that the Roman army was so impressed! Whereas, humanly speaking, the army should have remained horrified, and the execution should *not* have been a source of improved discipline.

VAN DOREN: Let's get back to Abraham and Sarah, Maurice. You denied that Adam and Eve were the first lovers in the Bible, that is, lovers in any sense that we can understand; and I think I do have to agree with you. But would you agree that Abraham and Sarah are the first lovers, in view of the fact that there is no love talk between them?

SAMUEL: There's just that one remark I mentioned in our last talk, when Abraham and Sarah go down to live in Egypt, and he says to her:

GEN. 12:11 *I know that thou art a fair woman to look upon.*

That's quite enough. The Bible doesn't have to expatiate on points. Incidentally, Abraham and Sarah are no longer
GEN. 12:4 young when this occurs. The Bible tells us that Abraham
was seventy-five years old when God called on him to leave Haran and go into the land of Canaan; and then famine drives the household down to Egypt.

What impresses me about this couple is their robust relationship and their many family problems. For example, Ishmael—the son of Abraham and Hagar—introduces the problem of juvenile delinquency into this

household. One sentence in the biblical text veils somewhat *see* GEN. 21:9
the nature of that problem, but it is clear that Sarah is greatly disturbed to see that Ishmael is playing with young Isaac, and is teaching him bad habits. The legends expatiate on that.[28] Ishmael is sent away, and turns out afterwards to become the universal symbol of the man who's against the world, and the world is against him.

Abraham and Sarah have a lot of problems in quite the same sense as human beings always will have, no matter how society improves, no matter how affluent we become, no matter how many planets we settle on or how many galactic systems we bring under our communications control. And going back to our theme at the beginning of this talk, it occurs to me that one of the reasons why people nowadays stand off from these deep, permanent human narratives is that they think the world is altogether different from the world in the Bible. They think that human beings have been changed fundamentally by our admittedly marvelous and exciting scientific achievements; and that the stories in the Bible are "old stuff." If they examine human beings at all, it is by means of all the latest devices of investigation—psychological, psychiatric, psychoanalytical. As for all the old wisdom, they say, "Oh, *that*! It belongs to the remote past!"

VAN DOREN: And of course, they're wrong! The very example of Ishmael whom you just now mentioned as a juvenile delinquent is a case in point. As all too many people say these days, juvenile delinquency frequently is a by-product of broken homes. In the story of Abraham and Sarah, the home hasn't actually been broken, but it's
been severely split. Sarah's long barrenness moved her GEN. 16:2

once to suggest that Abraham take Hagar, her own handmaid, for a second wife, so that through Hagar, she and Abraham might have a child to bring up as their own. That situation would cause domestic difficulties in any age. Sarah's suggestion was taken up. Hagar's role in the household changes. She conceives and bears Abraham his first son, Ishmael; but Sarah is not at all happy about that. She had apparently thought she could be, but it was a strain to put upon a woman, and Sarah could not endure it. She was, to say the least, mean to Hagar. She spoke against her.

GEN. 16:4 SAMUEL: Yes, but the text tells us that the moment Hagar knew she was pregnant, she began to despise her mistress. That we must accept.

VAN DOREN: That's true, yes.

SAMUEL: It's interesting that this method they used was a rather primitive child-adoption system. Instead of going out to find a child somewhere, the husband would beget children by the maids, and these children would be part of the family, having been born into it. You'll remember that Jacob, too, begot children by the maids, as well as by his two wives.

To use that phrase again—not too seriously—"juvenile delinquency": Esau, the son of Isaac and Rebekah, was a problem. Jacob had a good many such problems, beginning with his two sons, Simeon and Levi, whom we'll discuss in a later talk. All the Patriarchs had these problems, and here they begin in their fullness. It's as though here is the human theme, starting with Abraham and Sarah. We're going to continue telling these immensely revealing and absorbing stories throughout the remainder of our conversations.

VAN DOREN: If I'm smiling a little bit, it's because of the word "fullness" you just used. I think it's a perfectly proper word. But there are those who would say that there's no fullness here because there is no talk, no logical or psychological chopping, no analysis, no discussion of motivation.

SAMUEL: In our next talk—on Isaac—we're going to find a fullness based on a stunning and most revealing silence.

VAN DOREN: Isaac is the most silent of them all.

VI

ISAAC, THE SUFFERING, SILENT SERVANT

VAN DOREN: Maurice, we've touched briefly on the narrative style of the Bible, and that topic becomes particularly pertinent when we consider Isaac, the second of the three Patriarchs. The narrative style is distinguished by extreme simplicity and brevity. It lacks anything excessive, anything that isn't truly necessary—we've called it "psychology," "motivation," "analysis"—and confines itself to action, that is, talk about what people *did.* The Bible for the most part is content to tell you *what* they did, and does not explain it. You are expected either to understand it at once, or to spend the rest of your life trying to understand it. Now in the case of certain great persons in the Bible, and particularly in the case of Isaac, there is an especial gift for silence. It isn't *literally* true that Isaac never says anything, but in thinking about him, one has the impression that he almost never talks.

SAMUEL: The Bible in general is not verbose. It deals with an immense world which was implicit to the minds of its readers in the ancient days. The writers and editors of the Bible took it for granted that the Jews knew what the tradition was, and they threw in a word here and there just by way of a reminder. Now, Isaac himself, as you intimate, is the outstanding example of pregnant silence. His not speaking is full of significance. This is not the silence of a man who doesn't know what to say, but of one who has so much in him that he leaves you to guess and to reconstruct from the condition of his life what he must have gone through. Isaac was not an adventuring man, unlike his father, Abraham, and unlike his son, Jacob. Abraham's family is traced back to Ur of the Chaldees, that is, to southern Mesopotamia.[29] The family and Abraham move to Haran, in northwest Mesopotamia. Abraham and his family then travel to the land of Canaan, the Holy Land; famine drives them down to Egypt. They come GEN. 14:14–15
north again; Abraham and his "trained men" pursue the kidnappers of his nephew, Lot, almost to Damascus. These are just a few of Abraham's adventures. Jacob, of course, was born in Canaan, went after his wives in Mesopotamia, and at the end of his life, moved down to Egypt, where he died. Isaac was actually forbidden by God to leave the GEN. 26:2
land for Egypt. He was not a man of action. He was a man whose being and ideas had to impregnate, as it were, all of the conceptions that we have of him.

VAN DOREN: In other words, Isaac is almost the specimen Patriarch, isn't he? That is, we think of a Patriarch as somehow *doing*, rather than saying.

SAMUEL: Yes! But it's odd that in the Jewish tradition, we refer in our prayers very frequently to "Abraham, our father"—*Avraham avinu*, in Hebrew—and to "Jacob, our father"—*Ya-akov avinu*—but we don't talk of *Yitzhak avinu,* "Isaac, our father." He is between those two figures, silent, imposing, suffering, and in a sense, imposed upon, except that the negative aspect of this phrase is lost, because it is God's will that is imposed on him. Isaac is thought of always as the accepter of circumstances.

VAN DOREN: But his name is never forgotten, is it? It's always "Abraham, Isaac, and Jacob," when you speak of the Patriarchs?

SAMUEL: No. Isaac's name is never forgotten. Our prayers speak of "God of Abraham, God of Isaac, God of Jacob." I meant, a moment ago, references to the individual Patriarchs: we single out Abraham and Jacob, but somehow, Isaac is not usually mentioned alone.

That name, Isaac, has in it a peculiar incongruity for me. The name itself is based on the Hebrew root meaning "to laugh," and *Yitzhak*, or Isaac, means "he will laugh." You remember, of course, how that name came about: when Abraham was ninety-nine years old, God told him that he and Sarah would be blessed with a son, and the Bible says:

> *Then Abraham fell upon his face [in gratitude], and laughed, and said in his heart: "Shall a child be born unto him that is a hundred years old? And shall Sarah, that is ninety years old, bear?"* GEN. 17:17

Sarah overhears the news later, in her tent:

> *And Sarah laughed within herself, saying: "After I am waxed old shall I have pleasure, my lord being old also?"* GEN. 18:12

She's so overwhelmed by the very idea that she laughs, and in the very next sentence, she is rebuked:

> *And the Lord said unto Abraham: "Wherefore did Sarah laugh . . . ?" Then Sarah denied, saying: "I laughed not"; for she was afraid. And He said: "Nay; but thou didst laugh."* GEN. 18:13–15

Finally, when the son Isaac is born, Sarah says:

> *"God hath made laughter for me; every one that heareth will laugh on account of me."* GEN. 21:6

In other words, everyone will rejoice *with her* over this blessed event. There's a double meaning of "laughter" in these passages: Sarah laughed first in disbelief, and afterwards she laughed with joy. A name connected with "laughter," however, is peculiarly unfitting for this silent, suffering, repressed man Isaac.

VAN DOREN: Yes, because he isn't funny in any sense of the word. I mentioned before that Isaac almost never speaks. The first time he utters any words occurs on that famous occasion when his father takes him up on the mountain to carry out the command to sacrifice the boy. The two servants are left behind, while the father and son make their way up the mountain to the place of the

GEN. 22:7 altar. The boy suddenly asks his father: ". . . but where is the lamb for a burnt-offering?" It's a natural question. They were carrying up the wood, the fire, and the knife, but the sacrifice was normally an animal, and where was it? Abraham, out of embarrassment or necessity, replies:
GEN. 22:8 "God will provide Himself the lamb for a burnt-offering, my son." And that has a double meaning, too, for at the critical moment, the Lord provides an animal for the sacrifice, a ram which has been caught by his horns in a nearby thicket. Isaac seems to be satisfied with his father's answer. It could be that he doesn't understand it. But never again in that fearful episode does he speak.

SAMUEL: The thematic tenor of his life is that he accepts and has faith. He suffers and believes that things will come out well as long as he doesn't struggle against them. All his life, from the beginning to the end, he accepted. As a grown man, when he is living in Gerar and his flocks and his lands are unusually fruitful, the king of
GEN. 26:14–18 the Philistines comes and tells him, "Go from us; for thou art much mightier than we." Isaac departs without a word of protest. Without Isaac's knowledge, Abraham sent old Eliezer, his steward, to Mesopotamia to bring back a wife for Isaac. Isaac not only accepted that action, but we're told that when he saw his bride, "Isaac brought her into
GEN. 24:26 his mother Sarah's tent . . . and he loved her."

VAN DOREN: In other words, he doesn't protest in the beginning, with any statement like, "But I don't want anyone to choose a wife for me! I want to choose my own wife!"

SAMUEL: Or, "I wasn't consulted!"

VAN DOREN: Nor does he protest at the end of the mission. He's walking in the field at sunset when the camels bearing Rebekah and Eliezer approach—and not a word! He doesn't rush to meet them, he doesn't ask any questions, "Who is this? Where do you come from? What's your name? May I look at you under your veil?" No words whatever, but he takes Rebekah and loves her!

The most we ever hear Isaac speak is during that famous episode toward the end of his life when he is blind and feeble and he instructs Esau to go out and get some fresh venison. He feels that death is approaching, and he GEN. 27
wants "savory food" before he transmits the blessing to Esau, the older of his twin sons. Everybody knows what happens: Rebekah hears the instructions and arranges things so that Jacob brings in the savory food, and blind old Isaac gives the blessing to the younger son. When Esau returns with the venison and asks for the blessing, it is characteristic of Isaac, I think, that he "trembled very exceedingly," and said, "I have blessed him . . . and what then shall I do for thee, my son?" In other words, "I have already given my blessing. It cannot be changed, and I don't know what to give you, Esau."

SAMUEL: This is the suffering man, and it is my feeling there is something in him of a forecast of the suffering servant described in the Book of Isaiah—the man *see* ISA. 52–53
who takes oppression and pain upon himself, "opened not his mouth," and who therefore is a redeemer. In the Jewish tradition, Isaac is always thought of as the great redeemer because of the *Akedah*, the binding, the incident

of the sacrifice. He surrendered everything without a protest, without a murmur, and because of that, the Jewish people have regarded him as a special redeemer.

What is especially interesting to me is that Isaac suffered deeply over Esau, the son whom he loved. We read:

GEN. 26:34–35 *And when Esau was forty years old, he took to wife Judith the daughter of Beeri the Hittite, and Basemath the daughter of Elon the Hittite. And they were a bitterness of spirit unto Isaac and to Rebekah.*

He loved Esau, even though as a boy and as a man, Esau was always contrary to the spirit of what Isaac stood for.[30] I spoke of him as a problem of juvenile delinquency, although as a man of forty, Esau was still afflicting his parents. Jewish legends tell that Isaac's blindness began during his youth: as he was lying bound on the altar, the angels began to weep, and their tears fell upon his eyes, weakening them for the rest of his life. Then, in his later years, he lost his sight entirely because Esau's idolatrous wives insisted on burning incense to their idols in Isaac's home, and the smoke offended his eyes, and made them smart. All of this Isaac accepted without a word.

VAN DOREN: I hadn't come across that legend. Let me ask you, Maurice, a question about the blessing. On the basis of any knowledge that you may have, would it have been unthinkable for Isaac (or for anyone else in his position), once he had become aware of the mistake, to have done anything about it? Could he have done anything? Isaac discovers from Esau that the blessing has been given to Jacob. He has a fit of trembling, as the text tells us. But he doesn't rage, tear his hair, rend his garments, or curse anybody. Nor does he say, "Well, we shall begin all over again, since it was not done properly. Now it shall be done properly." There is a sense in his mind that this ritual, having been performed, cannot be re-performed. Is that his own character speaking there, or is it something else?

SAMUEL: I must say, Mark, I haven't thought of it. I don't remember any such suggestion anywhere in the biblical commentaries, although it might exist. However, what speaks against it is the whole tenor of Isaac's life.

VAN DOREN: Yes, that's true.

SAMUEL: And also, there must have been in Isaac an unacknowledged—what we call now an unconscious —love for Jacob, which was overridden, overlaid, by his weakness for Esau. His weakness for Esau was human, emotional and nervous; and his love for Jacob was much more deeply rooted. It was connected with his sense of the destiny which he bore as the carrier, the continuer, of the line. The episode of the blessing occurs in the Bible text *after* Esau, the hunter, married pagan women and embittered the spirit of his mother and father. After they had seen how Esau went after these pagan ways, Isaac took an affirmative step—one of the few affirmative steps that he took. In conformity with Rebekah's wishes, he called in Jacob, blessed him again, and told him to go back to the "old country," as it were, to Rebekah's family, and get
himself a wife there. From the text, we can very well GEN. 27:46
imagine that the idea came from Rebekah.

There's something very human about this proposal, something very reminiscent of the wanderings of families.

Many Americans today, the descendants of immigrants, remember how their grandmothers and grandfathers used to talk about "sending for a wife" from the old country. They felt more secure, somehow, and there was a nostalgia in it. Also, there was a distrust of the new world. They had come to America as immigrants, and the strangeness of the world distressed them. They were confident of the deep and abiding values which existed in their native land, and so they thought of sending for a bride—to Ireland, to Germany, to Poland, to Italy, wherever. We mentioned in our last talk that the modern generation doesn't understand what the old biblical stories are all about. But they also don't know what the old generations went through, nor can they possibly imagine what future generations may also have yet to pass through. They wouldn't understand somebody sending to the old country for a bride for the son, or a bridegroom for the daughter. Yet, this was in the mind of Isaac and Rebekah, although fantastically enough, the Laban they were thinking of was just no good! According to the Bible and the tradition, Laban was not only an idol-worshiper—he was a bad person.

VAN DOREN: Laban was a deceiver. But to return to Esau: you said a moment ago that there was something especially human about Isaac's love for Esau. Of course there was. But there was also something animal. Isaac's interest in Esau attaches to his interest in Esau's pursuits. Esau is a hunter; he lives in the open, in the fields. His very clothes smell of grass, and of the animals with which he's had contact—tended, perhaps, or killed and cut up. There is something about all of that which peculiarly touches Isaac. However, I quite agree, his love for Jacob is there all the time, and finally it is demonstrated in a way that reveals Isaac at last seems to understand what *we* understand—the line was intended to have been carried on, and must now be carried on, by Jacob. Isaac's love of Jacob finally has to become a human love—that is to say, he has to be interested in Jacob not as a human being having also an animal existence, but as a human being having an intellect, feelings, and a discriminating intelligence. Esau is never represented as having that; his hairy exterior is a kind of symbol, wouldn't you say so, of a certain roughness. He is furred, like an animal.

SAMUEL: Yes. The Bible says he was born "ruddy, all over like a hairy mantle." GEN. 25:25

VAN DOREN: And there's always been to me something very touching about Isaac's devotion to Esau, for that reason. The suggestion could be either that Isaac was something like that himself (there was something primitive about Isaac); or that he was moved pathetically by the primitive in his son.

SAMUEL: The fact that it's almost impossible to fathom what went on in Isaac's mind with regard to Esau is just one more demonstration of the multiple subtleties in these biblical narratives. Sometimes I see the story as the thinking man's admiration for the man of action, or the philosophic man's admiration for the hero. Perhaps Isaac was "sicklied o'er with the pale cast of thought"; and as he looked at Esau, he thought to himself, "Now *there's* a man! He's not worried by ideas; he goes out and hunts, he gets his food, and he brings it in!" On the one

hand, he admires this strange son; and on the other hand, he is also rather repelled by Esau, because Esau was a throwback to the very primitive—not only in his personality and manner of living, but also in religious feeling. Imagine a grandson of Abraham marrying idol-worshipers! Isaac was a thinking man with problems that must have
GEN. 24:63 been gnawing at him all his years. On the evening when Rebekah arrived, he was out walking in his fields, meditating.

VAN DOREN: Of course, I dare say you're right. I'm only amused to think that if I wanted to—and rather perversely!—I could maintain the opposite. He was walking in the fields, meditating, because he loved to be there —as *Esau* did. He wanted to be close to the ground.

SAMUEL: You wouldn't be contradicting me. You would simply be using another instance to illustrate the complexity of these apparently simple stories.

VAN DOREN: It isn't what I necessarily believe, mind you! But I am in complete agreement with you when you say that there are an infinite number of ways of understanding these "simple" stories. I suddenly see Isaac in yet another way: he himself had been a kind of throwback. He was not like his father, or like his son-to-come, Jacob. His character was of the utmost simplicity; and this simplicity made it difficult for him to play his role. He played it, but it was so hard for him that he's silent about it. That could explain his silence, by the way: he was struggling all the time to understand his role so that he had no energy, or perhaps the ability or inclination, to speak. But I'm not too serious about this.

SAMUEL: No, no—that might be it! There are a hundred ways of interpreting these matters. Do you remember that line from Kipling's poem "In the Neolithic Age"? It goes:

There are nine and sixty ways of constructing tribal lays,
And—every—single—one—of—them—is—right!

VAN DOREN (*laughing*): Yes!

SAMUEL: There's nothing wrong in the contradictory interpretations we make. As a matter of fact, in the *midrashim*, the Jewish legends, you will find innumerable completely contradictory interpretations of single chapters of the Bible, and each one of them is an illumination. But with regard to Isaac's submissiveness—perhaps a silently rebellious submissiveness—it was that of a man who has surrendered, saying: "God knows better what I really want and need than I do, myself." It began with the sacrifice, it continued with the wife who had been given to him, and with the deception (some have called it a swindle!) practiced on him by his wife and younger son. It strikes me that there is something symbolic in the fact that he was smitten with blindness. He refused to *look* at the world, thinking that it was a fraud, that all that appears to us in life is a hallucination, and that the realities must be seen only in meditation—for which reason this half-willed blindness came upon him, and he said, "Let things take their course." There's a saying in the Talmud: "Every man gets the wife he deserves." I don't know exactly what the Rabbis meant by it, but Isaac must have taken that point of view, and he loved the woman who was brought to him.

VAN DOREN: And by the way, she loved him. She was of a more complicated nature, I'm sure. There was something most interesting about the alacrity with which she decided to leave her mother and her brother, Laban, and to go along with the old steward.

SAMUEL: Rebekah didn't waste a moment. "I will go," she said, the minute they asked her, although she had never met Isaac!

VAN DOREN: Yes, Eliezer found Rebekah at the
GEN. 24 well after his long journey. It was evening, and they proceeded to Rebekah's house, where Eliezer explained his mission, and handed out precious gifts. The next morning, Eliezer was ready to return home, but her mother and her brother said, "Let her stay a few days, at least ten!" But Eliezer insisted, and they decided to call in Rebekah, and let her decide. "Will you go with this man?" they ask, and she answers immediately, "I will go."[31] Now there's no evidence that Rebekah does not love Isaac; and she must have respected him, too, because of all the effort she went to in order to deceive him in arranging for Jacob to get the blessing.

SAMUEL: She more than respected Isaac.

VAN DOREN: He was not nobody in her eyes.

SAMUEL: Oh, no! She looked through his weaknesses. She was, if I may so put it, a masterful woman. She had made up her mind, and apparently it was in the Plan, so to speak, the Divine Plan, that she was to be the instrument of the fulfillment. She knew very well that that blessing could not go to Esau; it had to go to Jacob. And there's no evidence of any distress or repudiation on the part of Isaac. He accepted her, and he probably knew from the beginning: "What she's going to do for me is the right thing. She knows better than I. She's been better instructed than I. She is much more specific."

VAN DOREN: I suppose the most famous story about Rebekah, or rather, the most famous image, is that of her at the well. It just occurs to me that when old GEN. 24:7
Abraham instructed his steward to go out and find a wife for Isaac, Abraham said that God would send an angel with him, to help in the search. That's the first and the last time we hear of an angel guiding this particular mission. I imagine we are to understand that the angel is assisting Eliezer, and perhaps giving him ideas. It's as if the angel had suggested to Eliezer: "Very well. Now you've GEN. 24:10–29
arrived here at the well outside of the city of Nahor. Why not say that you will be especially interested in any maiden who comes out and is willing to give water not only to you, but also to your camels?" And Eliezer does exactly that. By the way, there are innumerable pictures of Rebekah at the well.

SAMUEL: Innumerable and most of them very poor.

VAN DOREN: Very poor, indeed.

SAMUEL: Every amateur has tried his hand at painting that scene.

VAN DOREN: It's a very famous scene. But what interests me is that all of these activities and preparations and questionings are not of Isaac's doing at all—everything is being done *for* him. He's waiting back home for the results—if there are any—of the search. It's remarkable how little Isaac does, just as it's remarkable how little he says. And yet, for me, Isaac remains one of the outstanding figures in the Bible. I see something monumental in him.

SAMUEL: This is what has happened in the Jewish tradition, too. Here is a man who apparently does nothing to direct his own life, and does nothing in protest; yet he stands up as a gigantic figure of a fulfillment without a protest, and you might almost say, without any effort on his part—beyond, of course, the tremendous effort of acquiescence. To acquiesce requires a tremendous effort, too.

VAN DOREN: Yes! You said earlier in this talk that Isaac is not a laugher. I suddenly remember that I had a very cheerful great-uncle named Isaac. The names Abraham and Isaac were frequent in my family.

SAMUEL: They don't use these names much nowadays in American life, do they? They used to. We've had a lot of Abrahams, Isaacs, and Jacobs in American history of the past.

VAN DOREN: No, those names aren't used anymore. Abraham was the third generation before me, and as I said, I had a great-uncle Isaac, I saw him once, but I've never forgotten him. I can still see him. He was a short, thick-set, bald man—his head was not only bald, but shiny—and his face was always broken into smiles. He was a very merry old soul. (*laughing*) I remember meeting him when I was a very small child, and being terribly taken by him because he was so merry.

SAMUEL: But not at all like the biblical Isaac. Your uncle was a man who laughed.

VAN DOREN: That's right. He was a laugher.

SAMUEL: And the Isaac of the Bible is one who was laughed *for*, as it were. But we'll talk of Isaac's son, Jacob, and of his many grandchildren next time. We won't find *them* very silent. As a matter of fact, one grandson in particular gets into trouble for having too much to say.

VII

THE CONFLICTING LOVES OF JACOB

SAMUEL: Mark, I wonder if you agree with me that the person most heavily ladened with love in the Book of Genesis is the third of the Patriarchs, Jacob?

VAN DOREN: Oh, by all means!

SAMUEL: I think of Jacob as a refutation of that antinomian idea that love is the only guide in life, and that it's a trustworthy guide. Jacob was torn by the multiple, conflicting loves of his life, loves that tormented him, led him into error (one might almost say sin) and into tragedy. His love for Rachel was so predominant that he was unjust to Leah. His love for Joseph and Benjamin led him to slight the other sons. Through all of his life, Jacob was, in a sense, a prisoner of love, almost misdirected by it—an illustration that you can't trust love by itself.

VAN DOREN: Jacob is the first of these persons in the Bible of whom you can say that he is represented as having fallen in love. (Isaac before him had simply accepted his bride, "and he loved her," the Bible says, "and GEN. 24:67
. . . was comforted for his mother"—which is quite a different thing.) When Jacob went to Laban's house, at the direction of his father, he already knew that his uncle had daughters, but he had never seen them before and didn't know what he would find. He kissed Rachel, the younger GEN. 29:11
daughter, at their very first meeting, and evidently fell in love with her at that moment. He met Leah, the oldest daughter, but he did not love Leah. Later, when he has twelve sons (not to mention a daughter), he looks at all of his sons, and he is in love with one of them, Joseph. He loves Joseph with a love which is in excess of his parental obligation, and indeed, of many other obligations. We can eventually wonder whether his obvious preference for Joseph was not the first example of that kind of special favoring which can lead to so many ills.

SAMUEL: That leads back to the problem we discussed in our third talk: whether one can love not merely one's neighbor as oneself, but also all men, indiscriminately; and now we're extending that to ask whether or not a parent can even love all his children equally. In the days of polygamy, there certainly was an inclination for preference among one's wives; and now we have two of the three Patriarchs—Isaac and Jacob—showing preference for a particular son. (I exclude Abraham because he obviously loved Ishmael, as well as Isaac, and it was Sarah who forced Ishmael out of the family.) Mark, let's go to the Bible for a description of Jacob's display of favoritism. Here is the passage which opens up the whole subject of a preferential love, a love that is unjust in its way:

GEN. 29:16–19 *Now Laban had two daughters: the name of the elder was Leah, and the name of the younger was Rachel. And Leah's eyes were weak; but Rachel was of beautiful form and fair to look upon. And Jacob loved Rachel; and he said: "I will serve thee seven years for Rachel thy younger daughter." And Laban said: "It is better that I give her to thee, than that I should give her to another man; abide with me."*

Let me interrupt to say what an ungracious reply that was!

VAN DOREN: Yes, yes it was!

SAMUEL: Laban was saying, "Oh, all right—you're a relative, you're better than a stranger; I'll give you a break!" There was coarseness in this man, Laban. The text continues:

GEN. 26:20–22 *And Jacob served seven years for Rachel; and they seemed to him but a few days, for the love he had to her. And Jacob said unto Laban: "Give me my wife, for my days are fulfilled . . ." And Laban gathered together all the men of the place, and made a feast.*

We know what happened after that: in the night, Laban substituted Leah for Rachel, and Jacob didn't know it until the morning. When Jacob complained about the deceit, Laban passed the whole thing off as local custom, extorted a promise from Jacob to serve another seven years for

Rachel, and told him he could marry Rachel the next week. The wedding takes place, and Jacob "loved Rachel more than Leah." Then, the Bible tells us:

> *And the Lord saw that Leah was hated, and He opened her womb; but Rachel was barren.* GEN. 29:31

That was the punishment. Leah conceived, and bore a son, Reuben. Then she bore Simeon, and then Levi, and then Judah. The fantastic thing here is the obstinacy of Jacob's love for Rachel, who is barren; and of his hatred for Leah, who bears him one son after another. In those days—and nowadays, too—to have children, and to them, particularly sons, was the greatest blessing in life. But Jacob *hates* Leah, and goes on loving Rachel! How do you explain that obstinacy?

VAN DOREN: You remarked before that love is not enough, that love even can have something the matter with it if it results in this kind of favoritism. Let me say this: maybe the outstanding fact is not that Jacob loved Rachel, but that he did *not* love Leah; not that he loved Joseph, but that he did not love any of the other eleven sons as much as he loved Joseph. You see, you could put it that way. There was a failure of love towards the other sons, towards Reuben, for example, who took it very hard that he was not loved by his father as much as Joseph was. In his great rewriting of the Joseph story, you'll remember how eloquent Thomas Mann was in his account[32] of Reuben's bitterness and his melancholy, which nearly verged on being a disease. Now, I'm putting it negatively, you might say. Maybe there is not that much love in any man; maybe no man has enough love to distribute it equally with the intensity that was characteristic of Jacob among twelve sons. But I would stick to my theory that love *is* enough. I would merely point out that in this instance, love was lacking in eleven cases—or, if you add Leah, and his daughter, Dinah, and the two maids who were his secondary wives, in fifteen cases.

SAMUEL: Somehow I think that a mother could love her twelve sons equally, and all with an almost infinite amount of love, but it isn't in the father. That's probably a prejudice of mine gained from personal observation, not from any statistical data.

VAN DOREN: There's an interesting question here: it could be that the duty of a parent—if he feels in himself a preference for one child over another, or over several others—is to act as if that were not true.

SAMUEL: Yes, I'm glad you brought that up. I've been waiting to discuss it, and somehow the occasion never presented itself until now. You know, the moralists tell us that if you don't love a person, act toward him *as if you did love him.* Is that possible? Doesn't it lead to a distortion of your behavior? Supposing I detest a certain man; the best thing for me to do, I imagine, is to keep away from him. But everything in religion, certainly in the Bible, warns against this. Proverbs, for example, advises:

PROV. 25:21 *If thine enemy be hungry, give him bread to eat,*
And if he be thirsty, give him water to drink.

In other words, behave toward your enemy as if you loved him. Is that humanly possible? Doesn't it lead, instead, to a man doing violence to his own feelings, and therefore, to an intensification of the hatred?

VAN DOREN: All civilization does violence to our feelings. Civilization is the repression of many desires, emotions, and impulses. If we choose not to be civilized, all right. But we *have* chosen to be civilized, and it means that we do a great many things that we wouldn't do naturally. For instance, say a teacher many, many times would prefer not to go to class. He wakes up in the morning, and he would rather spend the day by himself, doing nothing perhaps, and doing something other than teaching. But the mere act of his going to class as if he wanted to is what makes him a member of society. And by the way, once he gets to class, he may enjoy it after all!

SAMUEL: Here's a very personal question that suddenly occurs to me. I've never been a teacher, in the formal sense that you have been. I've been invited to teach. I made one or two attempts, and discovered that when I taught, I played up to the best of the students, and ignored the poorer students. I was having a good time, and I comforted myself with the thought that if I were to slow down for the sake of the poorer students, I would be doing an injustice to the better ones. What have you done about that problem, which fits in with this topic of favoritism we're dealing with?

VAN DOREN: I did exactly the opposite. I never considered that some students were better than others. It seems to me that the whole policy of a teacher must be to assume equality among his students. To an astonishing extent, they then become equal——

SAMUEL (*interrupting*): Mark, it wouldn't occur to you to mention it, but I will: you have a great reputation as a teacher.[33]

VAN DOREN: Well, if I do have one, it's exactly for that reason. I did not think that I had poor students.

SAMUEL: I don't know. I do a lot of lecturing[34] and I address what I imagine to be the best part of the audience. If the rest don't want to listen, they can go home, and don't have to come again.

VAN DOREN: Yes, but you don't know who those are. I quite agree with you that as you're speaking to a hundred, or five hundred people, you say the best thing you have to say. But I think you must assume they all can understand it.

SAMUEL: No, no, I'm pretty sure that many of them don't.

VAN DOREN: Yes, but you don't know which ones don't.

SAMUEL: That's true, I don't.

VAN DOREN: You don't pick them out beforehand, and say, "I shall disregard you." No, you talk to all as if they were equal. The principle of equality is what makes civilization; it's what makes law. A judge doesn't pretend that he thinks that man *A* is equal to man *B*. He acts as if he *knew* he were, and that is how he proceeds. I think that everything that makes life good, makes life tolerable, comes out of our being willing and able to act as if men were equal.

SAMUEL: If that is the proper point of view—and probably it is—Jacob's actions were not in consonance with it. Apart from the fact that he did love Joseph and Benjamin, the children of Rachel, more than he loved his other children, at the end of his life—in his famous blessing—he shows discrimination. Of course, that deathbed statement is not only a blessing; it's a series of injunctions to his sons to remember what they are. He singles out two sons—Judah and Joseph—for long and eloquent blessings; but in his dying moment, he remembers the evil done by two other sons—Simeon and Levi, who had destroyed the city of Shechem—and he repudiates them:

Simeon and Levi are brethren; GEN. 49:5–7
Weapons and violence their kinship.
Let my soul not come into their council;
Unto their assembly let my glory not be united;
For in their anger they slew men, . . .
Cursed be their anger, for it was fierce,
And their wrath, for it was cruel;
I will divide them in Jacob,
And scatter them in Israel.

It's not a blessing at all. At that last moment in his life, even Benjamin—little Benjamin, the youngest, whose birth brought death to his mother, Rachel—Jacob dismisses with an offhanded and conventional promise of triumph:

GEN. 49:27 *Benjamin is a wolf that raveneth;*
In the morning he devoureth the prey,
And at even he divideth the spoil.

Of the three Patriarchs, indeed, of nearly all the fascinating figures in the Bible, Jacob is the man most dominated by emotion, and least by reason and by a disciplined sense of what he ought to do. Does he ever strike you that way, Mark?

VAN DOREN: Oh, yes! Let me make a distinction between what I suppose any man ought to be—namely, perfect—and what the heroes of stories actually are. We would not have story unless men were imperfect and passionate. Stories are about men who make terrible mistakes, and let their feelings, as we say, control them. The understanding exists in men's minds that their reason, not their feelings, should control them. But actually, in life, it doesn't happen that way: no man keeps a balance between his feeling and his thought. And stories are always about people whose feelings were dominant, and who made gross errors—or maybe beautiful errors—but they were errors. It isn't that I'm making Jacob the subject of a sermon. I'm glad he did just what he did, because the story we have of him is so interesting and reveals so much, and in fact makes it possible to preach a sermon to oneself, if one pleases. Jacob is utterly human in that he has the weakness to which human beings are prey: their feelings can overcome them.

But to go back just for a minute to the subject we touched on, acting *as if* something were true. You cannot conceive of civilization without courtesy, and what is courtesy except the habit that one may form of assuming that all other persons are courteous, too? As far as I know, courtesy consists in nothing except my assuming that you are courteous. I do not say that *I* am a gentleman; I say that *you* are. But let me get away from the personal pronouns, and use *X* and *Y*. *X* assumes courtesy on the part of *Y*, and *Y* may laugh to himself: "Ha, ha, ha, *X* thinks I'm a gentleman! Isn't that a joke!" Well, of course, the joke is on *Y*. *X* is imperturbable. He passes on to the next person, *Z*, and acts as if he thought *Z* were a gentleman, too. Now *X* has trained himself to do that. Maybe his natural observation does not suggest to him that all men are gentlemen, but he doesn't permit himself to make those discriminations.

SAMUEL: There's a very specific series of injunctions to Jews about treating people with courtesy in the *Ethics of the Fathers*. One of those injunctions is: "Receive all men with a cheerful countenance."[35] Treat them with what you've called courtesy. But when you get down to deeper relations, to carrying out the command to love your neighbor as yourself, then you must love all your children equally, presumably at least as you love yourself, and even perhaps *more* than you love yourself. You see the difficulty of it. Probably the greatest appeal in the human sense in the Bible is that men are shown as defective. The Hebrew Bible does not pretend to present a number of utterly stainless and perfect saints.

VAN DOREN: Oh, by no means!

SAMUEL: It shows men struggling with themselves as, in fact, the whole of the Hebrew Bible is the story of the struggle of a people with itself to find its personality, and to crystallize its relationship to cosmic principles, to God, call it whatever you want. This is illustrated over and over again in the behavior of those who are held up as the forebears and the prototypes of the people. We are actually asked to remember that they had weaknesses, and regretted them, and were punished for them. The lesson to us is: study these men who were so much more than you. Learn from them that you have weaknesses, and you must struggle with them.

VAN DOREN: I think that's what I was trying to say. The profound importance of story can be stated very simply as this: it is the record, or the display of weakness and error, from which we ourselves can learn a great deal—not, of course, that we shall not repeat those same weaknesses and errors ourselves. You could not have story about a stick; from the point of view of the artist, a perfect man might seem to be a stick. The people of the Bible are of every kind, and they make every conceivable kind of mistake—and that's why the Bible is such a stupendous book. The people in the Bible are being asked by God all the time to act *as if* they loved Him. He not only tells them to love Him, but He also tells them how to do it: "Keep My commandments. Have no other gods before Me. That is how you should act if you are to prove that you love Me." You know, much of life, maybe 99 and 99/100ths per cent of it is acting like a man. What does it mean when I tell you, "Act like a man"? I don't actually tell you to deceive anybody, do I?

SAMUEL: No.

VAN DOREN: I'm asking you to do the most diffi-thing there is—act like a man.

SAMUEL: There's a confirmation in Jewish tradition about acting "as if" in respect of a man's relations to his wife—and hence to his children. Jewish legends tell that marriages are made in heaven. Shortly before every male child is born, a voice echoes through heaven, saying that such-and-such a woman has been destined for him. God is the great matchmaker; He began with Adam, and has continued ever since. All marriages, according to the legends, are recorded by Elijah the Prophet, and God puts His seal on them. Whatever may be a man's specific feelings about his wife and the children she has borne him, he must be mindful that his marriage was ordained. In the days of polygamy, a man may have felt a preference for one of his wives, but he had to behave as if all his wives were of equal status in his eyes.

VAN DOREN: Yes, behave *as if*. I suppose, from our own point of view, we ought to be thankful that Jacob did show favoritism to Joseph, because if he *had* been able to conceal his love for the boy, we wouldn't have the story which is, I dare say, perhaps the best-known story in Genesis, and we wouldn't have Thomas Mann's great book about it. Joseph was most lovable himself; he was so brilliant, so charming, so beautiful, and so extraordinary a boy that Jacob could not resist showing preference. The favoritism *causes* the story: Joseph is spoiled, he's very proud of his brilliance, and he becomes a showoff. His arrogance takes on such proportions that he's willing to make that unpardonable remark not once but twice to his *see* GEN. 37 brothers: "I dreamed that you bowed down to me." One can't blame the brothers for feeling bitterly about that. But quite apart from any consideration of the justice or injustice of the father's actions, Jacob's utterly human, utterly lovable error of favoritism—if it was an error—caused everything that followed.

SAMUEL: It suddenly occurs to me, Mark: do you ever think of Joseph as a *loving* person?[36]

VAN DOREN: No, he's a person who loved to be loved. He assumed that people loved him.

SAMUEL: Yes, he doesn't show any outgoing love. But here's another question that comes to me: when we moderns talk about love between men and women, we often think about it as an explosive incident in the life of a couple. They meet, they confront each other, and there's a great burst of emotion. That does occur now and again in biblical descriptions of love—sometimes for good, as in the case of Jacob and Rachel; and sometimes for ill. That calls to mind the many love stories outside the Bible—the great love stories: Paolo and Francesca, for example.

VAN DOREN: Tristan and Isolde.

SAMUEL: Romeo and Juliet. And in real life, Héloïse and Abelard. What strikes me is that almost all of these great stories of love are disastrous; but I can think of only a few in the Bible in this category. I mention it now since we're talking about Jacob and his children, because a very bitter love story affects nearly the entire family. It's the story of Dinah, Jacob's only daughter, and what happened to her when she meets Shechem, the son of Hamor.

VAN DOREN: Let's talk about that next time.

SAMUEL: Meanwhile, let's consider this element of love, which nowadays we have made into a specific thing by itself. We speak of love as being the determinant and self-contained—almost self-justifying—element in male-female relations. A man meets a woman; love bursts out; there's the end of it. That's not biblical, is it?

VAN DOREN: No, because the inference, I think, in all biblical discussions is that love between persons is a part of a greater love. As a matter of fact, it is suggested in the Bible, is it not, that Jacob's love of Rachel was not a sin, of course, but was unfortunate to the extent that Jacob loved Rachel *in herself*, rather than in God.

SAMUEL: Now that's it. Incidents like that occur. There was the tragic episode between Judah and his daughter-in-law, Tamar—a moment's passion which, strangely enough, was a love commanded in order that there might be offspring from her. And yet it was an illicit love, which the commentators of the Bible have struggled with to justify. They've told about Judah's reluctance to have this affair with this woman that he didn't know, or at least recognize in her disguise at the time. There was desire, which was wrong in itself; and yet it was part of the Divine Scheme. What is so interesting to me is that the Divine Scheme includes for men things that not only they are reluctant to fulfill, but which, on the surface, it seems wrong for them to fulfill.

VAN DOREN: Yes—as if they could fulfill the entire purpose of the universe through anything they *individually* felt and did. I suppose what we're suggesting all the time, Maurice, as we talk more and more about this subject is that the people of the world are quite right in saying love is what makes the world go round. It is a subject of fundamental importance.

SAMUEL: Ah, but they mean it in another sense.

VAN DOREN: Yes, I know that.

SAMUEL: They don't mean it in the sense that God has instituted, as it were, this emotion as being the *prime mobile* of human relations and of history. They think it's their particular love.

VAN DOREN: That's true.

SAMUEL: It's not *their* love, really; it's the love that is infused into the whole world, and in which they are permitted to participate.

VAN DOREN: Yes, but they might mean all that, too, when they use those words.

VIII
THE TRAGIC LOVERS: DINAH AND SHECHEM

SAMUEL: Mark, one of the most tragic—although rather obscure—love incidents that occurs in the whole range of biblical literature is the story of Dinah, the daughter of Jacob, and Shechem, the son of Hamor, of the city of Shechem. Perhaps it is *the* most tragic love story of all.

VAN DOREN: Is it your impression, Maurice, that not too many people know this story?

SAMUEL: Not too many know it, and I rather think that it's half-suppressed also in the consciousness of people because it does not reflect at all well on the sons of Jacob. In my opinion, and in the opinion of many others, the episode is one of the sins that must be written down to the sons of Jacob. They committed sins, and they're reproved for it. This one in particular makes the chroniclers, the fabulists, and the commentators extremely uncomfortable.

VAN DOREN: Now this is interesting, Maurice. I agree with you, Jacob himself never forgot what his sons Simeon and Levi did in this connection. To him, it was as if *they* had committed a sin. On the other hand, they were avenging what *they* thought was a sin on the part of the prince of Shechem himself!

SAMUEL: Well Mark, let's go through the narrative so as to build up the background for our comments on it. The story begins at the opening of chapter 34 of Genesis:

> *And Dinah the daughter of Leah, whom she had borne unto Jacob, went out to see the daughters of the land. And Shechem the son of Hamor the Hivite, the prince of the land, saw her; and he took her, and lay with her, and humbled her.*

Let me stop for a moment. She "went out to see the daughters of the land"—that is to say, there was contact between the two groups, the sons of Jacob who had arrived recently and had purchased land, and the inhabitants of Shechem. They were on a social footing. Dinah couldn't have gone out otherwise, although the commentators already begin—rather cruelly, I think—to call her a "gadabout," and to blame her for the fact that she went out to visit. In any case, in my view, there was a social relationship.

VAN DOREN: Yes, but notice that social relationship was with the women and the girls.

SAMUEL: Yes. How are we going to interpret the statement that the prince "saw her and took her"? My impression is that they met at some festivity. Thomas Mann's retelling of this story in his *Joseph and His Brothers* describes Shechem's wooing of Dinah very charmingly: he makes the prince fall in love with her, desire her, and open suit for her in marriage. When negotiations break down, Mann has the impatient prince abduct the girl, and in his account, Dinah is not exactly unwilling. I don't get the feeling, either from the biblical account, or from Mann, that Shechem used force. What is your feeling about that?

VAN DOREN: I think he used force, and I'm going not merely by the language I find in translations other than the one you just cited. The King James translation says that he "defiled" her, and a modern translation I've consulted says that he "ravished" her.

SAMUEL: I quoted the English translation of the Hebrew Bible issued in 1917 by The Jewish Publication Society of America. The word there is "humbled,"[37] and my own feeling is that it fits better my conception of the story that Dinah fell in love with him, too.

VAN DOREN: Oh, I'm sure *that's* true. But what makes the story so interesting later on is Shechem's behavior. Evidently his original feeling about her must have been so powerful that it made him forget every scruple he had. He had to have Dinah, as we say nowadays, and I think the meaning of the story lies in the concept of this having been a ravishing; after which, instead of hating his victim, he fell in love with her. Perhaps he had fallen in love with Dinah in the first place.

SAMUEL: I have another interpretation which we'll discuss, but I think we can bring out the various points by disagreeing. The text then goes on:

GEN. 34:3 *And his soul did cleave unto Dinah the daughter of Jacob, . . .*

You agree that there was a deep and genuine love there?

VAN DOREN: Oh, yes!

SAMUEL: The text describes his feelings:

GEN. 34:3–5 *. . . and he loved the damsel, and spoke comfortingly unto the damsel. And Shechem spoke unto his father Hamor, saying: "Get me this damsel to wife." Now Jacob heard that he had defiled Dinah his daughter . . .*

VAN DOREN: There's the word "defiled." Jacob *heard* it.

SAMUEL: Jacob heard that Dinah had been defiled —meaning that Shechem hadn't married her. But Mark, you'll remember that there are two passages in the Hebrew Bible which refer to a situation of this kind; and the writers of the story could have had them in mind. We are told in those passages that if a man entice a virgin that is not betrothed, and lie with her, then he must pay a dowry for her. Deuteronomy says: ". . . She shall be his wife, because he hath humbled her; he may not put her away all his days," that is, he can never divorce her. In other words, it was not a criminal act; the man's action could be immediately redeemed. It's true that in this particular story, Shechem was a Hivite, but he offered to become circumcised, and indeed, all the men of the city consented to the ritual, as the text tells us a bit later on. My interpre-

DEUT. 22:28–29; EXOD. 22:15

GEN. 34:20–24

tation of the word "defiled" here is that an irregularity took place, not a great criminal act.

VAN DOREN: I'm quite willing to grant that. I think we shade it somewhat differently, and I don't want to stick to any one view of it. But I do want to point out that the peculiar and profound interest of this story does attach, for me, to the conception that there was some kind of violence in the beginning. It wasn't an ordinary courtship; it wasn't even perhaps an ordinary seduction. There is something in the story which suggests to me that Shechem "had his way" with Dinah regardless—at the moment—of her will. Now the text says nothing about how Dinah felt about him later on, but I agree with you that she loved him—which again is extraordinary.

SAMUEL: Yes. Let's go back to the story. Shechem has told his father, Hamor, to go to Jacob and arrange the marriage. We must infer that the young man had great influence over his father, or else the father saw that the young man's heart was dead set on the match.

VAN DOREN: Jacob's behavior on first hearing the news might be very important:

> *Now Jacob heard that he had defiled Dinah his daughter; and his sons were with his cattle in the field; and Jacob held his peace until they came.* GEN. 34:5

In other words, whatever Jacob heard had not been such as to make him want to do anything himself *immediately.*

SAMUEL: Which would speak of the interpretation I've just suggested: it was wrong, it was irregular, but it was not an irreparable crime. It could be straightened out according to the law. The later writers—that is, those who set down the books of Exodus and Deuteronomy—assumed that to be the case.

VAN DOREN: Yes, either that, or it could mean that Jacob, whatever his intentions, decided to wait for his sons to return, because if any action were to be taken, it would be taken by them, rather than by him.

SAMUEL: Then we read:

GEN. 34:7–10

And the sons of Jacob came in from the field when they heard it; and the men were grieved, and they were very wroth, because he [Shechem] had wrought a vile deed. . . . And Hamor spoke with them, saying: "The soul of my son Shechem longeth for your daughter. I pray you give her unto him to wife. And make ye marriages with us. . . . And ye shall dwell with us; and the land shall be before you; dwell and trade ye therein, and get you possessions therein."

The story is one of apparent genuine intermingling. The man saw almost nothing wrong in it. And there was the chance for a coming together of these peoples.

VAN DOREN: Notice, Maurice, how very much Shechem *did* love Dinah, because at this point, he takes up the appeal and makes his own plea:

GEN. 34:11–12

And Shechem said unto her father and unto her brethren: "Let me find favour in your eyes, and what ye shall say unto me I will give. Ask me never so much dowry and gift, and I will give according as ye shall say unto me; but give me the damsel to wife."

The young man is saying, "I will give *anything* for Dinah! Anything at all, I will give!"

SAMUEL: That's a very powerful passage. You see a man pleading; he's completely at the mercy of his love for Dinah, and ready to make any sort of concession. Then we read how the brothers respond:

> *And the sons of Jacob answered Shechem and Hamor his father with guile, and spoke, because he had defiled Dinah their sister, and said unto them: "We cannot do this thing, to give our sister to one that is uncircumcised, . . . Only on this condition will we consent unto you: . . . that every male of you be circumcised, . . ."* GEN. 34:13–16

It's all "with guile"! At this particular point, they have done something dreadful: they use the ritual of circumcision for their own evil purposes. They want to weaken the city. When the prince agrees to this condition, and he and all the men of Shechem have submitted to the ritual, and are "in pain" and vulnerable, then Simeon and Levi descend on the city, sack it, destroy it, and kill all the males.

VAN DOREN: Here's the full statement of what they did:

> *. . . Simeon and Levi, Dinah's brethren, took each man his sword, and came upon the city unawares, and slew all the males. And they slew Hamor and Shechem . . . and took Dinah out of Shechem's house, and went forth. The sons of Jacob came upon the slain, and spoiled the city, because they had defiled their sister. They took their flocks and their herds and their* GEN. 34:25–29

> *asses, and that which was in the city and that which was in the field; and all their wealth, and all their little ones and their wives, took they captive and spoiled, even all that was in the house.*

It was a complete conquest.

SAMUEL: Yes, it was a terrible thing. Thomas Mann, when he expands this story, goes so far as to suggest that the unfortunate incident concerning Dinah was practically a pretext in the minds of these young men. They had already thought about plundering the city before the abduction. They were still young; they were in their teens, and they were wild. Immediately after their ghastly deed, Jacob orders the household to move away from the scene and, deeply grieved, he tells his sons and the entire house-
GEN. 35:2 hold: "Put away the strange gods that are among you"—
by which he no doubt meant not only the actual teraphim and figurines, but also—more importantly—their false ideas, and the contradiction between their outlook and his outlook. This is the way Thomas Mann describes the sons of Jacob at the time of the Dinah episode:

> *Shepherds and sons of the steppe they were, running almost wild since infancy; ready with bow and knife, used to encounters with lions and wild bulls and also to wholesale brawling with strange herdsmen over pasture rights. Very little of Jacob's mild and pensive piety had come down to them—their concerns were strictly practical, their minds full of the youthful spirit of defiance which forever looks for insults and seeks out quarrels. They were arrogantly proud of their race, though knowing naught of the spiritual nobility upon which its true greatness rested.*[38]

VAN DOREN: That's a very fine statement, and you know, it reminds me once more of the unspeakable importance of the Patriarchs. Just as these sons of Jacob did not understand what Jacob understood—his relationship to God, his election to carry on the great line—so even his son Joseph never quite understood, either. You remember, Mann also points out that for all of Joseph's brilliance, for all of his peculiar power to understand what most people do not understand, even Joseph never participated in his father's simple and deep vision.

SAMUEL: Mann's passage throws me back on the thought that there have been many Jews—then and now—who have been arrogantly proud of being Jewish, without knowing anything about the spiritual grandeur upon which the heritage rested. It's a reminder to the Jews that comes from a lover of the Bible, and a lover of the Jews—a reminder which is very well taken, at least by me.

VAN DOREN: And this is true of all peoples. There is no people that doesn't have members who fail to understand the true distinction of their own people, who are unfamiliar with their own tradition. When we wince at the behavior of Americans abroad, perhaps what really disturbs us is that these Americans do not understand all that an American can be. It can be true of Englishmen, or Frenchmen, or anyone else. It used to be true of Greeks, I dare say. Whatever Greece most profoundly meant was not always understood by every Greek.

SAMUEL: And by the Greek travelers abroad. Yes, I suppose this is universal. Did the pompous Englishman of the Victorian era understand the glory of England; or does the unthinking American of our day remember what America stands for? But let's get back to Dinah.

VAN DOREN: Maurice, notice how Jacob speaks to Simeon and Levi after they have destroyed Shechem. He doesn't speak to them in terms of some violation they have done to the proper meaning of their spiritual heritage. He talks, instead, in terms of the danger they may have brought down upon the family:

GEN. 34:30–31 *Ye have troubled me, to make me odious unto the inhabitants of the land, even unto the Canaanites and the Perizzites; and I being few in number, they will gather themselves together against me and smite me; and I shall be destroyed, I and my house.*

To which Simeon and Levi make a very simple answer, which ends the story, as far as it goes here:

And they said: "Should one deal with our sister as with a harlot?"

SAMUEL: Thomas Mann implies that Jacob knew he couldn't talk to these fellows on the level that would represent his outlook. When they use those words, "Should one deal with our sister as with a harlot?" Mann makes Jacob scream in a quite un-Jacobean fashion, "Yes! Rather that than endanger our lives and the blessing!" He can't *get* at them, he's unable to penetrate to them. He despairs of them, and he carries his bitter memory of their action until his dying day. In our last talk, we mentioned that scene in Egypt, when at the very end of his life, Jacob portions out the destiny of all his sons who are gathered about his bedside. He reserves his harshest words for Simeon and Levi:

Cursed be their anger, for it was fierce, GEN. 49:7
And their wrath, for it was cruel;
I will divide them in Jacob,
And scatter them in Israel.

That sounds almost hopeless. He divides and scatters their tribes: Levi never got a territory when the people returned from Egypt, and Simeon got only a part of Judah's territory.

Now that we've rehearsed this incident, Mark, you've dealt with a number of these biblical personalities and incidents—permit me to say it to your face—in some fine and lovely poems years ago. You have one on Dinah, which is a particularly apt recapitulation of the story. Won't you read it, Mark?

VAN DOREN: Yes, I'd like to, and thank you for speaking of it. I wrote this poem and others on the Bible in the early 1950s, and even before, because I was interested, and even troubled, by a fact which you and I have often mentioned in our talks: the narratives in the Bible are so brief as to be tantalizing. For instance, what struck me as I was reading chapter 34 of Genesis was this: nothing, or almost nothing, is said about Dinah herself. We hear about Jacob and his sons, and about Shechem and his view of Dinah, whatever it was, and his action toward her, whatever that was—and you and I have somewhat disagreed in our interpretations. But nothing whatever is said about Dinah herself. I think I wanted to assume, as I wrote this poem, that Dinah was in love with Shechem, too, once this thing—whatever it was—had happened, although the poem doesn't much more than raise that question. It goes this way:

DINAH[39]

For Dinah ravished, all of Shechem's city
Paid with all its blood. Shechem's, too,
Its chiefest prince, who longed for Dinah so—
To keep her, whom he ravished—he could smell
No craft in Dinah's brothers till they smote
And smote, and every house, red with the horror,
Died; even Shechem's, where in silence
Dinah sat. But her they rescued. And
She wept. Was it for joy? Or walking slow,
Did Dinah weep for justice—all the blood
Of all that lover's people drying now
In sunless rooms behind her? Did she turn
And look, and was it well that Shechem's face
No longer hoped for kindness in these eyes?
For afterward-consent? Shechem's hands—
Did Dinah shudder? Nothing tells of this,
Or anything she thought that bloody day
Her brothers bore her home, and she could hear
The captive herds about her—all the sheep,
Bewildered, and the beaten asses braying.

SAMUEL: I think it's very moving. That poem does assume more or less that there was violence at the beginning, that she was taken against her will—although you do leave it open with a subdued query. Perhaps it might have been otherwise. But you know, the legends of the Jews about Dinah are very confused, as though the commentators didn't quite know what to make of this incident. One legend tells that she married her own brother Simeon (although marriages between brother and sister were impermissible); and another legend says that Dinah was married to Job.[40]

VAN DOREN: Oh *no*!

SAMUEL: One legend about Job makes him the grandson of Esau, Jacob's brother. Esau married before that episode of the blessing, you'll remember, before the time Isaac told Jacob to go and find a wife in the home of his uncle Laban. If you accept the premise of this legend, the time factor could make Job and Dinah contemporaries. But there would be something strange about that marriage: a woman who had gone through this harrowing and crushing experience, herself to become the wife of a man who is the symbol for all the Western world of the patient and the suffering. Dinah would make a companion for Job.

VAN DOREN: Well, Maurice, do you agree with the poem—and therefore with me—in supposing that Dinah's own response to Shechem was somehow at last favorable? Or do you think it's necessary to assume it?

SAMUEL: The poem justifies itself. It's there, complete in itself. If you ask me, as it were, outside of the poem, how do I envision it—who knows what actually took place?

VAN DOREN: Of course.

SAMUEL: All the interpretations are useful, inasmuch as they lead us to consider the human motives and the human actions. I'm inclined to the view that this was a very miserable incident. Here she is, one girl among twelve brothers, and in the biblical chronology she is the third youngest in the family (Joseph and Benjamin are the last two to be born). We would presume that Dinah would be the darling of her ten older brothers, and perhaps this was what led to their ferocity. But how much she must have longed for someone to marry! There was only this one family of worshipers of God, so she *had* to marry outside—there was no one else. Then this episode with Shechem, a prince, occurred, and she saw that she was the possible instrument of a great reconciliation between her family and the people among whom they lived. They were willing to undergo the ritual requirement, even though their motive was questionable; certainly it wasn't a genuinely felt spiritual conversion. At any rate, Dinah could have seen herself playing the role of the pacifier, the reconciler of peoples; and there must have been more in her in the way of suffering, and of ultimate love for Shechem than is apparent in the narrative, which suddenly cuts off.

VAN DOREN: What interests me so much about all these narratives is that they are bare; they give only the facts, although granted, some of the facts, even, are difficult to state. But we are face to face always with the question—are we not, Maurice?—of what it means to call these stories "legends." I dare say that neither of us dismisses a thing that has been called a legend—insofar as it *is* a legend—as untrue or unbelievable. On the contrary, a legend is the most believable of all things.

SAMUEL: A legend that has been embedded in a people for centuries isn't, strictly speaking, a legend; it is a historical force. I've long waited for someone to write a history of the Jews in a new spirit—not from the point of view of the credibility or incredibility of the early stories, but rather, from the point of view of the time when these beliefs began to be rooted in the Jews, and therefore, to affect their behavior. With this approach, there would be no question, and no dispute as to whether the stories are true or untrue. But when did the Jews begin to believe these stories passionately, and when did they become factors in the shaping of the lives of the people? I've read quite a number of Jewish histories, from the very famous ones written by Heinrich Graetz and by Simon Dubnow to less illustrious ones; but nowhere do I find Jewish history treated in that fashion, and I'd like to see it done. If there's a historian eavesdropping I give him the suggestion.

VAN DOREN: Well, you know the question of the credibility of legends is in one sense very simple: I tend to believe a legend if it is very interesting to me. I can imagine, for instance, a child who has been spellbound by a fairy story being told, "Why, that's nothing but a fairy story!" What difference would that make to the child? None at all! He would *still* believe it, and as you say, live with it, and be molded by it.

SAMUEL: Yes, it's wrong to be rational too early.

VAN DOREN: That's right—and I dare say it's just as wrong to be rational too late!

IX
THE FRIENDSHIPS OF MEN: SAUL, DAVID, AND JONATHAN

VAN DOREN: We have before us now three fascinating figures: Saul, David and Jonathan. They are the central figures in a set of love stories. The relations of these three men are very complicated; so that this set of love stories might also be called a complex of love relationships. But the love relationships now have nothing but men in view. These are the loves, or the friendships, of men—a special aspect of love which has always interested me very much.

SAMUEL: There can be in purely masculine love jealousies and affinities; there can be torment in it, and I'm not speaking here of any kind of deviant, or any rubbish like that, that some people have rather hideously tried to inject into the story of David and Jonathan. There can be a lifelong struggle between men for the possession of each other's friendship. The case of David and Saul, particularly, is one of the most unhappy in world literature and even beyond that, in human memory. For me, and I know for you, too, their story has become a symbol of a tormented love. David and Saul loved each other, and I won't say hated, but had hostilities and repellent emotions towards each other as well.

VAN DOREN: Yes, and there's something about the whole relationship between King Saul and David which teases us as we attempt to understand it. I think the Bible is never anywhere more subtle in its narrative portions than in this portion which deals with Saul's jealousy of David, if that's what the emotion is. One is not quite willing, I think, to leave it with jealousy. There is an element of anger: Saul feels anger toward David, and it isn't simple brute anger. In both cases there is love. But David has fear of Saul, too, and he can be angry as well. I think David doesn't need to be jealous of Saul, but he could be outraged by him. The relation seems to change every minute; from one verse to the next, we have a new view. It's like changeable silk. I can understand very well why Robert Browning should have been moved to write that long and very interesting poem "Saul."

SAMUEL: Mark, have you ever considered how Saul, being the first king of the Israelites, began his rule under a cloud? You remember that speech made by Samuel the prophet when they asked him for a king.

VAN DOREN: Oh, yes!

SAMUEL: They wanted to be like all the other peoples, and Samuel made a very famous declaration to them warning them about what a king would be and would do. Saul must have heard about that warning, and therefore he began his reign under the cloud of being that which Samuel had *not* wanted, and which God had finally granted, as it were, almost against the Divine Will. Here is part of Samuel's warning:

I SAM. 8:11–18

> *. . . This will be the manner of the king that shall reign over you: he will take your sons . . . for his chariots, and to be his horsemen. . . . And he will appoint them unto him . . . to plow his ground, and to reap his harvest, and to make his instruments of war. . . . And he will take your daughters to be perfumers, and to be cooks, and to be bakers. And he will take your fields, and your vineyards, and your olive-yards, even the best of them, and give them to his servants. And he will take your men-servants, and your maid-servants, and your goodliest young men, and your asses, and put them to his work. . . . And ye shall cry out in that day because of your king whom ye shall have chosen . . . and the Lord will not answer you. . . .*

This must have been heavy in Saul's mind when he began the reign. Once he had established a royal line, a second king would not be under the same handicap, would not be carrying the burden of this denunciation. Saul began his rule—to put it colloquially—with a jinx on him. He must have been heavy-hearted when he was anointed, and must have said to himself, "So *I'm* the man that Samuel has been talking about! This is what the people will expect of me."

VAN DOREN: Samuel was warning the people against the institution of a monarchy, and particularly against the elevation of those oriental potentates. He was trying to give them a taste of what they would get; kings riding around in chariots, with great banners flying, who would assemble armies and take censuses of them, and brag about how many foot-soldiers and horsemen there were. Samuel was "displeased" about the people's demand for a king. When he was pressed, he unwillingly broached the matter to God. God told him that the people already had a king, namely God himself, and that he should "earnestly forewarn" the people about what they were in for if they persisted in their demand.

SAMUEL: The warning didn't do any good. The people refused to listen, as the Bible tells us:

> *But the people refused to hearken unto the voice of Samuel, and they said: "Nay; but there shall be a king over us; that we also may be like all the nations. . . ." And Samuel heard all the words of the people, and he spoke them in the ears of the Lord. And the Lord said to Samuel: "Hearken unto their voice, and make them a king."* I SAM. 8:19–22

It's almost a grudging concession to the popular demand. It wasn't done with that magnificent Divine generosity with which He gave them the Torah.

VAN DOREN: It's almost as if He were saying: "If you insist upon having a king, you may have one, although it can destroy you." It's as if God knew that; and in some sense, I dare say He did, because the deepest troubles of the people came after the three tolerable kings: Saul, David, and Solomon.

SAMUEL: After that, it was almost continual descent, with occasional restorations, as in the case of King Josiah and others, but the kingship was not a happy episode. Saul, the first king, begins to rule under inauspicious circumstances, and soon there appears this young man, David, who obviously—we can glimpse from the narrative—is more fitted to be a king than Saul. David has grace, power, and manifold abilities: he's a singer, a fighter, and apparently an administrator, too, because when Saul
I SAM. 18:5 sends him out on assignments, David has "good success" and the people love him. Saul himself is deeply, and one might almost say passionately, attracted to David, and we can imagine him sitting on his throne thinking to himself, "There is the *real* king, and what's going to happen to me and my line?" It's somewhat like Macbeth thinking of being king, but fearful that the line will descend through Banquo. Saul is fascinated by David; he can't help but admire him, he is soothed by David's music; and yet he begins to eye him in anger and in dread. There's an ambivalence all through the whole of the tempestuous relationship between them.

VAN DOREN: Of course, Maurice, Saul is picked by Samuel in the very beginning for a rather doubtful reason.
I SAM. 9:2 son. Saul "from his shoulders and upward . . . was higher than any of the people." Now it happens that Abraham Lincoln, who was a great president, was head and shoulders taller than most of the men about him, but that isn't why we call Lincoln a great man. Height has nothing to do with greatness.

SAMUEL: Yes, it reminds me of the somewhat sardonic or slightly ironic situation that's so often referred

to: a man goes out to look for his father's lost asses, and I SAM. 9:3
he finds a kingdom! There is something already not consonant with a great destiny in that sort of accidental and trivial circumstance.

VAN DOREN: To me, there is something terribly touching about the calling of Saul to this great office, of course to his surprise. He started out one day to search for the lost asses of his father, and suddenly he is called to this office which, I dare say, he didn't understand. The first few trials of him by Samuel don't turn out well. (Samuel as judge remains somehow—at least in the beginning, before he began to fear Saul—over the king, just as a counselor or a constitution can be over a king.) Saul is always making blunders in those trials, always misunderstanding. In one incident, Saul is in Gilgal, awaiting the I SAM. 13:8–14
arrival of Samuel in order to perform a certain sacrifice. Samuel fixed an appointment, and Saul waits and waits for him, and finally, when Samuel has still not arrived, Saul performs the sacrifice himself. As soon as he's finished, Samuel arrives, and says, "What have you done? *I* was supposed to offer the sacrifice. You shall be punished for this."

SAMUEL: It seems terribly unjust. There's a disproportion there between the action and the punishment. But it fits in with the unhappiness of all his career, and also with his vacillating character. There are some very marked differences between Saul and David. Saul is drawn into a prophetic frenzy at least twice in his life, and on
these two occasions, the people asked, almost derisively, I SAM. 10:11–12;
"Is Saul also among the prophets?" The saying became a 19:24
proverb. But when David danced before the Ark, there II SAM. 6:16

was something very exalted and inspiring about it, and nobody was derisive except Michal—but we shall talk about her later. To come back to the relationship between Saul and David, Saul evidently got much happiness and relief from David's music; but on two occasions, while
I SAM. 18:11; David was playing to him, Saul tried to kill him in a sud-
19:10 den convulsive fit of hatred.

VAN DOREN: We're not to understand at all, are we, that Saul had asked David to come and play for him just so that he could have him as a target?

SAMUEL: No, no! The deep love Saul has for David, and David has for Saul, comes out in two very moving passages, both of which describe episodes in which David spared Saul's life during the king's pursuit of him. David was able, in both instances, to reproach Saul for the sin of his enmity, and in both instances, Saul expressed
I SAM. 24 himself with the utmost tenderness. In the first episode, David and his men are hiding from Saul and his army deep inside a cave at En-gedi. Saul comes in, alone, David recognizes him, and cuts off a bit of the king's tunic. Instantly David feels shame, and he runs after Saul and prostrates himself: "Why do you pursue me?" David asks. "I could have killed you, but I will not put forth my hand against my lord." Then we read:

I SAM. 24:17–18 *And it came to pass, when David had made an end to speaking these words unto Saul, that Saul said: "Is this thy voice, my son David?" And Saul lifted up his voice, and wept. And he said to David: "Thou art more righteous than I; for thou hast rendered unto me good, whereas I have rendered unto thee evil."*

On the second occasion, David and his men come upon Saul and his army at night, when the king and his whole camp are sleeping. David goes down and steals Saul's spear, which is stuck in the ground at the king's head, and a cruse of water near the king. Then David goes up to a mountain overlooking the camp, and after shouting to awaken the king's men, he asks the same question: "Why do you pursue me?" And Saul answers:

> *"I have sinned; return, my son David; for I will no more do thee harm, because my life was precious in thine eyes this day; behold, I have played the fool and erred exceedingly."* I SAM. 26:21

David didn't return. He knew that the situation between them was hopeless, and it must have been aggravated, too, by the relationship of the children of Saul to their father: Michal, Saul's daughter and David's wife, who defied her father and saved the life of David; and then Jonathan, Saul's son, whose soul "was knit with the soul of David." Saul must have felt very bitterly towards Jonathan especially. He had to remind him:

> *"Thou son of perverse rebellion, do not I know that thou hast chosen the son of Jesse . . . ? For as long as the son of Jesse liveth upon the earth, thou shalt not be established, nor thy kingdom. . . ."* I SAM. 20:30–31

VAN DOREN: The seeds of jealousy were very deeply planted in the soul of Saul, and they grew; and the reason the story moves me so much is that it's so easy to understand why they might grow. But what moves me most of all is the fact that Saul continues to love David, and to admire his genius—even though he knows that he will lose everything to David in the end. If Saul had been nothing but a man head and shoulders taller than others, if he had been nothing but a gigantic Israelite——

SAMUEL (*interrupting*): An Israelite Goliath.

VAN DOREN:——If he had been nothing but that, nothing but ambitious or arrogant, he would not have been able to say these piercingly tender things that you've just now cited. He would not have been able to admit that he himself had been evil, and David had been good. No, there is a mixture in him at all times, and you never know which feeling is going to be uppermost, what he is going to remember, or what he is going to forget. I think that is why the story is so great. It is like all great love stories, for that matter, because all great love stories, surely—or all great loves—go in and out of understanding and misunderstanding.

SAMUEL: Yes, but the exception that I would make to that is the relationship between David and Jonathan. There doesn't seem to have been a single blemish, a single retreat from the intimacy and the love that they enjoyed. What is peculiarly striking about that relationship—and must have at moments been gall to the father—is the suddenness of it. There is such a thing, I suppose, as sudden friendship, as there is love at first sight. Here we have friendship at first sight.

VAN DOREN: Oh, by all means.

SAMUEL: And it wasn't perhaps at first sight that Jonathan loved David. Just after David has killed Goliath and has gone to tell Saul who he is (the king has one of his dreadful fits of amnesia and can't identify David, even though he had a long conversation with him before David fought Goliath), we read:

> *And it came to pass, when he [David] had made an end to speaking unto Saul, that the soul of Jonathan was knit with the soul of David, and Jonathan loved him as his own soul. . . . Then Jonathan made a covenant with David, because he loved him as his own soul. And Jonathan stripped himself of the robe that was upon him, and gave it to David, and his apparel, even to his sword, and to his bow, and to his girdle.* I SAM. 18:1–4

If Saul wasn't present at that moment, then it was certainly told him how his own son had abdicated his heirship in advance, and had passed it on to David. And by the way, "Jonathan loved him as his own soul": here's a pure instance of "Thou shalt love thy neighbor as thyself." It's a love that is steadfast and it never wavers. From the beginning, you have the feeling that no shadow will ever come between them.

VAN DOREN: One thing that favored the purity of the love of these two men—and by purity I mean the unbreakable nature of it—was that they were both young, both contemporaries. The relation between Saul and David was that between an older and a younger man, between a king, if you please, and a subject, even though an anointed subject; and that meant that there was a lack of equality between them of a sort that might endanger their relation. But between David and Jonathan, who are both young, possibly exactly the same age, there was at least an equality of age. I've always remembered Aristotle's analysis of friendship: he says that it cannot be real unless the status of the two friends is the status of equality. A difference in age, in rank, in wealth—anything that gives either of the friends an advantage over the other—tends to deprive the friendship of its perfection. As a matter of fact, Aristotle's analysis becomes so fine that you wonder whether two friends could ever truly exist. But David and Jonathan did have such a friendship, and David mourns Jonathan's death in a very famous lament.

SAMUEL: Yes, but in that same lament, David also expresses his love for Saul and his sorrow over *his* death, too. He loved Saul deeply.

VAN DOREN: Yes, very deeply. David utters the lament when word comes that both Saul and Jonathan have been slaughtered on Mount Gilboa in a battle with the Amalekites:

II SAM. 1:19–27

Thy beauty, O Israel, upon thy high places is slain!
How are the mighty fallen!

Tell it not in Gath,
Publish it not in the streets of Ashkelon;
Lest the daughters of the Philistines rejoice,
Lest the daughters of the uncircumcised triumph.
Ye mountains of Gilboa,
Let there be no dew nor rain upon you,
Neither fields of choice fruits;
For there the shield of the mighty was vilely cast away,
The shield of Saul, not anointed with oil.
From the blood of the slain, from the fat of the mighty,
The bow of Jonathan turned not back,
And the sword of Saul returned not empty.
Saul and Jonathan, the lovely and the pleasant
In their lives, even in their death they were not divided;
They were swifter than eagles,
They were stronger than lions.

Ye daughters of Israel, weep over Saul,
Who clothed you in scarlet, with other delights,
Who put ornaments of gold upon your apparel.
How are the mighty fallen in the midst of the battle!

Jonathan upon thy high places is slain!
I am distressed for thee, my brother Jonathan;
Very pleasant hast thou been unto me;
Wonderful was thy love to me;
Passing the love of women.
How are the mighty fallen,
And the weapons of war perished!

SAMUEL: One would say, reading that passage, that it becomes quite credible that the greatest psalms were written by David. People challenge it, and say that they were written much later than David's time. They may have historical arguments on their side, but they haven't got the spiritual argument on their side. I would say that here David set the pattern for threnody and praise, and for words that reach very deep into the heart.

Jonathan has always attracted me enormously for his modesty, and for his completely ungrudging surrender of the privileges he might have enjoyed. At one point, when David is in flight from Saul, Jonathan goes to meet his friend secretly, and he tells David: ". . . thou shalt I SAM. 23:17
be king over Israel, and I shall be next unto thee." That wasn't said out of ambition, as we today might say, "I want to be your right-hand man." He meant simply, "I want to be near you. Don't drive me away when you become king." And something of the sweetness of Jonathan comes through in another connection, in the battle with the Philistines. In our fifth talk, you'll remember that story about the brutal attitude of Torquatus, who actually sentenced his son to death for a breach of discipline. Now Saul

I SAM. 14:24–45 is ready to do that, too. He had ordered the people to fast on a certain day when they were going out to fight the Philistines. Jonathan hadn't heard about it, and with the tip of his rod he dipped into a honeycomb, and he got a taste of honey. Saul heard about it, and was ready to put him to death. But the people refused to allow it. "Shall Jonathan die? Far from it; as the Lord liveth, there shall not one hair of his head fall to the ground," they told Saul. Obviously, Jonathan must have been very deeply loved. As a matter of fact, Jonathan is shown in this particular battle as being very valiant. There's something in Jonathan almost of medieval knighthood.

VAN DOREN: That's right! That's a very fine image!

SAMUEL: The touch of the chivalresque!

I SAM. 20:18–42 VAN DOREN: And you'll remember that episode of the arrows, when Jonathan arranges to report to David on whether David should flee or return to the king's household. There's a perfect suggestion of a communication between these two boys.

SAMUEL: And there's something else that has a touch of the romantic about their relationship: the friendship didn't survive into old age because Jonathan died in his youth on Mount Gilboa. Let me interrupt myself: that curse David placed on Gilboa lasted down to very recent times. The peaks of Gilboa remained barren, and swamps covered the flat lands at the foot of it over many centuries until, in the early 1920s, young Jewish pioneers in Palestine (now Israel) determined to redeem the blighted area. In spite of the malarial conditions, they drained the swamps and built two very lovely colonies at the foot of the mountain.[41] It's as though this had been a cursed place, and perhaps that provoked some of this literature.

VAN DOREN: Maurice, let me go back to something you said earlier. The friendship of David and Jonathan was of course a normal friendship of that great sort that can exist between men, and I quite agree with you that there's to be no nonsense spoken about it. The friendship of men can be so deep and lasting that even the wife of one of the men can be jealous. I have known, and I dare say you have known, of a wife who was jealous of her husband's best friend merely because perhaps he could say things to the friend that he could not say to her; or because they like to be together. To be sure, that does not mean that the husband doesn't like to be with his wife, either, but there is something between those two men, some understanding that she does not share. This could be a bitter thing, although the wisest sort of wife, I'm sure, is happy to have her husband possess so good a friend.

SAMUEL: She may be happy that he has such a friend, and at the same time suffer a little from a sense of exclusion, aware that there are areas of her husband's life to which she has no access. Let me go back to what I call that "romantic" notion that Jonathan had to die young. I can't imagine these two men—with David's tempestuous life afterward, and with the punishment he meted out to certain members of the house of Saul—growing old together. Can you?

VAN DOREN: No!

SAMUEL: They have to be young. You find that same characteristic in the case of unhappy loves between man and woman. The perfection of the David-Jonathan friendship lies in the fact that it was never—I put it rather oddly—tainted with old age and any of the grumblings of old age.

VAN DOREN: It's something like the famous friendship between Roland and Oliver, the medieval knights in the *Song of Roland.* The two of them were like David and Jonathan in many respects; and death came early there, too.

SAMUEL: And there's Damon and Pythias, too. The beauty of these friendships is that they set a pattern, and the pattern disappears. You're not told a long, long story as you are in the case of men-and-women love. What you've just said about the relationship between David and Jonathan also gathers force from the fact that David was a great lover of women.

VAN DOREN: Oh, yes!

SAMUEL: David, and *not* Solomon was the great lover, in spite of The Song of Songs that we shall talk about later. As an offset to David and Jonathan, let's talk about David and his wives in our next conversation.

X

DAVID, THE UNIVERSAL MAN OF THE BIBLE

VAN DOREN: The time has come—and I for one have been looking forward to it—to discuss that person of the Bible about whom more love stories are told, I believe, than about any other, namely, King David. He was a lover of God, first and last, and such a pure and profound lover of God that God always returned that love without question, although David sinned and had to win forgiveness. David not only loved God, however: he loved women and his sons. He had a number of wives; the Bible gives us several love stories concerning some of them, and each story is of the greatest and deepest interest. Then, of course, there is that archetypal father-and-son love which David had for Absalom. Do you agree that David is the prime lover of the Bible?

SAMUEL: He's not only that, Mark, but there's something about David that makes me think of that phrase we use of Leonardo da Vinci, the *uomo universale*; David is the most universal man in the Bible. He was, as you said, many things: fighter, friend, lover, singer, man of God, and an altogether tempestuous character; and in each of these capacities, he was archetypal, outstanding, unique. Here's a man who could present himself in a duality many times, whereas certain other personalities famous in literature and legend—Paolo and Francesca, Damon and Pythias, Tristan and Iseult—are exhausted by a single linking. They have one relationship, and that's all. But we have in David a great many universal phrases: David and Bathsheba, David and Jonathan, David and Absalom, David and Goliath.

VAN DOREN: Yes, and last time we spoke of David and Saul.

SAMUEL: When you examine David's relationships to his wives, as you said, every one of the important women in his life stands out. Actually, David had eighteen wives and concubines—which is quite a large number, although
I KINGS 11:3 it doesn't begin to compare with the seven hundred wives and three hundred concubines ascribed to his son, Solomon. Solomon's reputation as the great lover of the Bible is founded on this numerical superiority, so to speak; and the fact that he is credited with writing The Song of Songs, although that is a lyrical experience which you think of as having occurred only once in the man's life. But Solomon's loves aren't at all like the loves of David, each one of which is solid and a bedrock experience; around each of them a book can be written.

VAN DOREN: In the case of Solomon, the only woman whose name is connected easily with his is the Queen of Sheba's—and that isn't a love story.

SAMUEL (*laughing*): I wonder what one would call that, since you've mentioned it? It's a sort of minuet,
an intellectual minuet. She comes to find out how wise he I KINGS 10;
is, and he shows off to her. II CHRON. 9

VAN DOREN: She also comes to find out how rich he is!

SAMUEL: Yes! I wonder what she had in mind. None of the great, wonderful riddles that he is supposed to have solved for her is mentioned. Her visit is just a bit of oriental pageantry thrust in, and the story illustrates, really, the difference between the passions of the two men. In Solomon's case, it was decorative rather than fundamental; and in David's case, the feeling goes down deep. You feel the blood boiling in every one of the love incidents in his life.

VAN DOREN: Yes, another way of saying that might be this: David is always *personal* in his love. His love is for a *person*, who for the time being is everything to him. Each one of his principal wives seems to have been that; and maybe several of them were concurrently. But when David loved, he gave all of his love to the person in question. There was Saul, who seemed to hate him, and didn't; there was Jonathan, to whom he was bound in that beautiful relationship; there was Absalom, his son, whom David, according to some, loved excessively. "Excess of love" is difficult to define, because love, I suppose, ideally cannot exist "in excess." But let's consider now, if you please, at least some of David's wives. The stories of just three—Michal, Abigail, and Bathsheba—are very different from one another.

SAMUEL: The one that interests me in a peculiar way is the daughter of Saul, Michal. I always think of her, by the way, by her Hebrew name, which is pronounced *Mee-khál* in English.

VAN DOREN: I dare say; otherwise, people can confuse her with Michael, the archangel.

SAMUEL: Is there any evidence that David loved
I SAM. 18:20 Michal? The story goes that Michal saw him and fell in
love with him. The indication is that she wanted to do
I SAM. 19:11–17 great things for him. She certainly helped to save his life
when Saul was after him: she let him down through a window, and put a figure in his bed to fool her father's men and thus gain time for David's escape. But there's no indication that he was enchanted by her, or loved her. I get the impression that she was the imperious type. She was the princess who was patronizing the shepherd boy who had made such a success at court, and she wanted to play the great role in his life, and it irked him. I don't think there was love on his side for her, and on her part, there was the kind of love that wants to direct somebody else's life.

VAN DOREN: David was eager to marry her, even though nothing is said about any love he may have had for her. When there is talk about the marriage, David seems to be thinking mostly of becoming Saul's son-in-law, rather than Michal's husband. He says: "Who am I that I should be son-in-law to the king?" and "Seemeth it a light thing to be the king's son-in-law, seeing that I am a poor man and lightly esteemed?" And the text says: "It pleased David well to be the king's son-in-law." Later, however, Saul in his anger at David gives Michal to a man named Paltiel. After Saul's death, David sends out an order: "Deliver me my wife Michal." Michal is returned to him. Now he remembered her; she didn't pass out of his mind like something discarded—he wanted her. It could be that he wanted her again only as a piece of property that Saul had deprived him of.

I SAM. 18:17–26

II SAM. 3:14

SAMUEL: It might be more than that.

VAN DOREN: Yes, I think it was more than that.

SAMUEL: I don't mean more than that in any emotional sense, but in the political sense. He may have wanted the daughter of Saul in order to establish his connection with the first dynasty, and to show the world that Saul's daughter was with him. There was a deep cleavage of temperament between them. You remember that when David brought back the Ark up to Jerusalem and danced before it with religious abandon, how she sneered at him, and reproached him for having shown himself off to the servant girls. David retorted bitterly that he would show himself the worshiper of God before everybody, and he put her away; he couldn't stand that bitter sarcasm of hers—she was too aristocratic.

II SAM. 6:20–23

VAN DOREN: After David rebukes her, the text says: "And Michal the daughter of Saul had no child unto the day of her death." That is to say, presumably as a result of this criticism, Michal ceased to be his wife from that point on.

SAMUEL: The legends tell that during the period Michal was the wife of Paltiel, the marriage was never consummated—they slept with a sword between them. I suppose it's an attempt by the commentators to vindicate the purity of her relationship to David.

II SAM. 3:16 VAN DOREN: Of course, let's not forget poor Paltiel. David sent his general, Abner, to bring Michal back from Paltiel. Instead of saying, "Very well, it is the will of David, and I must relinquish her," and instead of closing the door as she left, Paltiel followed after them for a long, long time, weeping all the way. When they got to Bahurim, Abner suddenly turned around to this poor man who hadn't said a word all this time—he just wept in longing—and said abruptly: "Go, return!" The Bible says: "and he returned." That's the last we hear of Paltiel.

SAMUEL: I remember that when we discussed this story before,[42] you thought that I was rather harsh on Paltiel for being (*laughing*) well, they call it in Yiddish, being a *shmate*, just a rag. He should have had the manhood to give her up when he had to, not to go (as I conceive it) sniveling along as if to say, "Aw, please don't do this to me!" until the very last moment, when Abner figuratively gives him a kick, and tells him, "Beat it!"—and Paltiel beats it! You were much more sympathetic toward him than I—and I'm still unsympathetic. I find him a rather paltry character; I don't know why he lingers there, except as some sort of exhibition of the little man pushing his way in among people with whom he doesn't belong—a hanger-on of history.

VAN DOREN: Although his behavior may indicate that Michal was desirable, and that somewhere or other in David's feeling toward her, there was love and desire, I don't know.

But of course, Abigail is another story altogether, isn't it? She was married to the rich farmer, Nabal, and Nabal had insulted David's young men—his band of outlaws hiding out from Saul—who were seeking free provisions. David grew very angry on getting that news; he and his men armed themselves and set out on an expedition against Nabal. I dare say they were going to seize his property and even put him to death. Abigail, on getting the news of this, acted very quickly:

> *Then Abigail made haste, and took two hundred loaves, and two bottles of wine, and five sheep ready dressed, and five measures of parched corn, and a hundred clusters of raisins, and two hundred cakes of figs, and laid them on asses. And she said unto her young men: "Go on before me; behold, I come after you." But she told not her husband Nabal. And it was so, as she rode on her ass, and came down by the covert of the mountain, that, behold, David and his men came down towards her, . . . And when Abigail saw David, she made haste, and alighted from her ass, and fell before David on her face, and bowed down to the ground.* I SAM. 25:18–23

She tells David, in effect: "You must not proceed and commit murder, which I believe you have in mind. I have come, as a matter of fact, to save you from the guilt of murder."

SAMUEL: There's a very high theme in this episode. Abigail tells David that he must not take the law into his own hands. She forecasts a time when he will be the king, and he must not have this stain on his record. The encounter has an aura of great nobility, although, to be sure, there is behind it also the shimmer of a romantic relationship. The setting itself calls for it: here is this lovely woman (the text describes Abigail as "of good understanding and of a beautiful form") come out to warn this young warlord, still an outlaw.

VAN DOREN: He's certainly very handsome himself, we can assume.

I SAM. 17:42 SAMUEL: Yes! The Bible describes him at one point as "ruddy, and of a fair countenance." Apparently that was a rarity among the Israelites of that time. So here is David, surrounded by his band of soldiers of fortune, and this young wife who has rushed to tell him to relinquish the notion of taking revenge on Nabal (whom she calls a "base fellow" and a "churl"!) and of wiping out the whole household. David is in such a fury of resentment against Nabal that he has already said he won't leave a single male alive in that house. They confront each other, David and this handsome, intelligent woman; and in the Jewish legends, there is a hint of the fact that David is very deeply stirred by her, and Abigail is aware of it. In a touch of prophetic foresight, she foresees in a far-off time a day when David would kill for the sake of love. In this first encounter Abigail's is the restraining hand. Altogether, it's a very exalted picture.

VAN DOREN: Yes, I'm sure that just as she was beautiful to him, so he was beautiful to her. David accedes to her request that he desist, and tells her, "You've saved me from blood guilt, and I'm turning back." Abigail goes home, arriving when her husband is giving a great feast and is very, very drunk. She waits until the next morning, "when the wine was gone out of Nabal," to tell him about all that had happened—the danger that he'd been in, how she saved him; and evidently she's so eloquent about it that the *ex post facto* fear kills him: "his heart died within him, and he became as a stone," and ten days later, he dies.

I SAM. 25:37

SAMUEL: It occurs to me that among the other capacities of David, he was a great hater, too. He could love tremendously, and he could hate tremendously. I'm always impressed, in a very depressing way, by the fact that on his deathbed he remembered two men whom he had hated. The first was General Joab, who had killed Prince Absalom, among others. The second was the old man Shimei, the son of Gera. When David was fleeing from Absalom, the old man had cast stones at David and his entourage, and had flung curses at David: "Thou man of blood!" he'd called him, and it was not an unjust appellation: David *had* been a killer. David at the time restrained his men from killing Shimei: "Let him alone, and let him curse," David had said. But on his deathbed, David had a change of heart. The thing rankled, so that in a most unworthy way, David instructed his son Solomon: ". . . bring his hoar head down to the grave with blood."

See I KINGS 2

II SAM. 16:5–13

I KINGS 2:9

I KINGS 2:36 Solomon didn't follow those instructions exactly. He told old Shimei to build a house in Jerusalem, and to stay there. It was a kind of house arrest. Solomon warned Shimei: "If you leave this house, then you'll be put to death." Three years later, two of his servants ran away to Gath, and Shimei made the mistake of going after them. It may have been a pretext, but he was put to death. But as I was saying a moment ago, David's capacity for hating as well as for loving is absolutely extraordinary. He's lying on his deathbed, an old man with all the warmth gone out of him, all passion spent after a tremendous and multi-colored life. Suddenly there boils up in him a recollection of rage! He couldn't resist it; but if you look at him over the span of his entire life, I think the love in him overwhelmed the hatred in him.

VAN DOREN: Yes, now, in the case of Abigail, David—who never forgot anything—remembered *her.* As soon as David learns about the death of Nabal, he sends
I SAM. 25:39–42 for Abigail to come and be his wife. I'm always interested in the fact that the Bible represents her as obeying with complete alacrity: she's been thinking of *him,* too! I'm sure that if the phrase means anything, she fell in love with him in the mountains that day, too, and so instantly she gathers her things and hastens off to marry him. That is about all we hear of her.

SAMUEL: That is something that the rabbis have commented on with disapproval. At the very moment when she's bringing this critical message to David—that he is not to stain his record with shedding the blood of Nabal—she tells him, "When you come into your own," meaning, when you become king, "don't forget me!" The

Rabbis made an adverse comment on it; in their view, she had something in her mind which was unbecoming, and it detracts from the loftiness of her approach to him.

VAN DOREN: I hadn't thought of that. But now we've come to Bathsheba, whose story is the most complicated of all. It involves that complete experience of love at first sight of Bathsheba, when David catches sight of her as she is bathing one evening, and decides that he must have her at all costs—even though one of those costs will be the life of her husband, Uriah the Hittite, whom David secretly puts in the forefront of the hottest battle.

SAMUEL: I'm afraid it's even more discreditable than that, in a way—*in a way*, I say, because David would have been glad to have Uriah think that the child Bathsheba was carrying was *his,* Uriah's. You remember that David sent for Bathsheba while Uriah was off fighting in the army, and she conceived. David then dispatched an order for Uriah to come back to Jerusalem. Uriah returned directly to the palace, and David urged him insistently to go home. But Uriah very nobly refused to go home, saying, "The whole army is encamped in the open field. Shall I go home and be comfortable with my wife? Shall I go home and make love to her?" David sees that he can't get anywhere with him, so he writes a letter to General Joab, ordering that Uriah be set in the forefront of the battle—and he even gives this letter to Uriah, to transmit to Joab! David as the intriguant here is very painful for me to consider. His attempt to manipulate Uriah into a visit home isn't often commented on by the Rabbis because, of course, they were overwhelmed by the dark crime of blood guilt that rested on David. What is interesting to me about the

See II SAM. 11

love story of David and Bathsheba is that it began illicitly and, in the end, it was redeemed. David was denounced by the Prophet Nathan, he suffered his punishment and sincerely repented, and then the love between him and Bathsheba became sanctified to the extent that of Bathsheba was to be born Solomon, in a certain sense the most illustrious king of ancient Israel. The love story is a progression from a sin to punishment, repentence, and redemption.

VAN DOREN: The punishment, by the way, is very acute: the child by their first adultery is not allowed to live. Solomon was the result of their true union later.

SAMUEL: Sometimes I think that the outstanding episode in that relationship—the episode on which the redemption hinges—is the fashion in which David took the rebuke from Nathan. We're speaking here of an absolute monarch. David had no formal or legal restrictions upon his power: he could do whatever he liked. The prophet was attached to the court; he was, if you like, an employee,
II SAM. 12:1–18 a retainer, of David's, and an intimate. The prophet came before him, and in one of the most powerful denunciations that have ever been uttered—it's one of the most powerful passages in the Bible, and that already places it in a class by itself—told him this story of the rich man with great flocks and herds, and the poor man, with only one little ewe lamb. A traveler comes to visit the rich man, and whose lamb is slaughtered to feed him? The poor man's. David flies into a rage against the rich man, and tells Nathan: "That man deserveth to die!" Nathan points the finger of accusation at King David: "Thou art the man!" What is so astounding is that David doesn't strike him

down, doesn't fly into one of his characteristic rages; instead, he cowers away from him, acknowledges that he has sinned, and he listens to the flood of denunciation which pours from the lips of Nathan: that the things David had done in secret would be done to him in the open; that David had taken another man's wife, and now David's wives would be taken in the light of the sun, before all the people; that David had used the sword against Uriah, and now the sword would never depart from his house. All of this pours out in a torrent, and David doesn't strike back! Here is David, the great warrior, ready to go up and kill Nabal and wipe out the household, David who kills two hundred Philistines, instead of one hundred, for the hand of Michal, David who is so explosively ready to sentence the mythical rich man to death—*David stands there and takes it!*

VAN DOREN: Stands there and *listens*! I'd like to say "listens." David years before had stood on the mountain and listened to Abigail. After all, he was a man, among other things, of intellect; and the clearest sign of the presence of intellect in anyone is his power to listen, to receive in his mind something that wasn't there before. You know, the person who can't listen to anything, who can't hear anything, and can't take in any new thing, is, in all people's minds, I think, the very symbol of stupidity. David had listened to Abigail; he had listened to Saul, for that matter; now he listens to Nathan the prophet. And let's remember, too, how he listened to Joab, when Joab reproved him for his overlong (overlong, in Joab's mind!) II SAM. 19:6–9
lamentation over Absalom. At that point, David, feeling as he did, could have risen and had Joab removed.

SAMUEL: Yes!

VAN DOREN: In a sense, David never did forgive Joab, either for that or for killing Absalom. It's curious, this image of David isn't accented. It's a negative thing as far as words go, but I'm not sure but what it's the most powerful thing we ever learn about David: he is sitting in his chamber, after that marvelous outbreak of lamentation for his son, Absalom, weeping in grief, his head bowed, not saying a word, not doing anything, hour after hour. Suddenly Joab comes to him and berates him bitterly, and tells him he's got to stop this behavior. David immediately obeys. He doesn't even say "I heard you," or "Yes," or "No."

SAMUEL: The knowledge, as it were, had ripened in him.

VAN DOREN: That's a sign, isn't it, of very great intelligence?

SAMUEL: Yes, but it's more than intelligence.

VAN DOREN: Yes, I would agree that it's more.

SAMUEL: There's a depth in David which responds at the right moment, just before it's too late. He risked his soul for the sake of Bathsheba, and redeemed it. He risked his kingdom for the sake of Absalom. He knew the kind of young man Absalom was. He could see him preparing this rebellion; and David's weakness for his son, his overweening fondness for him, made him close his eyes to what was a tremendous danger for the kingdom. There's very little doubt that if Absalom had raised the standard of rebellion, the other sons of David would have fought it, and the kingdom would have been rent into pieces long before it actually fell apart. Yet in these movements of his soul, David's capacity for love outran his discretion, outran his duty, outran his sense of justice—but in the end, he was brought 'round. What is so deeply moving about David is the fact that he was capable of these extremities of feeling that were actually sinful in their apparent uncontrollability; but at the last moment, before the irretrievable had been done, he was recalled—in one case by Nathan, in another case by Joab; or they were the instruments of that recall.

VAN DOREN: You know, it's interesting suddenly to me, Maurice, to remember how many love stories we've told in our conversations thus far that were the stories of love on the part of the fathers for their sons: Abraham and Isaac, Isaac and Esau, Jacob and Joseph, and now David and Absalom. The love of a father for a son probably may always exceed the love of a son for the father, the father being older and richer in his experience. I'm not sure but what those are the true archetypal love stories of the Bible.

SAMUEL: It may be. But now that we've brought up Absalom, it reminds me that the Bible has more disastrous love episodes than the one story of Dinah and Shechem we've already discussed. Next time, let's consider these disastrous stories.

XI
FOUR DISASTERS— AND ONE COMEDY

SAMUEL: Do you know, Mark, when we were talking of the calamitous love story of Dinah and Shechem, some lovely lines from Wordsworth[43] kept echoing in the back of my mind: "Old, unhappy far-off things,/ And battles long ago." There *was* an unhappy thing in that story, there *was* a battle—the sacking of the city; and those lines re-echo now when I think of what I've called the "disastrous love episodes" in the Bible that we have before us. All of them have that far-off, melancholic twilight effect of a sadness that can recur, but belongs to a legendary time. Their unhappiness is almost not human; it's like some everlasting dirge of the capacities of human beings for suffering.

VAN DOREN: And the pain that was then undoubtedly felt is not felt now. There is a cushion of time, a chamber, so to speak, through which time brings word of these things, and the cries change to a kind of music. Homer speaks of that somewhere in the *Odyssey*; he mentions tragic events of long ago as things that now give pleasure, when beautifully sung.

SAMUEL: Pleasure—in a way. I'm thinking, for example, of Samson's love for the Philistine women. There is in it a recollection of things that went very badly at a certain time, and yet fitted into a pattern. Now Samson had not one but two disastrous loves: the woman of Timnah, and Delilah. By the way, you've noticed, of course, that most people don't know anything about the woman of Timnah in his life.

VAN DOREN: Yes, even though her story in relation to him is exactly like the story of Delilah in relation to him. Both of them were asked by the enemies of Samson to betray a secret that he had; both persuaded him to reveal the secret so that they could inform his enemies. There's no failure in the parallel.

SAMUEL: Except we remember Delilah because she was, as it were, in at the kill; she was the instrument of the final betrayal which resulted in the capture and the blinding of Samson. As I look back at that story, I see a fascinating element. Samson was ordained to love; he betrayed himself, and that, too, was ordained. He was caught up in historical or in Divine purposes, and wasn't aware of it; while his story was being played out, there was nothing but sorrow and anguish in it. But let's look at the story as the Bible tells it:

JUDG. 14:1–4

And Samson went down to Timnah, and saw a woman in Timnah of the daughters of the Philistines. And he came up, and told his father and his mother, and said: "I have seen a woman in Timnah of the daughters of the Philistines; now therefore get her for me to wife." Then his father and his mother said unto him: "Is there never a woman among the daughters of thy brethren, or among all my people, that thou goest to take a wife of the uncircumcised Philistines?" And Samson said unto his father: "Get her for me; she pleaseth me well." But his father and his mother knew not that it was of the Lord; for He sought an occasion against the Philistines. Now at that time the Philistines had rule over Israel.

VAN DOREN: His father and his mother did not know that "it was of the Lord," and of course, neither did Samson.

SAMUEL: Here is one of the riddles of the Bible. A man is involved in a purpose beyond his seeing, beyond his intentions. His passions are used; he is a pawn in some great—let's say a great chess game, if that isn't derogating from the seriousness of the issue. He is being used: the thing was "of the Lord." You see the imperiousness with which Samson speaks to his parents: "Get her for me!" There's no argument here; he doesn't say, "Well, I've looked for somebody else. You know I've been trying to find a bride among my brethren, but there wasn't anybody who pleased me." He simply says flatly, "Get her for me!" and that's the end of it.

VAN DOREN: You know, Samson, who is visibly the least spiritual and intellectual, I suppose, of all the heroes of the Bible, behaves here just like the young savage which, to all intents and purposes, he was.

SAMUEL: By the way, you've hit on something. The Rabbis and the commentators say that he was among the three least important of the Judges.[44] They do put him on a low level of the men who ruled over and judged Israel in that period; and yet, you see, he was an instrument of God's purpose.

VAN DOREN: In our first talk [*see* pp. 4-5] we had occasion to mention that turbulent period of the Judges. Throughout that whole time, the people were in constant peril from their enemies. Whenever the children of Israel did that which was evil in the sight of the Lord, and He wanted to punish them for their backslidings and their wickedness, He would deliver them over into the hands of the Philistines or the Midianites for seven years or forty years, or whatever. From time to time, after a generation or two, a mighty man of valor—called a "Judge"—would arise among them to save them. God was the punisher, and God was the savior; just as He at certain times allowed the enemies to have their will with the Israelites, so at other times He "raised up" someone to save them. I quite agree with the commentators; Samson is the least distinguished among these persons. He is a man of gigantic strength, he is a person purely primitive, whose passions, as you say, are being used. I dare say that that is the special distinction of his story: he is always being used; he never knows what he's doing.

SAMUEL: There is something more about him: he is aware of something wrong with him once he retires into solitude. Apparently there was a tumult in his soul; all of this was too much for him. It's as though you had taken this primitive—to use your description— and had involved him in matters which were forever beyond the reach of his intelligence. Or he's like a child who is being used by grownups in some immense and far-reaching play of power. Now this woman of Timnah, this wife his parents unwillingly get for him, betrays him. You remember that strange episode of the riddle which he put to the young Philistine men at his wedding feast.

JUDG. 14:8–18 VAN DOREN: He challenged them to answer his riddle within the seven days of his feast, and put a high wager on it. It was an odd riddle, involving a slain lion, a swarm of bees, and honey.

SAMUEL: They accepted his challenge, and of course couldn't solve it. When the seven-day period is about to expire, they threaten Samson's wife to find out the answer or else they'll burn her up, and burn down her father's house. She goes to Samson, and begins to weep and to cajole him for the answer to the riddle—and he gives in and tells her. He's furious when the Philistines come to him with the answer just before his deadline expires, and utters that striking phrase:

JUDG. 14:18 *If ye had not plowed with my heifer,*
Ye had not found out my riddle.

Now, notice how Samson is compelled to do the same thing again with Delilah. This is a form of what they call "dittology" in another sphere of the Bible, dittology, or repetition. If a man is doomed to do a certain thing, he can't struggle against it. Delilah torments him in a much more serious matter, the secret of his strength and of his status as a Nazirite, that is, a man devoted to God. In the first episode with the woman of Timnah, there was bitterness enough to have taught him a lesson. He should have learned from it that the Philistines were ready to betray him and to kill him at any time.

VAN DOREN: And they were willing to use his wife.

SAMUEL: Both wives. The pattern is repeated, and there is the man trapped, as it were, in this compulsion which is not of his own making.

VAN DOREN: Now, of course, whereas the woman of Timnah is simply said to have "pressed him sore," nothing is said about any wiles—she apparently weeps and weeps during their wedding feast, and that's all. But Delilah uses wiles we can easily recognize as such. The text says:

And she made him sleep upon her knees. JUDG. 16:19

His head is on her lap, in other words.

SAMUEL: The legends are very specific about the way she torments him with her caresses, refusing him satisfaction until the man was driven—this is a peculiarly apt phrase—out of his senses. The Bible says, "his soul was vexed unto death," and that's exactly what she did with her maddening, continuous pleadings—drained the life out of him! And he yielded to her. But I say, what has always haunted me about this, and has given sadness to the story is this: a man may have to perform what seems a sin, or do wrong in some way; he is aware of it, and yet he is serving a purpose. That this is "of the Lord" is one of the riddles, the mysteries, of the Bible, as I mentioned. I've asked myself: How are we to understand it? The Bible was edited. We don't know when the parts we now have were actually written. They were collected afterwards and edited in order to serve a moralistic purpose. Sometimes I think to myself that in the editing, the Rabbis had to put in some things which they themselves could not answer. They were stories or passages that had become sacred in the memory of the people; they had become folklore that couldn't be divorced from the national history and the national consciousness. This particular story of Samson remained as a riddle, with which they struggled, but to which they never found a satisfactory answer.

VAN DOREN: In other words, they were stories that could not be suppressed. You know, Maurice, I suddenly think of a parallel in our own life. Secular history tends to be written in the same fashion; that is to say, a great person—a king, a prime minister, a president, a general or the like—is often discussed by historians as if he represented a force, a trend of the times, or a tendency in all history which was working through him, although he is not supposed to understand that altogether. You're aware, aren't you, of how historians may present figures—military, political, or indeed religious—in this way?

SAMUEL: Well, it's almost inevitable. We can't assume that men know completely what they're doing.

They know what they *want* to do, but they can't take account of all the forces which are involved, and the issues which will result from their actions. It's not an unjust way of dealing with these matters, except that a historian, too, may be shortsighted.

VAN DOREN: Of course he may! He may be wrong, too. But he is in effect representing men also as being used —but in this case, being used by history rather than by God.

SAMUEL: You've just said something pregnant with meaning: "by history rather than by God." The distinction of the Bible is: there is no history apart from God.

VAN DOREN: That's true.

SAMUEL: And I suppose that a profound difference between the Jews, looked upon as a people, and other peoples is that the Jews have no history except what happened in their struggle with God. Take American children, and Jewish children in their quality as American citizens. They're learning American history in the public school, and they can say, "This is history." Then, on certain days, at other schools, they learn religion. But among Jewish children, if they are learning their Jewish history, they are learning their religion. They have nothing but a sacred history.

VAN DOREN: That's why I slipped in the word "secular" when I did. Well now, Maurice, let's have another example of a disastrous love. The phrase interests me very much; it was a phrase you yourself proposed.

SAMUEL: I would call Ahab and Jezebel a disastrous love, even though earlier in our talks [*see* pp. 49-51] we were much exercised with the question as to whether "love"—genuine love—could be applied to their relationship. Jezebel is, I suppose, the arch-egotist of the Bible. I don't know of another biblical personality who is so self-centered, and has this ferocity of his or her desires.

VAN DOREN: And ferocity of purpose, which never changes.

SAMUEL: Yes, she is completely unscrupulous, without a sense of inhibition as to the rightness or the wrongness of what she's going to do. Here is this man, Ahab—no great shakes as a moral figure himself; nevertheless, not evil incarnate as she is—letting himself be used by her. She is for me the symbol of the alter egotism of human beings.[45]

VAN DOREN: Ahab, as you say, is of course not a figure of moral stature; nevertheless, he is capable somehow of understanding how much force is hidden in the prophet Elijah, who is the figure who will destroy him. The prophet Elijah, that quiet, excellent man—in whose very quietness and excellence there is a force that never will be in Ahab and Jezebel put together—can terrify Ahab just by appearing from time to time, just by letting Ahab know of his presence and of his intention to come to a certain place. Ahab is capable of hearing; in other words, he's one of those listeners.

SAMUEL: Yes. There is a moment when God expresses His approval, shortly after Elijah had confronted

Ahab in the garden of Naboth (the rightful owner, who had been "framed" and murdered so that Ahab and Jezebel could get possession) and had uttered those three Hebrew words. Unfortunately, in English, they have to be expanded, but in Hebrew, the prophet confronts Ahab with:

> *"Ha-ratzakhta v'gam yarashta?"*[46]*—"Hast thou killed, and also taken possession?"* I KINGS 21:19

Just the uttering of those words—it's like a thunderbolt or a lightning flash! Ahab shrinks back, he goes and puts on sackcloth, and he fasts, and he goes "softly"—he's terrified by what he's done. God says to Elijah: "Seest thou how Ahab humbleth himself before Me?" In other words, "Do you see how Ahab has repented!" Of course, Jezebel could not be reached by anything like that. She reminds me of those people who use love as the pretext for expressing impulses in which they themselves have been frustrated: parents who show off their children as an extension of their own vanity, or who force their children to undertake enterprises which the children are not fit for, saying: "You've got to do thus-and-thus, you've got to be better than I was." What they're doing is *not* expressing love, but their self-love, using somebody else as the instrument, or the mirror, of their self-love. All this is contained for me in the picture of this Jezebel, whose husband, the king of Israel, is her tool for self-aggrandizement. She is going to be the queen—and behind the scenes, the manipulator —of the most powerful man in the kingdom.

I KINGS 21:29

VAN DOREN: Yes, you almost can suppose that it doesn't make any difference for her what her husband's name happens to be, Ahab or something else; her love of the man himself—if it's love at all—is not personal. I can't help thinking in this connection—and I referred to it in our fourth talk, when we first mentioned Jezebel—of the parallel in Lady Macbeth and Macbeth. Macbeth is a man who can be shaken; who, when the witches speak at the beginning of the play, trembles all over, and his heart is too big for his body. It's as if he were dying from anticipation of terror and disaster. And of course we all know how, once he has committed the murder that he should never have tried to commit because it was not in his nature, he is shattered by it, and he goes to pieces scene by scene before our very eyes. Lady Macbeth, at least until the very end, is utterly unperturbed. She has this ferocious singleness of purpose.

SAMUEL: But when she breaks down, it's complete!

VAN DOREN: That's true. There's nothing like that in the case of Jezebel. She never breaks down. Years later, she is killed.

SAMUEL: She's chucked out of the window. That's the first case we have of execution by defenestration.

VAN DOREN: Years after the chief events of their story, Jezebel is there looking out her window, her eyes "painted," and her head "attired"——

SAMUEL: The hideous old harridan, just as fresh in evil as when she was a young woman!

VAN DOREN: ——and Jehu, king of Israel, looks up, sees her at the window, and calls out to his men, who have come up behind her: "Throw her down." They throw her down, and she's eaten by dogs. II KINGS 9:30–37

SAMUEL: Machiavelli has a famous saying that suddenly occurs to me. He warns people: if you're not an evil person, don't try to do evil. If you haven't got the stomach for it, stay good! It's a very wise remark.

VAN DOREN: Have you got another disastrous love affair, Maurice?

SAMUEL: Yes, the love affair—or is it a love affair? —between Amnon, one of David's sons, and Tamar, his half-sister. He violated her, took her against her will; and that affair is all the more incomprehensible to me because Tamar was not averse to him, you'll remember.

VAN DOREN: Oh yes, how could I forget that story?

SAMUEL: It's one of the grim stories of the Bible, and it's made all the grimmer when we speculate on what might have been. When he expresses his passion for her, and shows that he is ready to go to any length to satisfy it, Tamar pleads with him:

> *". . . I pray thee, speak unto the king; for he will not withhold me from thee."* II SAM. 13:13

That's a strange statement, implying that David would allow a marriage between his first-born son, Amnon, whose mother was Ahinoam the Jezreelitess; and a daughter of another of his wives, Maacah. Leviticus 18:11 ap- II SAM. 3:2

pears to prohibit marriages between the children of the same father and different mothers; even so, the legends take the view that Tamar, strictly speaking, wasn't David's daughter.[47] In any case, Tamar's remark at that point leads one to speculate that perhaps there could have been a straightforward love and marriage between them. But Amnon would not listen to reason; his passion swept him on to take her forcibly. Immediately after that scene of violence, the text says:

II SAM. 13:15 *Then Amnon hated her with exceeding great hatred; for the hatred wherewith he hated her was greater than the love wherewith he had loved her. And Amnon said unto her: "Arise, be gone."*

He's finished with her—out! Here's an instance in the Bible of an appetitional frenzy—the *id*, as they call it nowadays in psychoanalysis, taking hold of a man so that he doesn't know what he's doing.

VAN DOREN: Your term "disastrous" fully applies here. Not only is the story itself, the action, dreadful; but the deception, the connivance, the maneuvering are all repugnant. He pretends to be sick, and he insists that he wants no one else other than his half-sister, Tamar, to come and bring him food and wait on him. That seems an innocent desire, and his father David actually orders Tamar to go and serve him—and then that act of force, and suddenly he hates her. (By the way, this is the exact reverse of Shechem's feeling for Dinah after *his* act of violence.) All of these things are disastrous in themselves; but the consequences are terrifyingly calamitous. Absalom, David's third son, and the full brother of Tamar, never forgives
II SAM. 13:23–29 Amnon. He waits two years, hating him all the while, then

arranges to kill him. That, in turn, I've always supposed, somehow leads to the eminence that Absalom attains among his brothers, and among the men of the kingdom. It's his first taste of blood; if you please, his first taste of power.

SAMUEL: It might very well be considered as a contributory factor in the embitterment of Absalom, or the awakening of the lust for power in him. But let me go back to what I was talking about a few minutes ago when I spoke of men apparently being forced to sin in order to fulfill a purpose. You remember, I've already mentioned another Tamar [*see* pp. 105-106] and her illicit relationship with Judah, Jacob's son, her father-in-law. She de- GEN. 38
ceived him into thinking she was a harlot; he was tempted and went with her.

VAN DOREN: She wanted a child by him.

SAMUEL: She got twins. Thomas Mann treats her story in magnificent fashion. He says that Tamar "was bent on pushing herself into the great history, and she did it, with amazing strength of purpose."[48] She felt that Jacob's family carried the religious destiny of the world, and she was determined, at all costs, to be in it. Now the Rabbis are disturbed about this situation; they talk of Judah as being reluctant—he *didn't* want to do this thing, and after he did it, he was contrite. When the woman tempted him, he is supposed to have turned away, and he was actually compelled by an angel sent by God to turn back again![49] This is what he *had* to fulfill! In the Judah-Tamar story again is that riddle coming out from ancient days, and leaving in our minds an echo of situations in which we find ourselves when we have done wrong, and it has turned out well. We've done something against our conscience, and in the end we see that we didn't understand what we were doing—as the contrary, too.

VAN DOREN: Well, you remember that great reconciliation scene betwen Joseph and his brothers, when Joseph identifies himself and the brothers are speechless with
GEN. 45 fright. Joseph says, "Don't be frightened or angry with yourselves that you sold me. God sent me before you to preserve life, to save you." That whole story was "of the Lord." Yes, that theme is always coming through. There are various names for it; for example, it has been called "Providence."

SAMUEL: Let me interrupt, Mark. It suddenly occurs to me: perhaps when a man repents for a wrong that he's done, he should also pray, "Maybe it served a purpose that I didn't know. I was wrong, but I pray that good will come out of it, even though I mustn't forgive myself for it."

VAN DOREN: By the way, "providence" means, etymologically, "foreseeing," doesn't it? "Seeing beforehand."

SAMUEL: Yes.

VAN DOREN: In other words, it is assumed that there is One who foreseees the consequences of all acts; although, as you yourself said a few moments ago, perhaps no man ever knows all that is involved in any of his own actions. No man, in other words, completely knows what he is doing.

SAMUEL: You know, Mark, this conversation has rather depressed me, thinking of all these disastrous stories! I'd like to wind up on a lighter note. You're aware, of course, that there's a ridiculous love story in the Bible, too.

VAN DOREN: What's that?

SAMUEL: The story of the love of Ahasuerus for Esther. There's something quite ridiculous about it.

VAN DOREN: How is that ridiculous?

SAMUEL: It's ridiculous because of the circumstances under which he chooses her. He gets drunk at a banquet, and asks his wife, Vashti, to come and show herself in all her beauty, and she refuses. He flies into a rage, and then he starts looking for a replacement. The way he does it is to send out messengers to all his 127 provinces: "Find me the nicest girls!" They're to be brought to him, and they're perfumed, and they're rubbed with oils; and he's got to see every one of them! Suppose there were, say, *two* from each province. So he's got to examine . . .

ESTHER 1:10–12

VAN DOREN: Two hundred and fifty-four.

(*laughter*)

SAMUEL: Thank you! He's got to decide from at least two hundred and fifty-four, and finally he picks out

Esther. It's a ridiculous story! The Rabbis actually say that Esther never consummated the marriage with him. They call him "the fool king," the *melekh tipesh*—he's a fool of a man.

VAN DOREN: Although once more, maybe in a somewhat grotesque context, the same thing happens, doesn't it? That is to say, Esther's adventure is one of the ways in which once more the people are saved.

SAMUEL: Yes, that is the great role which she plays. The Book of Esther, by the way, was looked on with suspicion by the Rabbis. They were of half a mind to keep it out of the Bible. The name of God isn't mentioned in it once, even though a good many passages in the text seem to demand it. Well, I'm glad we've got through this subject—disastrous loves—which I had to bring up.

VAN DOREN: Well, it was your subject.

SAMUEL: Yes, it was. As we draw toward the end of our conversations, let's talk about some very beautiful love stories of the Bible. Let's discuss Ruth and Naomi and Boaz next time.

VAN DOREN: That will be a relief!

XII
THE LOVELIEST OF THE LOVE STORIES

SAMUEL: Mark, I'm glad the tragic loves of the Bible are behind us.

VAN DOREN: Well, they were interesting, Maurice.

SAMUEL: Yes, but they were heavy going for me; they were dispiriting, and we're coming now into broad and shining uplands. We've reached what I consider—perhaps you do, too—the loveliest of the love stories in the Bible. Although it is love between two women, it constitutes perhaps the most famous personal love episode in all biblical literature.

VAN DOREN: Now wait a minute, Maurice. Yes, it is about the love of two women; it is also—perhaps we shall disagree about this—about the love of a woman and a man, Ruth and Boaz. We'll reserve the question.

SAMUEL: Yes. Since you've introduced the question in this fashion, I can see that we probably will disagree. But for the moment, let's go ahead with the Ruth-Naomi relation. You will admit that it is more significant, and has taken hold of the world's imagination much more strongly than the relationship between Ruth and Boaz?

VAN DOREN: Oh, yes! There's no question about that! Anyone asked to remember the Book of Ruth remembers the famous moment when Naomi is asking her daughters-in-law to return home. And Ruth refuses. It is merely that later on, I think we shall have something to talk about in connection with the other relation that develops, when the two women return to Israel.

SAMUEL: You know, Mark, writing about Ruth and Naomi once,[50] I called their story "An Idyll of Old Age." Now I think of it also as the great example of love in bereavement: how sorrow bound two women together in an everlasting love. The story has become, one might say, the symbol for all human beings—how a disaster is the prelude to an abiding relationship.

VAN DOREN: Do we need to remind anyone, Maurice, about what happened before the story begins? The first five verses of Ruth sketch in the background: years before, Naomi, her husband, and two sons had left their home in Bethlehem, during a time of famine, to live in the land of the Moabites. They had left their people and their country. Naomi's husband dies. Her sons—who had married Ruth and Orpah, two women of Moab—die. Naomi is left there only with her daughters-in-law. And now it is time to come home, "empty," she says; and the story proper begins in the first chapter with a description of Naomi ready to start out on her long journey home. There on the road, she tells Ruth and Orpah to return to their parents' homes, and she prays that both of them will find new husbands.

SAMUEL: Orpah turns back, but Ruth refuses, and she "cleaved unto her." There's reason to read and reread Ruth's immortal words as one sings a familiar and much loved melody. The fact that Ruth's answer is well known is no reason for not repeating them. Ruth says:

> *"Entreat me not to leave thee, and to return from following after thee; for whither thou goest, I will go; and where thou lodgest, I will lodge; thy people shall be my people, and thy God my God; where thou diest, will I die, and there will I be buried; the Lord do so to me, and more also, if aught but death part thee and me."* RUTH 1:16–17

Marvelous words! In Hebrew, they are incomparably more compact, even than in the admittedly magnificent English.

VAN DOREN: Can you read them in Hebrew? I'd like to hear them.

SAMUEL: Let me read them:[51]

Va-tomer Rut:	And Ruth said:
Al-tifg' i-vi l'az'veykh,	"Entreat me not to leave thee,
la-shuv mey-akharayikh;	and to return from following after thee;
ki el-asher tel'khi eleykh;	for whither thou goest, I will go;
u-va'asher talini alin;	and where thou lodgest, I will lodge;
ameykh ami,	thy people shall be my people,
ve'lohayikh elohay;	and thy God my God;
ba-asher tamuti amut,	where thou diest, will I die,
ve-sham ekkaver;	and there will I be buried;
ko ya'aseh adonay li,	the Lord do so to me,
ve'kho yosif, ki ha-mavet	and more also, if aught but death
yafrid beyni u-veyneykh.	part thee and me."

You'll notice it's shorter in the Hebrew. "Thy people shall by my people" consists of two words. It's a highly contracted form, and it has the immediate effect of piercing you with its intensity.

VAN DOREN: I don't know about that, to be sure. It could be that the ultimate effect, in English, is the same. "Thy people" and "my people" are four words only, technically.

SAMUEL: The others are intermediary words.

VAN DOREN: Well, that doesn't matter—I was interested to hear that passage in Hebrew. I'm reminded of an experience I've often had with persons who ask for advice about how they might learn to write stories, short stories in particular. I've always told them not to bother too much with rules, with books, and with teachers who would undertake to instruct them how to do it. I say, for instance, that this thing called "characterization" is all nonsense if you remember that one of the most famous persons in all story characterized herself by just one speech. Nothing else needs to be said about the woman who could say that. I'm speaking to you as a novelist, incidentally. Do you agree?

SAMUEL: Yes, that's very cogent. That can happen. Yet, I would ask you this question: doesn't the Book of Ruth gather much warmth from its background, its surroundings, and its implications? Admittedly, that speech alone could be—and indeed is—immortal. One could find it as a fragment of a poem, and say: "Some great person spoke that." Nevertheless, the effect of the book as a whole is compounded from a number of circumstances. Let's say the following are some: this is the story of the coming together of two peoples—the Moabites and the Israelites—who are often represented[52] as being hostile to each other; it is also a marvelous little episode—peaceful, pastoral, interpolated, episodic—in the midst of the very bloody time of the Judges. We are told in the Book of Judges at one point:

> *In those days there was no king in Israel; every man did that which was right in his own eyes.* JUDG. 17:6

There was no continuous leadership, a fact which led to the establishment of a monarchy later on, under Samuel. And in the midst of all this tumult, this rushing back and forth of armies, the shouting, the bloodshed, and the exploits of the heroes, we see that a quiet life in a little town did go on, and a lovely, idyllic incident took place. To me, all of that seems to be contributory to the immense effect of the Book of Ruth, without in any way derogating from what you've said.

VAN DOREN: Yes, of course. By the way, when the reader of history explores the past of a people afflicted with times of trouble, he is inclined to take the view that there was turmoil everywhere, and all the time. But only common sense can tell him that there must have been times and places where there was no turmoil, just as here, in the Book of Ruth, there is this little pool of peace. The book opens: "And it came to pass in the days when the judges judged. . . ." In other words, this was in the time of some of those figures we read about in Judges—Jephthah, Gideon, Samson—who had bloody and often terrible experiences. This, however, as you say, is entirely personal, pastoral, and domestic.

SAMUEL: It reminds us that life went on—the weaving of the creative side of life which lies in these daily domestic episodes, and not in the battles and in the ambitions of generals and princes. It also makes me think of the distorted picture we get very often from satirists, and even from prophets. Writing on Roman history, Samuel Dill makes the point that if what Juvenal said about life in Rome was anywhere near his satiric description, the whole of that society would have collapsed.[53] And if life in Judea was anything like what the prophets described it—a sinful nation, sick from top to bottom—then that people wouldn't have lasted a year, let alone centuries. Here in the Book of Ruth we have this reminder of the continuity of normal, good, loving people, even in the midst of very dreadful and destructive circumstances and events.

VAN DOREN: The story of Ruth is famous, among other things, for its brevity. All the things that you've been saying apply, but they are things that we say after we have been penetrated by the arrow of this tale. Notice what the storyteller says after Ruth makes that wonderful speech to Naomi:

> *And when she [Naomi] saw that she was steadfastly minded to go with her, she left off speaking unto her. So they two went until they came to Beth-lehem.* RUTH 1:18–19

This is all that is said about the journey from Moab to Israel. There's no discussion, no description.

SAMUEL: A novelist would have taken advantage of the fact that this was a wild country, and would have given us—very skillfully, no doubt—all of the solemn effect of the mountains and the caves, and the crossing of the Jordan. It's all gone here!

VAN DOREN: And the rising of the sun, and the setting of the sun . . .

SAMUEL: And their reflections and meditations, and throwbacks. He'd have made a Hollywood business of it!

VAN DOREN: Yes! The wonderful thing about this story is that nothing like that is done. Ruth speaks, and the two women go on.

SAMUEL: As a matter of fact, when Hollywood gets hold of a Bible story, all it does is to remind you how good the Bible is—if you go back to it!

VAN DOREN: There have been several novels in our day based on this little tale. I read one not long ago, called simply *Ruth.* As you say, the author was skillful and ingenious at realizing matters that are only implied here. But no amount of realization, it seems to me, sufficed. I prefer to do the realizing myself—as people always have.

SAMUEL: You mentioned the brevity of the Book of Ruth, Mark. There are two short books of the Bible—this one, and the Book of Jonah—which have made a great impression on the Western world. Now there are shorter books in the Bible—the books of the prophets Nahum, Habakkuk, and Zephaniah. They're shorter, but they give the effect of being fragments.

VAN DOREN: I was going to say that.

SAMUEL: Whereas these two are absolutely perfect! This is a whole world presented—if I may use the phrase—in a gigantic miniature.

VAN DOREN: The account of the arrival of Ruth and Naomi, for that matter, is marvelous too for its brevity, and yet for its fullness:

RUTH 1:19–22

And it came to pass, when they were come to Bethlehem, that all the city was astir concerning them, and the women said: "Is this Naomi?" And she said unto them: "Call me not Naomi,[54] call me Marah; for the Almighty hath dealt very bitterly with me. I went out full, and the Lord hath brought me back home empty; why call ye me Naomi, seeing the Lord hath testified against me, and the Almighty hath afflicted me?" So Naomi returned, and Ruth the Moabitess, her daugh-

ter-in-law, with her, who returned out of the field of Moab—and they came to Beth-lehem in the beginning of barley harvest.

SAMUEL: That's the cutoff, as it were and now the scene is set for the action. It's perfectly done! You've noticed, Mark, how the book insistently and repeatedly refers to Ruth as "the Moabitess"—always reminding the reader of Ruth's identity. It's as though the author had it in mind: "Now don't you forget that this is not a story just of two women; it is the story of two women of different peoples, of different backgrounds, of different nations which were always, or nearly always, hostile. And look how they built up between them an everlasting story of love!" I'm quite certain that the authors, or the editors, were deliberate in their purpose. It is for me one of the instances of the struggle that went on perpetually in the Israelites, the Jewish people, between two contending impulses: one, the narrow, provincial, and particularist impulse; and the other—which was later to triumph and to become characteristic of what we call "normative Judaism" —the universalist impulse. They were always lapsing into the egotism of being a "chosen people" in the wrong sense; and then striving through their prophets, and through books like Ruth and Jonah and other literature of this kind, for the big vision of being chosen not as a privilege and as a concession to their ego, but for burdens and responsibilities—being more a "choosing" people than a "chosen" people treading the wide path of the universal approach to mankind. This is what I read into this persistent "Ruth the Moabitess." Afterwards, when Boaz announces to all the people of the little town that he's going to take Ruth to wife, again it's "Ruth the Moabitess."

VAN DOREN: Now that you speak of Boaz, Maurice, let's argue—if we have to—over the question of whether the Book of Ruth is not equally the love story of Ruth and Boaz and the love story of Ruth and Naomi. No word of love is spoken anywhere in the book.

SAMUEL: That's it! I checked on it because I wanted to talk on it: the word "love" is not mentioned. Of course, it needn't be.

VAN DOREN: No. Let me say, neither was it spoken in the case of Naomi and Ruth. Ruth merely says, "I will follow you wherever you go, and your God will be my God. I shall dwell where you dwell." It is not said that Naomi then understood that Ruth loved her; she merely understood that she was never going to be able to persuade this girl to go back. So, just as there's no word of love spoken between the two women, there's no word of love spoken between the woman and the man. And yet to me, the story of Ruth and Boaz is one of the most interesting of all love stories.

SAMUEL: Let's look at the text. You remember, of course, that there was some sort of managerial play there. Theirs wasn't a chance meeting, except as Boaz happened to see Ruth gleaning in his field, was very much moved, and told her how he knew about her and about
RUTH 2:8 what she had done. In their first conversation, Boaz calls her "my daughter." From this we gather that he was an older man[55] and perhaps it never occurred to him that there would ever be an intimate relationship between them.

VAN DOREN: Perhaps.

SAMUEL: Perhaps. The fact is that old Naomi had to fall back on an ancient custom of appealing to the nearest kinsman of her dead husband and sons to discharge his responsibility as kinsman—to redeem the family land, marry the widow, and beget children to "raise up the name of the dead."[56] Boaz was not the nearest kinsman, he was the second nearest. Old Naomi was going to remind him of his responsibility in case the nearest kinsman defaulted. Naomi waited for a right moment, and it came during the barley harvest when all the farm workers slept out in the field. She sent Ruth to Boaz:

> *And she went down unto the threshing-floor, and did according to all that her mother-in-law bade her. And when Boaz had eaten and drunk, and his heart was merry, he went to lie down at the end of the heap of corn; and she came softly, and uncovered his feet, and laid her down. And it came to pass at midnight, that the man was startled, and turned himself; and, behold, a woman lay at his feet. And he said: "Who art thou?" And she answered: "I am Ruth thy handmaid; spread therefore thy skirt over thy handmaid; for thou art a near kinsman.' And he said: "Blessed be thou of the Lord, my daughter; thou hast shown more kindness in the end than at the beginning, inasmuch as thou didst not follow the young man, whether poor or rich. And now, my daughter, fear not; I will do to thee all that thou sayest, . . ."* RUTH 3:6–11

She hadn't said anything, of course! I suppose he meant "all that you imply."

VAN DOREN: Yes, imply merely by being there.

SAMEL: Boaz continues:

> *". . . all that thou sayest; for all the men in the gate of my people do know that thou art a virtuous woman.* RUTH 3:11–13

And now it is true that I am a near kinsman; howbeit there is a kinsman nearer than I. . . . if he be not willing to do the part of a kinsman to thee, then will I do the part of a kinsman to thee, . . ."

There is affection there.

VAN DOREN: No, no, wait a minute! I think there's more than that! You remember, Naomi had put Ruth up to everything that she did. Once the two women returned, Ruth assumes a passive role, as indeed she had assumed a passive role in the beginning: she was utterly in the hands of Naomi, just as later on, she will place herself in the hands—of if you please, literally, at the feet—of Boaz. Ruth has the courage to do what Naomi tells her, but it's not clear that she would have had the courage to do anything by herself. Naomi plans the whole thing. Once she hears that Ruth has found herself among the reapers and the gleaners of Boaz, it seems to be clear to Naomi that this is an opportunity. She gives Ruth explicit directions about that evening on the threshing-floor. And I have always been especially interested in what she says when Ruth returns and reports how kind Boaz had been. Naomi says:

RUTH 3:18 *"Sit still, my daughter, until thou know how the matter will fall; for the man will not rest, until he have finished the thing this day."*

In other words, "I know what is happening!" Now Boaz did not need to do all that he did do. He could have been merely polite, distant, and formal; he could have been courteous and omitted giving Ruth the gift of six measures of barley. I think Ruth interested him a great deal. She interests you and me—and every reader. It's one of the mysteries of love stories how it is that the reader becomes convinced that someone in the love story is lovable. You know how much we want persons in love stories to fall in love with one another! What does the storyteller do in order to make us have that desire—because our desire is just as strong as theirs, the characters in the story. So we are for Ruth. We think she's beautiful—although, by the way, she is never called beautiful.

SAMUEL: No, she's not!

VAN DOREN: She's merely called "good"—although, I suppose, goodness is the supreme form of beauty.

SAMUEL: As a rule, it radiates the features.

VAN DOREN: Now here we are given—and I don't think I'm reading too much into this—to understand that Boaz looked at this strange girl who had suddenly come among his people, asked who she was, kept on looking at her, kept saying to himself, "Everything that she does is good; everything that she does is comely," and he does these favors for her. He sees to it that she is safe among the women; he orders his young men not to molest her; he goes to the trouble of commanding his young men to pull out from their bundles some sheaves of barley for her "of purpose"—deliberately. "Help her out!" in other words. "Do everything for her!" He doesn't need to do all that. When he was disturbed by her presence in the night, he could have said, "I am disturbed. You are doing too much."

SAMUEL: Perhaps, Mark, it may be that one of the reasons that I see this not primarily as a love story, although it is full of good affection——

VAN DOREN: By the way, I'm not saying "primarily."

SAMUEL:——or let me say, the reason I play it down—at least in comparison with you—is my vision of their being involved in a drama. You know the Jewish belief that the Messiah will be descended from King David—descended therefore from Ruth and Boaz.

VAN DOREN: Yes, because David and his father Jesse are descendants of the child of Ruth and Boaz.

SAMUEL: Yes, so that there is here an intimation of more than human relationships, which gives the story a solemnity which—I won't say drowns out, but like a louder strain of music, subdues the individual melody. There's a remarkable passage on which I lean for this—what shall I call it?—this historic choreographic effect:

RUTH 4:13–14

> *So Boaz took Ruth, and she became his wife; and he went in unto her, and the Lord gave her conception, and she bore a son. And the women said unto Naomi: "Blessed be the Lord, who hath not left thee this day without a near kinsman, and let his name be famous in Israel."*

Now you see, there is already an intimation of a grand theme, in which these loving people, Ruth and Boaz, stand at the center of something greater than themselves.

VAN DOREN: Well now, Maurice, I'm not denying the great dimension of the story; and in the whole context of the Bible, that dimension is clear and terribly important. I'm merely saying that the Bible is the great book that we say it is because we don't have merely grandeur here. You see, I can imagine a book written by persons who did not have the genius to blend both grandeur and intimacy. Everything that you say is true about the whole tenor of this tale, about the whole meaning of it. Yes, it looks forward and backward; and as we've been saying, too, it has as its context the terrible time of the Judges; and the peace of it is eloquent because of the contrast. And yet the writers did not fail to make it naturally *right,* also. They did not fail to give it that warmth, that particularity, and that intimacy which would save it from being merely inflated and empty grandeur. This book is both grand and true, as you and I know very well. It would not seem as true to all the people who have read it. I think, if it were nothing but grand gestures and the drawing of huge, broad outlines. Whenever we enter it, we find some individual doing something which fascinates us.

SAMUEL: The choral blend of the individual and the historical—like a melody against a background of woodwind and brass!

VAN DOREN: That's right!

SAMUEL: Again, it appears in the passage preceding the one I've just read—when Boaz stands in front of the people and the elders at the gate and says:

> *"Moreover Ruth the Moabitess, the wife of Mahlon, have I acquired to be my wife, to raise up the name of the dead upon his inheritance, that the name of the dead be not cut off from among his brethren, and from the gate of his place; ye are witnesses this day." And all the people that were in the gate, and the elders,* RUTH 4:10–12

> *said: "We are witnesses. The Lord make the woman that is come into thy house like Rachel and like Leah, which two did build the house of Israel; and do thou worthily in Ephrath, and be famous in Beth-lehem; and let thy house be like the house of Perez, whom Tamar bore unto Judah, of the seed which the Lord shall give thee of this young woman."*

There's a grandeur in that scene which—I don't say forbids but makes one forget the undoubted tenderness, the kindness of the relationship, lifts it into something almost cosmic!

VAN DOREN: Yes, but you say "lifts *it*."

SAMUEL: Lifts *it*—yes, the thing is there.

VAN DOREN: It is there. We're not told what Ruth thinks of Boaz. It is quite possible that up to some point—maybe after the story ends—Ruth is nothing except the obedient daughter-in-law. She is doing just what Naomi had told her to do, and she is looking for a husband, to put it all too simply. But Boaz is touched by the fact that she came to him in the night, in that incident of the threshing-floor. He is touched by the fact that she did not follow the young men.

SAMUEL: I've often pondered on what the relationship was between them afterwards. Did they live "happily ever after," and did their marriage have the domestic sweetness of the incident we're going to discuss next time in the story of Tobit?

XIII
AN IDYLL OF DOMESTICITY

VAN DOREN: Maurice, you said last time that it was a relief and pleasure for you to move from the disastrous love affairs of Samson and Tamar and the others into the peaceful and personal love story—or perhaps love stories—that we find in the Book of Ruth. Today I feel an equal pleasure and relief in moving on to what I have thought for many years one of the most charming and most fetching of all stories connected with the Bible. To be sure, it is not included among the books of the Hebrew Bible; it's in the collection known as the Apocrypha.[57] Nevertheless, the Book of Tobit[58] tells a famous story: Tobit and his son, Tobias; Tobias and his angel; Tobias and the girl, Sarah, whom he marries; Tobias and his mother, Hannah; Tobias and his dog.

SAMUEL (*laughing*): And his dog—last, but perhaps not least! You know, it's the only place that I can remember in the Bible or the Apocrypha where a doggy comes in very affectionately, and hangs on!

VAN DOREN: Hangs on! He goes with Tobias, and comes back with him.

SAMUEL: Mark, I think you'd better tell a bit of the story so that this dog going with Tobias, and coming back with him, will be intelligible to those who haven't read Tobit.

VAN DOREN: It pains me to think that people do not know this story, if only because it touches me so much. Incidentally, Tobit has been a very famous story in art. Rembrandt painted or etched I don't know how many pictures based on the book. Among his works are a whole series of most moving renderings that he made of old Tobit and Hannah sitting in their little house, waiting for their only child, Tobias, to return. But here's the story, and I shall tell it all too briefly, drawing from the translation by Edgar J. Goodspeed. I shall leave out many things that we can pick up later on—and I shall probably forget the dog!

The Book of Tobit is named for its chief character, Tobit, an Israelite who lives in the time of the Assyrian Exile.[59] As a young man in Israel, before the Assyrian conquest, his tribe of Naphtali had revolted against their proper guides and leaders in Jerusalem; but Tobit personally had continued to be faithful to his religion. But all that is background. Now, here's the time of exile, and Tobit finds himself in Nineveh, an alien there, and a man put upon and despised, as all his people are. He is very faithful to all the ordinances of his people. He prays, he does good deeds, he gives charity, and he remembers everything that he should remember. He walks all the days of his life, as he says, in righteousness. And one thing that interests everybody around him—and interests us now—is that he feels a deep obligation to take care of the body of any Jewish exile who has been murdered or strangled in Nineveh, and thrown outside the city wall. As quick as a flash, Tobit will be out there, secretly burying that body!

It happens that on one occasion he does this at night, and being "ceremonially defiled," as he says, he must wait for a while before he can return into his house, and resume the business of his life. He lies down to sleep at the foot of the courtyard wall, not knowing that there are sparrows perched overhead. Sparrow droppings fall into his open eyes, producing white films over them, and from that moment on, Tobit is blind, and physicians can do nothing for him. TOBIT 2:9–10

Because Tobit is blind and cannot work, his wife, Hannah, has to support them, and the moment that happens, we have what is to me a very delightful bit of bickering between this couple. One day Hannah returns home with her wages and a bleating kid which she says has been given to her as a special favor by her employers. And Tobit, rather ungraciously, says, "I don't believe it. I think you stole it. You must take it back." Hannah is outraged, and retorts, "You seem to know everything!"

SAMUEL (*laughing*): That's exactly what the text says! Here's the dialogue, as Tobit tells it:

TOBIT 2:13–14 *"Where did this kid come from? Is it stolen? Give it back to its owners, for we have no right to eat anything that is stolen."*

But she said to me, "It was given me as a gift in addition to my wages."

But I would not believe her, and told her to give it back to its owners, and I blushed for her. Then she answered and said to me,

"And where are your charities? Where is your uprightness? Of course you know everything!"

VAN DOREN (*laughing*): This is a delicious story; it's so human, so true! Tobit becomes so outraged himself that he goes off alone to pray to God to take his very life. He says, in effect: "Here I have done all these good things. I've lived a good life, and people speak to me this way!"

SAMUEL (*laughing, interrupting*): Yes! "And look at my wife!"

VAN DOREN: Yes, "Look at how my wife talks to me with her false reproaches!" So he prays to God to take him.

Well, it happens that at that same moment in far-off Media, a girl named Sarah is offering substantially the same prayer. Sarah, the daughter of Raguel, lives in the city of Ec*ba*tana. (I pronounce it as Milton does in his *Paradise Lost*; he loves that name!) Sarah has been married to a bridegroom, and on the wedding night, a demon named Asmodeus has come and strangled the young man. She marries again, and again, and again—this happens seven times! Seven bridegrooms have died on their wedding nights in her chamber. Her father's maids have taunted

her, "Look, we don't believe any demon was involved; we
think *you* strangled your husbands! You're just a man-
killer, that's what you are!" Poor Sarah goes off to her
room to pray to God to take her life, because this is what TOBIT 3:10
people say about her.

The two prayers—Tobit's and Sarah's—are heard at the same instant by Raphael, the great archangel,[60] who sees to it that God hears them, and is given directions by God to go down to earth to take care of these persons—to cure Tobit's blindness and Sarah's loneliness by giving her as a husband no other than Tobias, the son of Tobit. The rest of the story is about how that happens.

I'll try to make this very brief now. Tobit at one
time had been a buyer and a businessman in Nineveh for
Shalmaneser, king of Assyria, and he'd made money. Before
he went blind, he had left ten talents of silver—a good
deal of money—with a kinsman in Media. Now the roads
are unsafe, he is blind, and cannot go for the money. Since
death is on his mind, he bethinks himself of how Hannah
and Tobias will live. He calls in his son, tells him to go get TOBIT 4:2
the money and to take care of his old mother as long as
she lives. Tobit tells his son to seek out a man to go with
him, and Tobias goes out on the street, looking. And lo
and behold! The first person he finds is Raphael himself,
who has taken on human form and uses the name Azariah.

Tobias reports that he's found a traveling companion. Old Tobit says: "Call him in. I want to talk to TOBIT 5:8
him. I want to find out if he is of good stock, and if he is
reliable. I want to discuss wages with him."

So now we have a very serious discussion of Azariah's forebears, the names of whom satisfy Tobit. The wages are established: a drachma a day, with all expenses paid, and a bonus if they come home safe and sound. And off they go, the tall, handsome stranger, the young man, and the dog.

SAMUEL (*laughing*): And Tobias's dog following after! Of course, Hannah begins to nag the moment they leave:

TOBIT 5:17–22 *And his mother Hannah wept, and she said to Tobit,*

"Why have you sent our child away? Is he not our walking-stick when he goes in and out before us? Do not let money be added to money, but let it be as dirt in comparison with our child. For while the Lord lets us live, that is enough for us."

And Tobit said to her,

"Do not be troubled, my sister. He will come back safe and sound, and your eyes will see him. For a good angel will go with him, and he will have a prosperous journey, and will come back safe and sound."

So she stopped crying.

(*laughing*): That's how the text goes!

VAN DOREN: Although later on, when a good deal of time has passed, and Tobias still has not returned, she then is perfectly convinced that the boy has perished. And nothing can change her mind. Of course she blames Tobit: "Don't deceive me," she wails. "My child is dead and you let him go!" Tobit says, "Be quiet. He is all right." And
TOBIT 10:7 she says, "*You* be quiet, He's dead!"

The relations between Tobit and Hannah are very delightful, and I love this little couple. I use "little" affectionately.

SAMUEL: It's properly used, because they're humble people. These are not heroic people at all; there's no great gesture among them. This is a good man, and a good wife, and a dutiful son, and a girl who's had many misfortunes. They are the "little folk."

VAN DOREN: That's what I mean when I say "little." Incidentally, in the passage you just cited, Tobit assures Hannah that "a good angel will go with him"; and when he blesses Tobias on his departure, he says, "God will prosper your journey, and let His angel go with you." He doesn't actually *know* that the traveling companion is Raphael. I'm reminded of that moment in Genesis when old Abraham is telling his servant Eliezer to go find a wife
for Isaac. Abraham says that God "will send His angel GEN. 24:7
before thee, and thou shalt take a wife for my son. . . ." It happens that we never see that angel; nothing more is said about him. However, we can merely assume that Tobit is saying something like this: "Good luck go with you. May some good eye watch over you."

Well, Tobias and Azariah—and the dog—leave Nineveh, and stop that evening to spend the night by the
river Tigris. A fish suddenly jumps out of the water, Tobias TOBIT 6:7
catches it, and Azariah instructs him to save the heart, the liver, and the gall for use later on. It seems that the heart and the liver, when burned in incense, will frighten off the demon who is killing Sarah's bridegrooms. He's going to fly away to the farthest reaches of Upper Egypt!

SAMUEL (*laughing*): Why to Upper Egypt, I don't know!

VAN DOREN: I've often wondered. The fish's gall is reserved to remove the white films from Tobit's eyes and cure him of his blindness. The angel and Tobias—and presumably the dog—go on from the Tigris, and everything turns out exactly right in this lovely story. They arrive at the house of Raguel. As they are approaching the house, Azariah tells Tobias that he's going to meet a
TOBIT 6:12 "beautiful and sensible" girl there, Sarah, who, as a matter of fact, is related to Tobias. Tobias is her only relative, and the angel keeps saying that Tobias, and no one else, has the right to marry her. Indeed, he *commands* Tobias to marry Sarah.

SAMUEL: Azariah is telling him, "Marry somebody in the family!"

VAN DOREN: It's always interested me that Tobias believes the angel implicitly. He *knows* that Sarah will be beautiful and sensible.

SAMUEL: In fact, he falls in love with her merely from the description that the angel, or Azariah, gives him. You have a poem on that subject, Mark. Now that we've reviewed the story, read that poem—it's a very fine condensed commentary on it.

VAN DOREN: The poem doesn't carry the story as far as we shall be carrying it. It refers only to this time on the way to Raguel's house, when Tobias, listening to Azariah speak as he does of Sarah, falls in love with her, although he's never seen her. The poem is called "Sarah of Ecbatana":[61]

Tobias, son of Tobit, felt desire
For Sarah, the sad daughter of Raguel,
Before he ever saw her. Could this be?
She was of his people, far away,
And destined for him, Azariah said;
And beautiful and sensible; but sad
Because of seven bridegrooms she had lost
On seven wedding nights—a demon's work,
Not hers, although the maids accused her so.
The angel Azariah said: "Go up
To her, Tobias, and possess her without fear;
For she is yours, and was from the beginning;
Pray with her, then draw the curtains close,
And sleep all night; I tell you it is well."
And so Tobias, with obedient heart,
Was full of love for Sarah long before
He ever saw Ecbatana, her city.
She was of his people; and was beautiful,
And sensible; and wanted to be dead
Because she did not know the very boy
Was coming who could save her, and whose bride
In truth, not lust, she was from the beginning.
So Azariah said, whose other name
Was Raphael; and obedient Tobias
Eagerly walked with him all the way.

SAMUEL: Yes! Do you know, Mark, what this story of Tobit makes me think of? It may sound a little incongruous to you: it makes me think of Sholom Aleichem! I'll tell you the particular reasons why. The name Tobit is close to the Hebrew name *Tuvia*, and of course *Tuvia* is practically the name of Sholom Aleichem's famous Tevye the dairyman, with his seven daughters.[62] Again, one thinks of Tobit as that "little" person, because he was of the folk; and in spite of that fact, as we get to know Tobit (as in the case of Tevye), he grows in our imagination until he is much more than one of the "little folk"—he is a representative figure.

The whole of this story, Mark, has a particular charm for me because it gives us a picture of the Jew in exile, managing as best he can, and longing for the return
TOBIT 13:1–18 to the homeland. There are some prayers of rejoicing toward the end of the book in which Tobit, his sight restored, his son safe at home with a good wife—a relative! —thinks only of the consummation of life's purpose, which is the restoration of the Jewish homeland and the rebuilding of Jerusalem. I'm terribly sorry that this book has not been accepted canonically as part of the Hebrew Bible.[63] Scholars differ as to the date of the authorship. Some place it two and a half centuries before the Common Era, although perhaps it was written earlier. It was written certainly as early, let us say, as the Book of Daniel, and perhaps even the Book of Esther. It's very strange, when you compare Tobit with Esther, to see the difference in spirit between the two. In Esther, as I mentioned earlier [*see* p. 168], God is never mentioned, nor is there any reference to the longing of the Jews to return to their homeland. Some of the Rabbis felt that Esther was too secular to be included in the canon; there was a great deal of discussion about it, and they finally put it in. But if it's true that Tobit was written, say, two and a half centuries before the Common Era, it should have gone in. I often think that there are three books which should not have been put out in the cold, among what are called in Hebrew the *Sefarim Hitzonim*, the "outside books": Ecclesiasticus, The Wisdom of Solomon, and this one, Tobit. If I called the story of Ruth and Naomi "An Idyll of Old Age," this could be called "An Idyll of Domesticity." It has all of the

coloring; it has the domestic squabbles. Tobit and Hannah aren't angels; their quarrels are small, but very lively. It's a kind of Darby and Joan picture on a Jewish background in the Exile.

VAN DOREN: Yes, it's one of the loveliest of stories, and I'm not the less fond of it because it makes me smile many, many times—and not only when Tobit and Hannah bicker. I always have to smile at the beginning of the book. Tobit is always rushing to bury the bodies of Israelites who've been killed by the Assyrians. An informer went to tell the king about his secret activities, and he got into terrible trouble: his property was seized, and he was a marked man. But he just can't stop doing that. One night as he is just sitting down to a festival meal, he learns another Israelite has been murdered. He rushes out to dig a grave, and his neighbors laugh at him, saying, "Here he TOBIT 2:8
is burying the dead again!" It's a grim subject, of course; and I don't want to minimize it. But here's old Tobit, he just can't help it; he's got to have a shovel in his hand!

Now there's another lovely scene with Raguel, Sarah's father. The angel has been telling Tobias that Raguel is his relative, yet Tobias cannot resist having a little recognition scene with him. He doesn't identify himself as he enters Raguel's house. Raguel looks at the young man and tells his wife, "My, how he resembles my cousin TOBIT 7:2
Tobit." Then he asks the two visitors where they're from. They reply, and Raguel goes on to ask if they happen to know his kinsman Tobit.

SAMUEL: Tobias and the angel answer, "We do" —and they stop. Raguel presses, "Is he well?" And they answer tersely again, "He is alive and well." But finally Tobias bursts out with: "He is my father!" And of course this is met with excitement and weeping and kissing and blessings. This is the art of the storyteller.

VAN DOREN: Raguel and his wife are good people, too. They rush out and slaughter a ram and make a great feast for Tobias and the angel—whom they don't know as an angel. But when marriage with Sarah is mentioned, Raguel insists upon telling them the truth about the seven dead bridegrooms, and about how they're now dead and buried.

SAMUEL: There's a lot of burying in this book!

VAN DOREN: It's got to be a habit! As a matter of fact, that night, when Tobias enters the fatal bedcham-
TOBIT 8:9 ber, Raguel goes out with a shovel. He's getting ready!

(*laughter*)

SAMUEL: Out to dig a grave. He says to himself, "Here goes another!"

VAN DOREN: Raguel says, "Perhaps he will die too."

SAMUEL: He digs the grave, comes back to the house, and sends a maid to go look into the bedchamber. The maid peeps in on them, finds them soundly asleep—and alive—and she rushes back to Raguel to report that everything's all right. Raguel then hurries out to see that the grave is filled up again! (*laughter*) I think it's rather what you call *Galgenhumor*—a grim humor—but it *is* funny, just the same.

VAN DOREN: Funny in a wonderful way!

SAMUEL: Because you don't take those deaths of the bridegrooms seriously.

VAN DOREN: No, it was a sort of ritual death. The return of Tobias home is wonderful. While the whole family is having a fourteen-day wedding feast in Raguel's home, Tobias remembers that the main purpose of his journey—as far as his father is concerned—is to get Tobit's money from the person who is holding it. He sends Raphael off to get it, and the angel does that without the slightest difficulty. He rejoins Tobias and Sarah in Raguel's house, and the three of them—and the little dog!—start home.

The moment of their return is done with great, great narrative skill. (Rembrandt made several drawings or paintings of this scene in particular.) The angel tells Tobias, "You and I will go ahead, and Sarah will follow. Be sure to have the gall of the fish in your hand, because I know that your father will have his eyes open, and you must rub the gall on the white films immediately, and he will see you."

As they come down the road, there is old Hannah. Every day, she's been going down the road by which her son had left, watching for him to return. Suddenly she
sees him coming, and she cries out to Tobit, "Here comes TOBIT 11:6
your son and that man!" Tobit comes running out the door, and he stumbles.

SAMUEL: Yes, blind.

VAN DOREN: That's exactly how the angel has foretold it. As Tobit stumbles, he opens his eyes, and Tobias runs up to support him at that instant, and is able to rub his father's eyes. The white films—what we would call, perhaps, cataracts—scale off, and Tobit sees his son. The joy of Tobit is inexpressible—except that he does express it!

SAMUEL: This book *should* belong to the Bible, really. I wonder how much good material must have been lost?[64] Hundreds and hundreds of books, possibly—some of them perhaps not of the same value, but undoubtedly many very good ones.

VAN DOREN: The genius of that people was unlimited, to be sure.

SAMUEL: The story of Tobit makes me go back to the thought which has been haunting me throughout these talks—and I've mentioned it before in connection with Adam and Eve, and Isaac and Rebekah in particular: there is this puzzle always about these happy marriages. They are made in Heaven, and sometimes they are contrived on earth, and when they are contrived, one must assume that this was the will of Heaven that they should be so manipulated. These are *prearranged* marriages, and Jewish tradition says that God is the everlasting matchmaker [*see* p. 103]. Yet this doesn't take away from the spontaneity of the meetings of these people! They seem to choose each other; of if they don't seem to choose—as, let us say, Jacob *chose* to love Rachel, or David *chose* to love Bathsheba—nevertheless, they fall in love. So you have here in this simple form, without going into the great, grim problem of destiny, predestination, and free will, this paradox: it's arranged, but they are free to choose; it's arranged, nevertheless they love spontaneously. Here in Tobit, the angel speaks to the boy about this girl and, in so doing, wakens a tremendous love in him for her. He's never seen her, doesn't know her. But the mere words of Raphael are enough to set off in him a burst of affection, and he's already in love with her! There's a curious romantic touch for you—a romantic touch in the midst of these practical, down-to-earth matrimonial-agency activities!

VAN DOREN: That's right. And Raphael—now that you speak of him—is very splendid in my imagination at the moment of his revealing *his* identity at the end of this book. It's even more splendid because of that rather comical scene in the beginning, when Tobit has told his son, "Go bring that man in, and let me cross-examine him to find out if he comes from a good family and is reliable." At the end, the storyteller does not stint to let us have the full force of a recognition scene, and it's all very much to the credit of both father and son. Once the young man and his wife come home and everybody is rejoicing at a seven-day marriage feast, Tobit calls in his son and says, "Now we must settle with this good man who went with TOBIT 12:2
you. We really must give him more than we first thought."

Tobias says, "I think he should have half of all the money I brought back, because think what he's done for us! He brought me back, he got me the money, and he's cured you and Sarah." And Tobit agrees, "It is due him." They call in the angel and say, "Accept half of all that you brought back." Then Raphael reveals all: "Thank you, but there is something that you do not understand. I am Raphael, one of the seven holy angels." That news —which of course they cannot doubt—prostrates them.

SAMUEL: Yes, the text says:

TOBIT 12:16–17 *And they were both confounded, and fell on their faces, for they were terrified.*

VAN DOREN: This is what Raphael says:

TOBIT 12:17–20 *"Do not be afraid; peace be with you. Bless God forever. For not through any favor on my part but by the will of God I came to you. . . . Now give thanks to God. . . ."*

Raphael takes no credit for himself: he is merely a messenger sent to do these things. There is something very moving to me about the humility of the angel at that point. To you, also?

SAMUEL: Yes, but of course in the Jewish tradition, we are told that man is placed above the angels because the angels don't act of their own will; they haven't the choice, the free will, that is given to the human being, and therefore Raphael's behavior is in keeping with the tradition.

The story ends very charmingly, too, like a real fairy tale. Just before he dies, Tobit makes a long speech to his son, telling him to go and live in Media because he believes that Jonah's prophecy about Nineveh is going to be fulfilled—namely, the city will be destroyed (and by the way, ultimately Nineveh was destroyed). Tobit attributes the happy ending to his life to the fact that he gave charity, and he says:

> *"See, my children, what charity can do, and how uprightness can save." As he said this, he breathed his last there in his bed. He was a hundred and fifty-eight years old; and they gave him a splendid funeral.* TOBIT 14:11

(*laughter*)

BOTH: "And they gave him a splendid funeral!"

XIV

THE SONG OF SONGS: LOVE LYRIC AND/OR ALLEGORY?

SAMUEL: Mark, with The Song of Songs we reach the climax of the subject of the treatment of love in the Hebrew Bible. It's one of the most precious of all the biblical books; many scholars have said that it is almost as beloved as the Psalms among the biblical writings. As many people know, there has always been a tremendous discussion about the significance of the Song. Was it intended to be simply a love lyric of the highest order?

VAN DOREN: A love lyric, or a group of love lyrics, we might say.

SAMUEL: Yes, let me rephrase that. Was it intended merely as a collection of love songs, some of them bucolic, others relating to the court; or was The Song of Songs originally intended to be that which the Rabbis have said it is—a very high allegorical representation between God and His people?[65] I think we might talk a little about this aspect before we do some reading of significant passages; afterwards, we can examine the allegorical side against the background of actual passages in the text.

VAN DOREN: In my view, it is very difficult to understand The Song of Songs as an allegory. I am quite content to take it as a love lyric, or as a set of love lyrics —lovely, by the way, beyond parallel. I find no signs in it anywhere that point to an allegorical design. Nothing seems to be in the text calling upon you to interpet it in the light of some further meaning. I'm sure that when an allegory is intended, some hints or other marks of that sort must exist. Another thing appears to be true, too: the natural sense, the literal sense, if you please, the love theme of The Song of Songs doesn't seem to be incomplete, or to call for interpretation. (Here I'm leaning upon some scholarship of which I've availed myself.) The text seems to speak for itself. For these two reasons, I have never been very sympathetic to the conception of this great and lovely book as allegorical.[66]

SAMUEL: I'm probably more sympathetic to it than you are, but we'll come to that later. It seems to me that this book (which never mentions the name of God at all!) is something that by all accounts should have been excluded from the canon, if there had not been in it something that profoundly affected the religious sensitivities of the editors of the Bible as long as 1,800 years ago, when the canon was fixed. But to set the background for discussion, let us first read those passages that are most characteristic. They are deeply—I won't say erotic, but deeply tinged with physical and with spiritual love.

VAN DOREN: I hope we have picked the right verses to illustrate the beauty of this book. I shall begin very near the beginning, when the Shulammite maiden is speaking:

SONG 1:2

Let him kiss me with the kisses of his mouth—
For thy love is better than wine.

SAMUEL: And she goes on:

SONG 1:5–6

I am black, but comely,
O ye daughters of Jerusalem,
As the tents of Kedar,
As the curtains of Solomon.

Look not upon me, that I am swarthy,
That the sun hath tanned me;
My mother's sons were incensed against me,
They made me keeper of the vineyards;
But mine own vineyard have I not kept.

VAN DOREN: The girl is still speaking:

SONG 2:1–5

I am a rose of Sharon,
A lily of the valleys.

As a lily among thorns,
So is my love among the daughters.

As an apple-tree among the trees of the wood,
So is my beloved among the sons.
Under its shadow I delighted to sit,
And its fruit was sweet to my taste.

He hath brought me to the banqueting-house,
And his banner over me is love.
Stay ye me with dainties, refresh me with apples;
For I am love-sick.

SAMUEL:

My beloved spoke, and said unto me: SONG 2:10–14
"Rise up, my love, my fair one, and come away.
For, lo, the winter is past.
The rain is over and gone;
The flowers appear on the earth;
The time of singing is come,
And the voice of the turtle is heard in our land;
The fig-tree putteth forth her green figs,
And the vines in blossom give forth their fragrance.
Arise, my love, my fair one, and come away.
O my dove, that art in the clefts of the rock, in the covert of the cliff,
Let me see thy countenance, let me hear thy voice;
For sweet is thy voice, and thy countenance is comely."

VAN DOREN: The girl is speaking:

By night on my bed I sought him whom my soul loveth; SONG 3:1–5
I sought him, but I found him not.
"I will rise now, and go about the city,
In the streets and in the broad ways
I will seek him whom my soul loveth."
I sought him, but I found him not.
The watchmen that go about the city found me:
"Saw ye him whom my soul loveth?"
Scarce had I passed from them,
When I found him whom my soul loveth:
I held him, and would not let him go,
Until I had brought him into my mother's house,
And into the chamber of her that conceived me.

"I adjure you, O daughters of Jerusalem,
By the gazelles, and by the hinds of the field,
That ye awaken not, nor stir up love,
Until it please."

SAMUEL: Now the lover is speaking:

SONG 4:8–10, 16

Come with me from Lebanon, my bride,
With me from Lebanon;
Look from the top of Amana,
From the top of Senir and Hermon,
From the lions' dens,
From the mountains of the leopards.
Thou hast ravished my heart, my sister, my bride;
Thou hast ravished my heart with one of thine eyes,
With one bead of thy necklace.
How fair is thy love, my sister, my bride!
How much better is thy love than wine!
And the smell of thine ointments than all manner of spices! . . .
Awake, O north wind;
And come, thou south;
Blow upon my garden,
That the spices thereof may flow out.
Let my beloved come into his garden,
And eat his precious fruits.

VAN DOREN:

SONG 5:4–9

My beloved put in his hand by the hole of the door.
And my heart was moved for him.
I rose up to open to my beloved;
And my hands dropped with myrrh,
And my fingers with flowing myrrh,
Upon the handles of the bar.
I opened to my beloved;
But my beloved had turned away, and was gone.
My soul failed me when he spoke.

I sought him, but I could not find him;
I called him, but he gave me no answer.
The watchmen that go about the city found me,
They smote me, they wounded me;
The keepers of the walls took away my mantle from me.
"I adjure you, O daughters of Jerusalem,
If ye find my beloved,
What will ye tell him?
That I am love-sick."
"What is thy beloved more than another beloved,
O thou fairest among women?
What is thy beloved more than another beloved,
That thou doest so adjure us?"

SAMUEL: The Shulammite continues her conversation with the "daughters of Jerusalem," that is to say, the ladies of the court:

"Whither is thy beloved gone, SONG 6:1–3
O thou fairest among women?
Whither hath thy beloved turned him,
That we may seek him with thee?"

"My beloved is gone down to his garden,
To the beds of spices,
To feed in the gardens,
And to gather lilies.
I am my beloved's, and my beloved is mine,
That feedeth among the lilies."

Now a man is speaking. Some of the commentators believe it may be King Solomon, who has fallen in love with the country girl, and is trying to woo her from her shepherd lover:

Thou art beautiful, O my love, as Tirzah, SONG 6:4
Comely as Jerusalem,
Terrible as an army with banners.

VAN DOREN: And now the Shulammite is reunited with her lover:

SONG 8:6–7

Set me as a seal upon thy heart,
As a seal upon thine arm;
For love is strong as death,
Jealousy is cruel as the grave;
The flashes thereof are flashes of fire,
A very flame of the Lord.
Many waters cannot quench love,
Neither can the floods drown it;
If a man would give all the substance of his house for love,
He would utterly be contemned.

SAMUEL: Those are the characteristic passages, and against them, we'll talk about the probability—or perhaps you would say the propriety, Mark—of looking upon this work as allegorical; not that the allegorical would exclude its other character: the two would go parallel with each other, and one would strengthen the other. The traditional Jewish view of this is that God here is speaking to His people, and the people are speaking to Him, with the Torah, the Law, alternating. Many of the allusions the Rabbis have made would certainly sound strained; the particular points they raise might strike us as incongruous. Let me dispose of them, so that we won't be talking pedantically, as it were, about specific references. Here are a few of the rabbinical interpretations, and I grant you: they *do* sound strange!

SONG 1:6

My mothers' sons were incensed against me,
They made me keeper of the vineyards;

The Rabbis say that this is a reference to the revolt in the desert against Moses—the famous rebellion led by

But mine own vineyard have I not kept.	Korah, described in Numbers 16.	
Thy cheeks are comely with circlets, . . .	One of the Rabbis says that these circlets, being two in number, refer one to the Written Law that is contained in the Torah—the Five Books of Moses—and one to the Oral Law that was handed down to Moses, and he passed it on to Joshua and the Elders and the Prophets, and the men of the Great Synagogue.	SONG 1:10

VAN DOREN: *That*, if I may be frank, seems to me perfectly absurd! I know, in some contexts, it isn't absurd; but that is the kind of thing I tend to resist in all discussions of this work. A moment ago, you yourself said the allegorical would "strengthen" the lyrical side of the work. There are those who find meanings in it which make it stronger. But I would begin by assuming that the poem is as strong as a poem can be. It needs no strengthening! I would have no objection to any allegorization of The Song of Songs which *did* enhance it, or which filled it with meaning over and above that which it has; but I would be very suspicious of the kind you quoted.

SAMUEL: Let me strengthen your argument for you by going on with some of these quotations. I'm giving you just a sampling that I've culled from a medieval Hebrew anthology called *Yalkut Shimeoni*:

SONG 2:2	*As a lily among thorns,* *So is my love among the daughters.*	The "lily among thorns" is Israel in Egypt; just as it is difficult to take a lily out from among thorns—said the Rabbis—so it was difficult to draw the Israelites out of Egypt.
SONG 2:8	*Hark! my beloved!*	That's supposed to be Moses calling the Israelites in Egypt to freedom.
SONG 3:1	*By night on my bed I sought him. . . .*	That's supposed to be Abraham looking for Isaac the night before he took him to the place of the sacrifice.
SONG 3:4	*I held him, and would not let him go, . . .*	That's supposed to be David buying the land from Araunah the Jebusite [II Sam. 24:21], upon which the Temple was later built.

Now, all of this I give you, so to speak, as a present. You can have it in order to strengthen your argument.

VAN DOREN: You give that to me, and of course I reject it! I'm aware of further highly strained efforts to put meaning into something that I think has plenty of meaning—and excellent meaning, too. I know there are those who say that this is an allegory of the relation between Solomon and his people, or Solomon and Wisdom. (King Solomon loved Wisdom; he prayed for it in II Chronicles. Very well, this is somehow Solomon and Wisdom singing to each other.) There's a theory that this is an epithalamium, sung at the marriage of King Solomon and an Egyptian princess, a daughter of one of the Pharaohs.[67] I hear it sometimes spoken of as a celebration of wedded love; or else it's Israel and her King, as you suggested; or the history of the Jews from Exodus to Messiah. All of these seem to me to be perfectly absurd.

see II CHRON. 1:10

SAMUEL: Supposing we grant all that—putting it on that extreme basis. Just the same, the Hebrew Bible is full of transpositions of the Divine love for the people into human terms of man-and-woman love. The prophet Jeremiah has some famous passages in which God is addressing the Israelites in such terms:

I remember for thee the affection of thy youth,
The love of thine espousals;
How thou wentest after Me in the wilderness,
In a land that was not sown.

JER. 2:2

Or just a bit later:

Can a maid forget her ornaments,
Or a bride her attire?
Yet My people have forgotten Me
Days without number.

JER. 2:32

The prophet Isaiah uses some of the same terms:

For thy Maker is thy husband,
The Lord of hosts is His name;

ISA. 54:5–6

And the Holy One of Israel is thy Redeemer,
The God of the whole earth shall He be called.
For the Lord hath called thee
As a wife forsaken and grieved in spirit;
And a wife of youth, can she be rejected?
Saith thy God.

Now in those passages, the reference to the relationship between God and His people in terms of man-and-woman love is indisputable, isn't it?

VAN DOREN: Yes, I suppose so.

SAMUEL: Without making use of those admittedly hairsplitting refinements of interpretations that I quoted before, can't you imagine a deeper meaning than what appears to be obvious, on the surface? Perhaps it wasn't written with any deeper meaning, but from very early on, it was seen by a great many as having a more than man-woman meaning.

VAN DOREN: Yes, I dare say. I merely want to hold out for the glorious poet—or poets—who wrote this. Nobody can tell me as long as I live that anything except just what appears on the very surface——

SAMUEL (*interrupting*): As long as you live? I'd like to meet you afterwards, Mark. Maybe we could reach a conclusion later?

VAN DOREN: No, no, I insist upon saying that!

SAMUEL: As long as you live!

VAN DOREN: Yes! Nothing on earth could convince me that the poet who wrote those lines we read was thinking of anything except what they plainly say. If he had had some more abstract weight on his mind, if he was carrying some heavier burden, I don't think he would have struck this stride:

Rise up, my love, my fair one, and come away. SONG 2:10–12
For, lo, the winter is past,
The rain is over and gone;
The flowers appear on the earth;
The time of singing is come,
And the voice of the turtle is heard in our land; . . .

Now, it's just *crazy* to ask that to mean any more than that. That's it!

(*laughter*)

SAMUEL: If you're so completely set, I don't know what I can do about it. All the same, we know that in a great many religions, there is a transposition of the human passion into a divine passion. And besides that, I think you'll admit that many great poets write *more* than they are aware of in the words which they utter. You used the word "absurd." It wasn't altogether absurd that the Jews saw allegory here. I go back to what I was saying. Supposing it wasn't so intended by its author or authors, or by the folk through which it issued. Nevertheless, because of the intensity of the passion, something more than human was read into it; and that something more than human had to be the relationship between the Divinity and man.

VAN DOREN: Yes, of course, that goes on forever. Words are written, and we shall never know why they were written, or what was in the minds of the men who wrote them. And men will read them as they will. I'm not objecting to anyone saying anything he pleases about this; I'm saying only that I for one am utterly happy to think of these poems (I think these are *poems* rather than *a* poem) as being love poems. There is nothing finer than that. And I for one respect the Bible, and adore it, because it contains this book—as well as for many, many other reasons. If it didn't contain this book, I think it would be poorer.

SAMUEL: Let's revert to a general consideration. Look at the way words are charged and double-charged with meaning. Think of the word "infidel" as opposed to the word "infidelity." How do you interpret these two words?

VAN DOREN: An infidel is one who does not have the faith. Infidelity is an act of unfaithfulness to a person.

SAMUEL: Usually to a woman.

VAN DOREN: Yes, usually.

SAMUEL: Or a woman to a man. But it's as between the sexes, isn't it?

VAN DOREN: The reference in the second case—the woman to the man—is much less great than in the first case.

SAMUEL: Then how is it that the two words are so closely linked that they become confused, as it were; they carry over from one into the other—that infidelity is the act, in a certain sense, of an infidel, and an infidel is one who has manifested infidelity?

VAN DOREN: I might ask you to consider the feelings of some woman to a man who's been unfaithful, or of some man to whom a woman has been unfaithful. If the love there is deep enough, the loss is something like the loss of any kind of faith at all. From the outside, we don't see that; we tend to say, "That's just another story. Those are just two other people!" It could be that to those lovers, the thing involved was as great as the loss of faith. There are those who say that Romeo and Juliet are just children in love. But try to see them from the point of view of children in love, and there's something terrific about that experience, which we have no right to condescend to. Please don't misunderstand me: I'm perfectly willing that anyone should say anything he likes about The Song of Songs, as long as the text is not changed, as long as the poems remain—and of course they *will* remain.

SAMUEL: You know, to this day it is the practice among Jews that at a certain season of the year, the man who is called upon in the synagogue to read a certain portion of Scriptures is called the *Hatan Torah*, the "bridegroom of the Law,"[68] and it's a very great honor. He is "wedded" to the Law. References abound in this as in other religions to the intimate link between the human expression of love, as between human beings, and the love of God. Very early in our talks [*see* p. 34] when we were discussing man's love for God, and his love for his fellow man, we saw a relationship there: in a certain sense, the two kinds of love are coterminous; there cannot be one without the other.

VAN DOREN: Wait a minute, though! When we spoke about the love of man for God, and of God for man, *that* was what the Bible was talking about: the words were perfectly clear. God says, "You must love Me." And men have said to one another, "We must love God." Here in The Song of Songs, there are no such words. A man loves a woman, a woman loves a man. They are country people —shepherds—and maybe they are quite young.

SAMUEL: What I was referring to was that man's love of his fellow men can be, if not entirely a substitute, then the next best thing to love of God; and perhaps for some it is the equivalent of a love of God. So in this case, when there is this intense feeling between a man and a woman, it transcends the human. If love between a man and a woman is something more than the passion of the flesh, if an element of the Divine exists in their relationship, then to me it is not an extravagance to translate their love relationship into the terms that the Rabbis used over many centuries—and that pious Jews still do—in speaking of God and His people. I'll admit that you can take one side of The Song of Songs and accept it. But for me, it is enriched by the other side, too. I suppose that love between a man and a woman is enriched when they imagine that an eternal principle, a significance which is beyond their own lives, is involved in their passion for each other.

VAN DOREN: Yes, that's true. I am only worried when I find discussions of this matter not enriching the original document, but impoverishing it. In searching for allegorical meanings in poetry or in anything else, I feel that strained analysis makes the work poorer rather than richer.

SAMUEL: Yes, there *are* people without any emotions at all who use this simply for a pedantic exercise of their ingenuity. They tell you, "This verse means such-and-such"; and "If you count up the letters here, and if you count up the letters over there, you'll find the same number in both passages, and therefore the two have a connected meaning." Admittedly, such persons have missed the content and its significance. But I'm also suggesting that part of it is missed if it is taken *only* in terms of human relationship, without an awareness of a resonance which seems to go into all space. This awareness transcends the two persons involved; it explains why lovers swear by the stars and by eternity, and by the everlasting forces. They feel that to speak only of themselves is inadequate. Now this, I submit, is what is felt in the power of The Song of Songs. It is the most marvelous of all love literature; and if love itself is to be referred to as something more than the human beings who are caught up in the passion, then we have to look here for something more than—I won't say the "literal" but the immediate sense that's given to us.

VAN DOREN: The immediate sense is so powerful; the language used by the lovers in calling upon so many objects of nature—the flowers, the mountains, the rains, the birds—is so rich; and the reference is so wide that it isn't as if these lovers were *little* people having a *little* love. Their love becomes very strong and deep, and I really agree with you: we can carry that to the skies if we please!

XV
THE LANGUAGE OF THE BIBLE

VAN DOREN: Maurice, we spent so much time in our last talk both agreeing and disagreeing about the possibility—or impossibility—of extending the meaning of The Song of Songs that we neglected to mention one view in particular which attempts to find structure in it where maybe no structure is. There are those who say that it is not an allegorization; it is a drama, a lyrical drama. A maiden has been brought from the country to the court of King Solomon, and there among the court ladies she is unhappy because she remembers her shepherd lover far away in the hills. The court ladies are addressed as the "daughters of Jerusalem," and Solomon himself is there in the background, soon to emerge to receive the girl into the company of his wives. But she keeps longing for her lover, and keeps remembering the particulars of their love. Sometimes she sings to the daughters of Jerusalem, sometimes to Solomon; and at other times she seems to be singing to herself or, by extension, to her lover; and she even imagines him to be singing to her. The drama ends with her refusal to remain. She rejects the king, he allows her to return home to her lover, and at the end of the book, the lovers are reunited happily. But Solomon loses the girl.

SAMUEL: Yes, Solomon reflects on her constancy in that famous passage toward the end:

Many waters cannot quench love, SONG 8:7
Neither can the floods drown it;
If a man would give all the substance of his house for love,
He would utterly be contemned.

The word "contemned" there is the shading that we would mean in our word "contempt." It's not our "condemned." We would say in that context, "treated with contempt." The act would be despised, or shown up as a gesture of the grossest coarseness of character.

The Song of Songs can be seen that way, as a drama. I see no harm in trying to re-form it, and to read those antiphonal exchanges into it. That wouldn't affect the deeper question of a higher allegorical content that we discussed last time. Nevertheless, I still believe that there are certain passages which it seems almost impossible to accept as an exchange of love expressions between young people. They are of such power, and have such implications of greatness about them that you withdraw for a moment, and say: "This is love, yes, but what is it that I hear like a subdued thunder in the background?" For example, here are two passages about the beauty of the girl:

SONG 6:4 *Thou art beautiful, O my love, as Tirzah,*
Comely as Jerusalem,
Terrible as an army with banners.

and:

SONG 6:10 *Who is she that looketh forth as the dawn,*
Fair as the moon,
Clear as the sun,
Terrible as an army with banners?

Now it may be that because I love the Hebrew so much, perhaps I see more in it than I ought to. We've talked about the highly condensed nature of Hebrew, and about its agglutinative character in connection with The Book of Ruth. The phrase, "terrible as an army with banners," has a peculiarly interesting structure that illustrates what I mean by this intensity of language. In Hebrew the phrase is expressed in just two words: *ayumah ka-nidgalot.* The first word is the feminine form of "frightening" or "terrible." The *ka* prefix of the second word stands for "as" or "like," and the rest of the word means "beflagged" or "embannered" things.[69] (The root is *degel*, meaning "a flag" in Hebrew; *nidgal* is the passive form, and *nidgalot* is simply the feminine passive plural.) With a genius which can never be surpassed, the King James translators —if they were the ones who first hit on this phrase—had this inspiration: "terrible as an army with banners." Now, the beauty of a woman can very well strike a man as having this overwhelming force; but when this allusion is packed into two Hebrew words, it's a bombshell! It makes you say, "This is not just lovers' talk!" There are echoings and reverberations which make it difficult to escape the implication that in the background, there *is* a resonance of a higher thing.

VAN DOREN: Yes, that's true. I only hold out for the possibility that the poet writing here was so great a poet that he makes you say things like that, the way Shakespeare makes you say things of Juliet's addresses to Romeo, or Antony's to Cleopatra. What lovers ever talked like that? None! Remember, in the course of their love, they don't talk about each other—they talk about the sun and the moon, about all the great things of the universe, none of which is too great!

SAMUEL: Yes, that tremendous phrasing by Romeo: "And shake the yoke of the inauspicious stars from this world-wearied flesh." It *is* superhuman!

VAN DOREN: I'm very happy that we have opposed each other to the extent that we have here, because we've managed to do two things: first, we've tended to state the possibility (it's a powerful possibility, I agree) that the preference in The Song of Songs, either intentionally or unintentionally, is to something transcendent; and second, in the course of our opposition we have hit upon a way of saying what poetry at its very greatest is.

But let me go back to that phrase, "terrible as an army with banners." I was interested to learn about the literal meaning of the Hebrew, because in looking over a certain new translation of the Bible, I couldn't find the phrase at all, or I thought I had found no equivalent of it. I found this:

You are as beautiful as Tirzah, my love,
As comely as Jerusalem,
As august as the most renowned.

And I rubbed my eyes!

SAMUEL (*laughing*): Genius! To maul that phrase into this piece of pedantry is also a kind of genius!

VAN DOREN: Your explanation of the Hebrew confirmed my belief that the original *did* mean something that the genius of the King James translators carried over into "terrible as an army with banners." When the phrase is repeated a second time, this translator changes it a bit more, and makes it even worse!

SAMUEL: *Worse*? That's very difficult to do!

VAN DOREN: A little worse! Just see if it isn't! Are you sure, by the way, that the Hebrew phrase is exactly the same both times?

SAMUEL: Oh, yes! *Ayumah ka-nidgalot* appears without any change whatsoever, so that he has no excuse.

VAN DOREN: All right. Now here is our translator —I say in vanity—changing it a bit:

Who is she that breaks forth like the dawn,
As beautiful as the moon,
As bright as the sun,
As august as the most distinguished?

(*laughter*)

VAN DOREN: I can't help laughing! "As august as the most distinguished!" Listen to all the *s*'s, the *t*'s, the *sh*'s—it sounds like, well, no poet at all, not even a good prose writer!

SAMUEL: Some people, I suppose, are tired of the standard translations out of the past. Great as the King James translation is, and good as some translations are for modern times, the fact is that we haven't got a translation that is in harmony with the language today—by which I don't mean a colloquial translation. One of the reasons is something we've deplored—the neglect of the Bible. Possibly "neglect" is not quite the right word. The Bible is read, it is known, but I don't think it's *enjoyed.* I don't think that it forms a part in people's lives, as it has done among certain groups in the past, and fewer in the present. Is it, do you think, that there isn't a translation which corresponds to times today?

VAN DOREN: The Bible is not *lived with* as it once was. Why? To me, this is a terribly interesting question. I am not one of those who think that no new translation of the Bible should be made. You know, there are those who hold up their hands in horror if one syllable of the King James Version is changed. I am not one of those at all, because I believe that this book is so living a thing that it must remain alive—and alive in the language, as Wordsworth said, that men use. There is every reason why we should be careful to keep it current, to keep it as "our book," and not as an antique.

SAMUEL: Not as a piety, a deliberate piety. People should read it not because they want to gather credits in heaven, but because it's a necessity of their lives.

VAN DOREN: But you see, the question is this: How shall we get that new translation without the genius to produce it? Just as it took genius to write this book, so it will take genius to translate it, and I think that all people agree: the translators of the King James Version were men of genius.

SAMUEL: There's something of a paradox in the problem we're facing here. I myself can't read a translation which hasn't got something of the archaic about it. I don't want it to be modern—I won't say with the slang—but with the locutions of today. And yet it has to be alive. That raises another problem: What is the translation supposed to do? Is it supposed to give us what that man meant when he wrote it? Can we know it?

VAN DOREN: We can't know that, of course.

SAMUEL: Is it supposed to mean what it meant to the Jews, let's say, of 2,500 or 2,000 years ago, when they read it? Or are we going to put new meanings into it (I guess it would be legitimate) as we reveal stretches of need in our own spiritual lives that this text would correspond to? I don't know what the acceptable basis for translation is here.

VAN DOREN: Why not put it this way, Maurice: the great versions made in English in the sixteenth century, culminating in the King James Version at the beginning of the seventeenth, were done with a view to making the Bible a possession of the people. As a matter of fact, men were put to death[70] for taking part in this enterprise, because the Bible was not supposed to be a possession of the people. These men went ahead to risk their lives to put the Bible into the English of the time so that people would think of it as *their* book—and they succeeded. But the English of their time—a glorious thing, in many respects—is not quite ours.

SAMUEL: Mark, you would know more about this than I; was it the English of their time? Was there no archaism in the language they used *as of that time?*

VAN DOREN: It's awfully hard to answer that. I agree with you, incidentally, with the greatest alacrity when you say that the Bible should *sound* as if it were an old book. On the other hand, I also agree that any word which has lost the meaning it had in 1611 should have the present meaning given to it. A famous illustration of an archaism is the word "prevent," which then meant merely "come before."[71]

SAMUEL: Yes, and "to anticipate."

VAN DOREN: And not "to provide obstacles." Let words like that be modernized, because there are those who, quite understandably, cannot comprehend them; but let the Bible *sound* like an old book. There's a parallel problem, by the way, in the translations of Homer, which keep on coming out one a year, almost. I myself am very unhappy whenever I read one that makes Homer sound like a detective story.

SAMUEL: Or a Western.

VAN DOREN: Or a Western written just around the corner, which doesn't retain what is undoubtedly there, distinguished and beautiful words.

SAMUEL: The Bible is now weighted with the association of centuries of human suffering and aspiration, so that it is not now what it was when it was written. And there's another difficulty: how to bring through this sense of historic accumulation that goes with it.

VAN DOREN: Let me say, Maurice, that when we discussed the Book of Tobit, both you and I read a modern translation of that book copyrighted in 1938. We both found the story very charming, and I suspect that was because it came at us immediately, entered our imaginations without any difficulty. Were you wishing as you read it that it were written in some other style?

SAMUEL: That's a very good observation. No, it was perfectly modern, perfectly simple, straightforward, colloquial, almost.

VAN DOREN: Which I suspect the original was.

SAMUEL: Yes, you get the impression that that's how the original was—artless, something told 'round a fireside, or a campfire, or by parents to children at home. However, this might not apply to the great books of the Bible—the heavy books, the magnificent books.

VAN DOREN: I'm afraid I would agree.

SAMUEL: It's very difficult to conceive of an adequate modern rendition of the great denunciatory passages in Isaiah; or for that matter, even the passages of immense comforting affection found in the Second Isaiah. People don't use language magnificently anymore, and the language of the Bible was magnificent. This is not an age of magnificent thinking.

VAN DOREN: No, it is not.

SAMUEL: That, perhaps, is the difficulty. Perhaps we're not ripe for a magnificent translation, because our relationship to language isn't serious enough.

VAN DOREN: Now *that* is a very illuminating remark. I myself lament that almost complete absence these days of people who value rich prose, or rich verse, for its own sake. We're afraid of such things; we shy away from them—although we didn't when Winston Churchill spoke. There were those who valued very highly a certain stately and even archaic style.

SAMUEL: Churchill dared to use that in his great speeches. You know, Mark, this seems to be the heart of the problem: people today appear to want a Bible rendered in—what shall I call it?—social-center English. They don't seem to understand that you cannot deal with all the everlasting, crucial, eternally important questions in the Bible in any other but a great language, however simple it might be. Take this one theme we've been discussing in all our conversations here—divine and human love as it runs through the Bible, with all these characters acting as its interpreters, instances, and illuminations; how can you transmit it if you reject a language which is in harmony with the grandeur and the width of the theme? Human beings have been seeking to understand the meaning of love ever since they stopped being animal, ever since they first became aware that a distinction exists between the kind of love they experience, and the simple attractions the lower animals have for each other. Human beings have been puzzling over the successive refinements of this emotion, trying to define or somehow to grasp the nuances of love relationships—and here is the Bible expressing it in the finest and the most glorious language. We haven't got a love poetry, or a poetry of friendship today that should give us the hope that a superb translation can either be made, or be accepted, by a public which is tone-deaf to the music of language.

VAN DOREN: I dare say, Maurice, that it would be absurd to expect that a translation satisfying all of our requirements would come along very soon. I for one am content that the effort is being made; and I shouldn't be surprised if it took longer than our lifetimes for such a thing to appear. It might take centuries! But if you take a long enough view of it, and think of, say, the King James Version as having done what it did when it did it for the first time, and if you're willing to look ahead a thousand years, there might need to be a translation different enough so that it was contemporary to its own time, and yet like enough to the original so that it preserved the sense: this was an *old* book.

SAMUEL: It's possible, Mark, isn't it, that the time is out of joint? People aren't thinking of the Bible and the great themes it presents with the seriousness that they have merited and will merit; and for the time being, we're caught up in an immense evasion. We think we've found clues and answers and devices which will make it unnecessary for us to examine an emotion such as love. Instead of examining the intrinsic emotion, we speak of a man's "ego needs," and of his "responses"—an evasion of that fundamental which is bound to be a concomitant of the sense of immense ingenuity which pervades the contemporaneous world.

VAN DOREN: People aren't lacking for religion today; we have a great many religions. We have "political" religions (sometimes called "ideologies"), and "social" religions. We even have "moral" religions promulgated by those who say that morality itself is enough, that you can build an ethical culture upon nothing except what the reason finds in human behavior. Of course, we also have "art for art's sake," which is the foundation of "aesthetic" religions; and then there are those who make science a kind of religion.

SAMUEL: Oh, yes, but they forget one fundamental which great scientists themselves have realized, namely, that science doesn't teach the *use* of science. (Bacon foreshadowed this long ago, you'll remember, when he wrote in his essay *Of Studies* that books do not teach the use of books.) But these people nowadays who prattle about "ego needs" wouldn't think of doing what you and I have been doing in these talks—examining the theme of love which is so richly represented in the Bible. Instead, they are busy considering social effects: What is the social effect of doing this, or that? What is the satisfaction to the individual?

—looking at the human beings schematically, and making graphs and diagrams, almost as if these people were Skinner's rats. You know, there's a very ingenious psychologist at Harvard, B. F. Skinner, who has done remarkable things studying white rats[72]—and we're going to learn from *that* how human beings ought to behave! The responses of the rats are of immense importance to the human heart! All that sort of thing is for me in deep and calamitous contradiction to what is the essence of human relationships.

VAN DOREN: To despair of men ever returning to wisdom and sense is something that could always have been done. The very book that we've been reading has its moments of despair, has it not? God himself despairs of His people! There are great and deep troughs, as well as great high waves, even in this story, and the whole history of man is a history of ups and downs. I often think that we're in a down trough now. I quite agree with the things you are saying, but I do not actually despair in the sense of assuming that the good will never come again.

SAMUEL: Yes, if you despair in that sense, it means that you anticipate the collapse of the human species; because if there is a decline that has no ending, and human beings become automata or merely highly intelligent animals with infinite ingenuity at their disposal, then the human species—as we know it—ceases to be. When people talk about the ending of the human race, they usually envisage it as some great atomic devastation, which causes the human species to disappear. I see it in another form: the danger is even greater that we may become "sublimated" into another species—a species in which the pursuit of skills is the substitute for the pursuit of knowledge and of feeling.

VAN DOREN: I heard a terrible statement the other day that I shall probably never be able to forget. Almost everybody knows, I think, that in the nineteenth century, Nietzsche said, "God is dead." (That statement explains a great deal of modern history. Many people act as if He *were* dead; or to put that another way, they have ceased to believe in Him.) Someone said the other day, "If God died in the nineteenth century, man died in the twentieth." The speaker was saying just what you said. He didn't mean that man as a species, physically, disappeared, but that he ceased to have in him the depth, the tone, the meaning that he once had.

SAMUEL: Is it your feeling that in the day when men no longer read the Bible, it will not be the human species?

VAN DOREN: I'm quite willing to say that. It would be true.

SAMUEL: Yes, I would say that, too. The disappearance of the Bible—not merely its values, but the form in which these values have been put——

VAN DOREN: The words themselves.

SAMUEL: ——the words themselves, which are more than human—the disappearance of these as a factor in human relations would mean the emergence of a kind of creature that we couldn't call human.

VAN DOREN: When we say "the words themselves," we could come back for the final time to this question of translation. What *are* the words themselves? Since for most people they must be put into other languages than Hebrew, what *are* the words themselves? I would pray, and you would, too, that persons appear soon enough who have the genius and the profundity to discover those words which maintain the strength of the original. Let them render the whole of the Bible in language that will pierce the hearts of their generation; but if it is not given to them to do all of it, then let them, if nothing else, address themselves to those portions which have engaged us in these conversations—those portions of the Bible that illuminate the meaning of love, love of God for men, of men for God, and of men for men.

EPITAPH FOR MAURICE SAMUEL

When I was asked in 1952 to go to the Jewish Theological Seminary of America and meet a man who would be one of two with whom, if all went well, I might discuss the Bible in summer sessions of "The Eternal Light," I didn't know that this man was Maurice, nor had I ever met him face to face; I knew only his books, which I greatly admired and relished, but that was different from knowing him. The meeting when it occurred was one of the most important events in my life, and one of the most delightful. For there he was, and I shall never forget his voice as, after a few minutes of talk about a third man who might complete the panel—in those days it was assumed that three heads were always better than two—Maurice thumped the floor with his walking-stick and cried: "There will be no third, I can talk with this man forever!" I still can't imagine how he knew this; for it was true, as the next twenty years proved. Our conversation, either on the air or off, never flagged or stopped. His mind was a fountain of ideas, observations, memories, tales; his voice was musical with excitement over things it had just occurred to him to say—or sing, for it was a singing voice, as his mind was a singing mind, and in my time I have never known its like.

He was always serious and he was always humorous—by which I mean he was always ready to be either, as only the greatest persons have been. For example, Abraham Lincoln, whose gravity at times was equaled by his wit and grace at others. And for another example, Shakespeare, the secret of whose power is precisely that no door of life was closed to him, no sound of the world shut out. Maurice was the peer of such men as those; he was perfectly at home with greatness. Masterpieces of literature did not intimidate him; they were written for him, he thought, and he was right. His knowledge of the Bible was the knowledge of a poet, of a storyteller, of a scholar, of a historian, of a moralist all at once. It was his favorite book, and he read it as Lincoln did, naturally and happily. He was at home in it everywhere; his memory of it was immense. What I learned of it through him I shall never be able to measure.

He was at home in the Bible because he was one of its people. No man, I think, ever enjoyed being a Jew more than Maurice did. And I mean by enjoyment everything it is capable of meaning: dedication and delight, fear and trembling, awe and simple pleasure, wrath and loving-kindness, woe and merriment intermixed. What I learned from him finally was that there is nothing so wonderful as loving what one does—and what one is—with all one's heart, and with all one's soul, and with all one's might.

MARK VAN DOREN
Falls Village
Connecticut

May 8, 1972

NOTES

The informal notes presented here are for readers of inquiring mind who may care to have slightly fuller information or further reading on certain points raised in the conversations. The basic reference works consulted for these notes are: *The Legends of the Jews* by Louis Ginzberg, in seven volumes (Philadelphia: The Jewish Publication Society of America, 1913); *The Jewish Encyclopedia*, in twelve volumes (New York and London: Funk and Wagnalls Company, 1901 and 1912); and the new—and very beautiful—*Encyclopaedia Judaica*, in sixteen volumes (Jerusalem and New York: Encyclopaedia Judaica and The Macmillan Company, 1972). They will be referred to here as *Legends, J. E.* and *E. J.*, respectively. A one-volume edition of Professor Ginzberg's classic was issued by The Jewish Publication Society in 1956, under the title *Legends of the Bible.* General readers who have no urgent need for the exhaustive index and voluminous notes of the original edition will find the one volume highly readable and rewarding.

1 The supercilious "How odd" jingle, entitled "The Chosen People," is by W. N. Ewer and appears in *The Silver Treasury of Light Verse*, ed. Oscar Williams (New York: Mentor Books, 1957). Following immediately on Ewer's heels in this anthology is "A Reply" by Cecil Browne, which goes, "But not so odd,/As those who choose/A Jewish God,/ Yet spurn the Jews." The "Oh no" jingle is by *Anon.* A variation goes, "Oh no, it's not,/ The Jews chose God."

2 Robert Frost, "The Lesson for Today."

3 Jews refer to the Hebrew Bible as the *Tanach* (pronounced *tah-nakh*, the second syllable stressed and rhyming with the German *ach*). The word *Tanach* is an acronym, formed from the initial letters of the Hebrew names of the three major divisions of the Holy Scriptures: *T* for *Torah* (also known as the Pentateuch or the Five Books of Moses); *N* for *Nevi'im*, the Prophets; and *K* for *Ketuvim*, the Writings or Hagiographa. Even though the terms "the Hebrew Bible" and "the Bible" take the singular verb, the Hebrew Bible is not *one* book but a library of books —twenty-four, according to Jewish tradition.

4 The injunction against serving other gods and making images or idols is the Second Commandment in Jewish tradition; in the Christian tradition, it is reckoned as the First Commandment. Rabbi Solomon Goldman's all-too-brief commentary on the Decalogue, *The Ten Command-*

ments, ed. Maurice Samuel (Chicago: University of Chicago Press, 1956) discusses this and a number of other significant points, including some differing interpretations of the much misunderstood word "jealous."

5 For a brilliant essay refuting the recurrent charges of racialism—in this instance, charges against the Jews by H. G. Wells and George Bernard Shaw—read Hayim Greenberg's "The Universalism of the Chosen People" in *The Inner Eye*, Vol. I (New York: Jewish Frontier Association, 1953).

6 From "The Proselyte: A Responsum" by Moses Maimonides. Reprinted by permission of Schocken Books Inc. from *In Time and Eternity: A Jewish Reader* edited by Nahum N. Glatzer. Copyright © 1946, 1961 by Schocken Books Inc.

7 From Poem 1765 in *The Complete Poems of Emily Dickinson*, edited by Thomas H. Johnson. Copyright 1914, 1942 by Martha Dickinson Bianchi. Quoted by permission of Little, Brown and Co.

8 The command to love God is supreme in Judaism, and is regarded as the primary duty of the Jew. It is embedded in the *Shema*, the core Jewish prayer recited twice daily, and is the basic and indispensable element in Jewish worship. The *Shema* consists of three selections from the Bible (Deut. 6:4–9; then Deut. 11:13–21; and then Num. 15:37–41), and takes its name from the opening word ("Hear") of Deut. 6:4. The six Hebrew words in this verse affirm the unity of God, and after reciting this affirmation, the Jew states the command to love God. The theme is so important and so many philosophers and teachers have written on it that the inquiring reader would do best to consult the *J. E.* and *E. J.* and then to sample

anthologies like *In Time and Eternity* (*see note* 6) and *Faith and Knowledge: The Jew in the Medieval World*, ed. Nahum N. Glatzer (Boston: Beacon Press, 1963). Two lucid short books are *Basic Judaism* by Milton Steinberg (New York: Harcourt, Brace, 1947) and *Judaism: A Portrait* by Leon Roth (New York: Viking, 1960).

9 Isaac Loeb Peretz (1852-1915) is usually linked with Sholom Aleichem and Mendele Mocher S'forim as one of the three "greats" of Yiddish literature in eastern Europe of the nineteenth and early twentieth centuries. Peretz is particularly noted for his Hasidic and folk tales. Some of his best stories were retold in English by Maurice Samuel in *Prince of the Ghetto* (New York: Alfred A. Knopf, 1948). Included in this book are "Between Two Cliffs" and the famous "Silent Bontche."

10 Graham Greene, *The Potting Shed* (New York: Viking, 1956, 1957).

11 "The Toys" by Coventry Kersey Dighton Patmore (1823-1896) is reprinted in *The Viking Book of Poetry of the English-Speaking World*, ed. Richard Aldington (New York: Viking, 1945).

12 See Maurice Samuel's *The World of Sholom Aleichem* (New York: Alfred A. Knopf, 1943).

13 Questionings of God and His justice are not uncommon in the Jewish experience. Abraham sought to mitigate the punishment meted out to Sodom and Gomorrah (Gen. 18:20–33); Moses averted the extinction of the children of Israel after their sin of the Golden Calf (Exod. 32:7–14); the Book of Job, of course, is entirely devoted to this theme. The Hasid called the *Shpoler Zeyde* (the "grandfather from Shpola") dared to bring God to trial.

He was Aryeh Leib of Shpola, a little town south of Kiev in the Ukraine. The saintly and highly regarded Rabbi Levi Yitzhak of Berditchev (1740-1809) is a famous example of another Hasid who felt so close to God that he did not hesitate to question His ways. During solemn High Holy Day services one year, Levi Yitzhak addressed a musical plea to Him from the pulpit. The song is a favorite of modern cantors and opera stars and has been recorded many times. An English translation and the music appear under the title "The Kaddish of Rabbi Levi Yitzhak" in *Heritage of Jewish Music: The Music of the Jewish People* by Judith Kaplan Eisenstein (New York: Union of American Hebrew Congregations, 1972).

14 The prophet Jeremiah (Chap. 25) speaks approvingly of the sect which in his time (*ca.* 600 B.C.E.) refused to drink wine or strong drink, cultivate the vine or live in houses. The *J. E.* identifies them as the descendants of Jethro, the father-in-law of Moses.

15 From "The World of Those Who Love God" by Bahya ibn Pakuda. Reprinted by permission of Schocken Books Inc. from *In Time and Eternity: A Jewish Reader* edited by Nahum N. Glatzer. Copyright © 1946, 1961 by Schocken Books Inc. Bahya ibn Pakuda (Spain, eleventh century) wrote the first systematic presentation of Jewish ethics in a book called *Khovot ha-Levavot* or *Duties of the Heart*, which was very widely read and loved. A portion of it is included in *In Time and Eternity: A Jewish Reader.*

16 *Pirke Avot*, variously translated as *Ethics of the Fathers, Sayings of the Fathers, Chapters of the Fathers*, and *The Wisdom of the Fathers*, is a slender little treatise of the Talmud which Jews have been reading on Sabbath afternoons during the summer since at least the eighth century. It is a collection of sayings, maxims and aphorisms distill-

ing the teachings and outlook of the Jewish sages about life and human conduct. The "Fathers" in the book—some sixty in all—lived in the period from the end of the fifth century B.C.E. to the third of the Common Era. Many translations with expert commentary are easily available, among them: *The Living Talmud: The Wisdom of the Fathers*, ed. Judah Goldin (New York: Mentor, 1957); and *Sayings of the Talmud*, ed. Joseph H. Hertz (New York: Behrman, 1945).

17 A saying of Rabbi Hillel, *Pirke Avot 2:5.* Hillel is probably the best-known of the Rabbis, famous for his wisdom, patience and humility, who was active from 30 B.C.E. to 10 C.E. The story about Hillel that is taught to every Jewish schoolchild is this: One day an impatient scoffer burst in upon Hillel and demanded: "Teach me the whole Torah while I stand on one leg"—in other words, in a hurry. Hillel replied: "Whatever is hateful to you, do not do to your fellowman. Now, go and study." The reply is of course a restatement in very concrete and concise form of "Thou shalt love thy neighbor as thyself" (Lev. 19:18). For a lucid discussion of Hillel's Golden Rule and the problems inherent in "love thy neighbor as thyself," see *Judaism: Religion and Ethics* by Meyer Waxman (New York: Thomas Yoseloff, 1958, 1960, 1967).

18 Karl Marx's father, Heinrich—originally named Hirschel ha-Levi—was the son of a rabbi and the descendant of a long line of rabbis in the Rhineland. He was received into the Lutheran Church in 1817, a year before Karl's birth. Karl was baptized as a child and confirmed at the age of fifteen. His vitriolic essay *Zur Judenfrage*, "About the Jewish Question," was written in 1844. For more about Marx's venomous writings, see the article in the *E. J.* and *Karl Marx: His Life and Environment* by Isaiah Berlin (New York: Oxford University Press, 1963).

19 Leo Tolstoy, *War and Peace*, trans. Constance Garnett (New York: Random House), pp. 901–905.

20 Elizabeth Barrett Browning, *Sonnets from the Portuguese*, XIV:

> *If thou must love me, let it be for naught*
> *Except for love's sake only.*

21 The Rabbis of the Talmud tried to shed light on the contradiction by holding that Prov. 26:4 applies to foolish opinions about nonreligious matters—these can be ignored; while in the verse following, the fool has incorrect notions about religious matters—these must be refuted.

22 *Legends* has a delightful tale that Lilith deserted Adam very shortly after she became his wife because of his male chauvinism. She insisted upon full equality, by reason of their identical origin—dust. *Legends*, vol. i, p. 65.

23 One legend sees the Hagar episode as the hardest of all of Abraham's trials. God appeared to him in the night to comfort him and remind him that Sarah, after all, was his true wife. The next morning he awoke early, gave Hagar a bill of divorce, and sent her and Ishmael away. See *Legends*, vol. i, p. 264.

24 Is Mark Van Doren's suggestion in consonance with the United States Supreme Court decision of June 17, 1963, which banned the recitation of prayers and devotional Bible readings in the public schools? In the frequently acrimonious public debate over that decision, few Americans have read the decision closely or remember that the Court was *not* hostile to either the Holy Scriptures or religion. In delivering the Court's opinion, Mr. Justice Clark declared:

> *Nothing we have said here indicates that . . . study of the Bible or of religion, when presented objectively*

> *as part of a secular program of education, may not be effected consistent with the First Amendment. . . . One's education is not complete without a study of comparative religion or the history of religion, and its relationship to the advancement of civilization. It certainly may be said that* the Bible is worthy of study for its literary and historic qualities. [*Emphasis added. E. S.*]

In his concurring opinion, Mr. Justice Brennan stated: "The holding of the Court today plainly does not foreclose teaching *about* the Holy Scriptures. . . ." This point was again stressed in the concurring opinion expressed by Mr. Justice Goldberg, with whom Mr. Justice Harlan joined: "It seems clear . . . that the Court would recognize the propriety . . . of the teaching *about* religion, as distinguished from the teaching *of* religion, in the public schools."

25 *Legends* presents a very beautiful and poignant elaboration of the passage in Gen. 22:1–2, portraying Abraham as desperately trying to evade God's test of him. It goes:

> AND HE SAID TO ABRAHAM: *"Take now thy son."*
> ABRAHAM REPLIED: *"I have two sons, and I do not know which of them Thou commandest me to take."*
> GOD SAID: *"Thine only son."*
> ABRAHAM: *"The one is the only son of his mother, and the other is the only son of his mother."*
> GOD: *"Whom thou lovest."*
> ABRAHAM: *"I love this one and I love that one."*
> GOD: *"Even Isaac."*
> ABRAHAM: *"And where shall I go?"*
> GOD: *"To the land I will show thee."*

See *Legends*, vol. i, p. 274.

26 Livy, trans. B. O. Foster. (London: William Heinemann, 1926, 1948), vol. iv, pp. 23–29 (Livy, book viii, chap. 7).

27 The wife-sister episode appears three times, in Gen. 12:10–20, 20:1–8, and 26:7–11, twice in the case of Abraham

and Sarah, and once in the case of Isaac and Rebekah. The Rabbis disapproved of Abraham's deception; the medieval commentator Nachmanides called it a great sin. The late Bible scholar E. A. Speiser surmised that Abraham may very well have been Sarah's brother. Speculating on Abraham's statement in Gen. 20:12, he asserted that Sarah may have been Terah's daughter by adoption, hence the sister of Terah's son, Abraham. But going to extra-biblical sources, Professor Speiser examined archeological evidence relating to the Hurrians, an ancient people who lived in central Mesopotamia, in the area of Harran (the biblical Haran) contemporaneous with the Patriarchal Age. It was the custom of the Hurrians, especially in the top levels of society, that a woman given in marriage by her brother became legally her husband's sister. "Such a wife-sister had the advantage of exceptional socioreligious solicitude and protection which was not enjoyed by ordinary wives. . . . It was evidently a mark of superior status," wrote Professor Speiser. Rebekah lived in Haran; and in Gen. 24, Laban, her brother, played the authoritative role. This led Professor Speiser to conclude that Rebekah, too, was given in marriage according to the Hurrian legal practice, which placed her in the wife-sister category.

Why did Abraham and later Isaac make a point of telling their royal hosts that their wives were their sisters? Status, said Professor Speiser; they wanted to convey the fact that they had wives of distinction. And why are the episodes related in the Hebrew Scriptures? Because they testify to the high caliber of the women, Professor Speiser said, and also to the "purity" of their children. Since the biblical genealogies are greatly concerned with the carriers of the heritage, details about birth, lineage, social status, etc., are obviously of immense importance.

See Professor E. A. Speiser's informative essay, "The Wife-Sister Motif in the Patriarchal Narratives" in *Biblical and Other Studies*, ed. Alexander Altmann (Cambridge: Harvard University Press, 1963), pp. 15–28.

28 One legend relates that Sarah noticed Ishmael playing at making "toy sacrifices" to idols; another, that in playing with his bow and arrow, young Ishmael used to aim at Isaac—in jest, he always explained. See *Legends*, vol. i, p. 264, and vol. v, p. 246, n. 211.

29 For a clear and concise discussion of Hebrew origins and of geographical factors, consult *Ancient Israel* by Harry M. Orlinsky (Ithaca, N.Y.: Cornell University Press, 1954).

30 Maurice Samuel's firm view that Esau was neither qualified for nor destined to receive the blessing is presented at greater length in a diverting chapter, "The Manager," about Rebekah, the effective head of Isaac's household. It is in his *Certain People of the Book* (New York: Alfred A. Knopf, 1955).

31 Professor Speiser (*see note 27*) attached great significance to Rebekah's reply. The Hurrian "wife-sistership" marriage documents included a statement from the woman involved that she concurred in the legal action. In Gen. 24:58, Rebekah's wishes are consulted; she answers affirmatively and sweeps aside the suggestion about a waiting period. For Professor Speiser, the resemblance to the Hurrian custom was further emphasized by the fact that the word "sister" appears twice in the two verses following after "I will go."

32 Thomas Mann, *Joseph and His Brothers* (New York: Alfred A. Knopf, 1934, 1935, 1938, 1944, 1948).

33 Mark Van Doren retired as professor of English at Columbia University in 1959 after thirty-nine years on the faculty. Two years later the university established the Mark Van Doren Award, given annually to "a member of the faculty who has distinguished himself in showing

those qualities and virtues exemplified by Mark Van Doren —zealous scholastic leadership, devotion to intellectual development, and humility."

34 Maurice Samuel began his career as a "boy orator" on the street corners of Manchester, England, and became a professional lecturer when he immigrated to America in 1914. He thought of himself as a *maggid*, a wandering teacher-preacher of the kind developed in eastern Europe. He described his career and some of his experiences in *Little Did I Know: Recollections and Reflections* (New York: Alfred A. Knopf, 1963).

35 *Pirke Avot* 1:16; 3:16.

36 Mark Van Doren and Maurice Samuel were both fascinated by the Joseph story in Genesis and by the monumental retelling of that story by Thomas Mann. They discussed the subject in ten conversations in 1953; and in subsequent conversations over nearly two decades, they kept reverting to Joseph and discovering new facets of his complex personality. Both men agreed that Mann's trilogy was a work of art and "one of the greatest achievements of the human imagination," but each held his own view about the character of Joseph and wrote long essays about him. Mark Van Doren's is entitled "Joseph and His Brothers: A Comedy in Four Parts." It may be found in his book *The Happy Critic and Other Essays* (New York: Hill and Wang, 1961). Maurice Samuel called his essay "The Brilliant Failure" and included it in his *Certain People of the Book* (*see note 30*).

37 The translation of *The Torah: The Five Books of Moses*, issued by The Jewish Publication Society of America in 1962, renders Gen. 34:2–3 as: "Shechem son of Hamor the Hivite, chief of the country, saw her, and took her and lay with her by force. Being strongly drawn to Dinah

daughter of Jacob, and in love with the maiden, he spoke to the maiden tenderly."

38 Thomas Mann (*see note 32*), p. 102.

39 Reprinted by permission of Hill and Wang, A division of Farrar, Strauss & Giroux, Inc., from *Collected and New Poems: 1924–1963* by Mark Van Doren. Copyright © 1963 by Mark Van Doren, p. 425. A section of this volume called "The People of the Word" contains some charming, poignant and insightful portraits-in-poetry of biblical personalities, including Joseph, Abigail, Bathsheba, Rebekah and Samuel.

40 *Legends* (vol. ii, p. 225) identifies Dinah as Job's second wife. Another legend (vol. ii, pp. 37–38) relates that Simeon married her. This second legend goes on to declare that Dinah bore a child to the slain Shechem, a daughter named Asenath. Her brothers wanted to kill the child, but Jacob saved her. An angel then flew her to Egypt, where she was adopted by Potiphar. Years later, when Joseph became viceroy of Egypt he married Asenath—so the legend goes.

41 In 1921, Jewish pioneers established Kibbutz En-Harod at the foot of Mount Gilboa near the spring associated with Gideon (see Judges 7:1) and possibly with Saul (see I Sam. 29:1). The following year Kibbutz Bet Alfa was founded nearby. The land on which the first tents were pitched had been part of a large parcel of land, the "Nuris Block" purchased by the Jewish National Fund from the absentee Sursuck family. In one of his early books, *On the Rim of the Wilderness: The Conflict in Palestine* (New York: Horace Liveright, 1931), Maurice Samuel wrote:

> *Part of the 29,000 dunams of land known as the Nuris Block was barren hill. Sixteen thousand dunams were covered by swamp. In all, less than 6,000 dunams*

> *were under cultivation, having been leased to 39 Arab families who engaged in cereal growing. The land was treeless except for a few sycamores. The entire district was infested with malaria, from which practically all the Arabs suffered. . . . Within two years the Jewish colonists had drained the 16,000 dunams of swamp land. In the first year 35 per cent of the colonists were taken with malaria; in the second year 22 per cent; in the third year 14 per cent. By 1928 malaria had practically disappeared from the region.*
>
> *It was universally considered, among the Arabs, that this region could not be made generally habitable. By 1930 there were settled in this region 1,500 Jewish souls, divided into six settlements. The following branches of agriculture are pursued: cereals, grapes, apricots, almonds, pears, plums, cherries, dairy produce, market gardening and beginnings in citrus fruits. Twelve hundred head of breed cattle produce half a million litres of milk a year. The vegetables of the colonies are sold in Haifa and Jerusalem, and exported to Damascus and Cairo.*

In 1962, a new border settlement was founded on the crest of Mount Gilboa, overlooking on the one side the lush green Jezreel valley of the State of Israel, and on the other the still treeless land of the kingdom of Jordan. The soldier-settlers heard a message from the then Premier David Ben-Gurion: "Tell it in Gath and publish it in the streets of Ashkelon that Israel youth has settled in the mountains of Gilboa"—a paraphrase of David's lament in II Samuel 1:20–27.

42 Paltiel first came up in the 1954 conversations between the two men ("The Supporting Cast of the Bible"). They disagreed about him then, and in 1961 were still disagreeing.

43 William Wordsworth, "The Solitary Reaper."

44 The Rabbis considered Jephthah, Gideon, and Samson as the three "least worthy" of the Judges. See *Legends*, vol. vi, p. 201.

45 His special loathing of Jezebel is expressed in the chapter on her he entitled "The Hellcat" in *Certain People of the Book* (*see note 30*).

46 Transliterations can never successfully convey all the nuances of sound. In this famous Hebrew passage, all the *a*'s are pronounced as in "father." The accents fall very heavily on *ratzákh* and *yarásh*.

47 Legend has it that Tamar was born before her mother was converted to Judaism, so that strictly speaking, "she cannot be called one of the children of David." See *Legends*, vol. iv, p. 118. Why the makers of that legend should have sought to mitigate Amnon's guilt is a puzzle; perhaps the thought of incest was so horrifying that they looked for some way to soften the harsh facts.

48 Thomas Mann (*see note 32*), p. 1016.

49 Tamar kept her face covered in chaste modesty all during the time she lived in the house of her father-in-law Judah, *Legends* vol. ii, p. 34 relates. Thus Judah did not recognize her and took her for a harlot. God rewarded her for her modesty by making her become the mother of the royal line of David and the ancestress of the Prophet Isaiah as well. The legend goes on to tell that Judah actually passed her by on the way to Timnah, whereupon Tamar appealed to God, who sent an angel to turn him back. Tamar bore twins to Judah—Perez and Zerah. Ruth 4:18–22 traces David's ancestry to Perez, the grandson of Jacob.

50 *Certain People of the Book*, (*see note 30*).

51 The hyphens do not appear in the original, but have been inserted to assist reading. The transliteration gives the Sephardic pronunciation used in the State of Israel and in the modern teaching of Hebrew. As in the previous transliteration (*see note 46*), the *a* is pronounced as in "father." The *ey* combination is pronounced as in the English "prey," and the *ay* as in the English "aye, aye." The *i* is short, comparable to the *ee* sound in "deep," and the *u* is sounded as in "ruby." The *kh* combination is the gutteral *ch* heard at the end of the German "ach."

52 The Moabites, descendants of Lot and his daughters, harassed the children of Israel during their journey to the Promised Land (see the book of Numbers 22–24) and led them into idolatry (Num. 25). Deut. 23:4–6 forbids a Moabite from entering "into the assembly of the Lord for ever." The Rabbis of the Talmud, however, noted that since the masculine singular form was used in the passage in Deuteronomy, the prohibition did not apply to Moabite women like Ruth, who converted to Judaism and married Israelites. This interpretation may have been academic, however, since the Rabbis also declared that the prohibition no longer applied after the Assyrian conquest. In the turmoil of war, various peoples were forced from their ancestral homes, and the comingling of refugees prevented clearcut dilineations of lineage and nationality.

53 Samuel Dill, *Roman Society from Nero to Marcus Aurelius* (London: Macmillan, 1904), p. 67.

54 The Hebrew name *Naomi* means "pleasant." As Naomi herself explains, *Marah* means "bitter."

55 Boaz is seen as an octogenarian in *Legends*, vol. iv, p. 34, and Ruth as a woman of forty. Read through this filter of legend, the story ends on an even higher note of triumph and joy: a child born to the good Boaz in his old age!

56 The nearest kinsman had not only the right but the moral obligation to redeem family land, according to Deut. 25:25.

57 The term "Apocrypha" (from the Greek, meaning "hidden away") refers to a group of books excluded from the canon of the Hebrew Bible, thought to have been written in the period of the Second Temple, i.e., between the fifth and the first century, B.C.E. The Roman Catholic and Greek Orthodox Churches included those books in their canon. The Church Father Jerome (346–420) translated Scriptures into Latin (called the Vulgate) and included also the additional books. In his German Bible of 1534, Martin Luther separated these extra books and placed them as a group at the end of the Scriptures. The authors of the King James English translation of 1611 rendered the books of the Apocrypha into English; but within a decade or so, they began to be omitted from Protestant Bible editions. Today the Protestant Old Testament is the equivalent of the Hebrew Bible. The Douay Bible, the official Roman Catholic edition in English, published in 1582 and 1609–1610, is a translation of Jerome's Vulgate and retains the Apocrypha.

The *J. E.* and *E. J.*, the *Encyclopaedia Britannica*, and other standard references contain articles on the Apocrypha and the individual books regarded as apocryphal works. Among these books are Tobit, Judith, I and II Esdras (Ezra), I and II Maccabees, Wisdom of Solomon, and Ecclesiasticus (also known as the Wisdom of Ben Sira).

58 It is thought that the Book of Tobit may be the oldest of the apocryphal books. Some sources believe it was composed between 200 and 50 B.C.E., others believe it is older. The original language in which it was written is also unclear, perhaps Hebrew or perhaps Aramaic. Fragments were found among the Qumran scrolls in both languages. The extraordinary amount of burying of the dead

in the book is a testimonial to the piety of the Jewish hero, Tobit. The obligation to bury the dead was a very important religious duty; indeed, the Talmud says that the care of the unburied body of a friendless man takes precedence over all other religious duties.

Anyone who is interested in Bible translations will find absorbing information in *Our English Bible in the Making* by H. G. May (Philadelphia: Westminster, 1952). The book rehearses some of Jerome's own description of how he translated the Hebrew Bible into Latin. He went to Palestine, learned Hebrew so that he could refer directly to the Hebrew Scriptures, and he also consulted with the rabbinic exegetes of the time. The entire task consumed fifteen years, but he translated Tobit in one day and the Book of Judith overnight. It was a marathon feat: his Jewish Hebrew teacher read the books aloud from Aramaic manuscripts, translating into Hebrew as he went along. Keeping pace, Jerome translated from the oral Hebrew into the Latin, dictating his translation line by line and word by word.

The translation of Tobit quoted in the Conversation is in *The Apocrypha: An American Translation* by Edgar J. Goodspeed (New York: Random House, 1959).

59 The Assyrian army under Sargon II captured the city of Samaria, capital of the northern kingdom of Israel, *ca.* 722 B.C.E. This is how he boasted of it in his annals: "Property of Sargon, the great king, the mighty king, king of the world, king of Assyria. At the beginning of my royal rule I besieged and conquered Samaria. 27,290 of its inhabitants I led away as booty."

60 The archangel Raphael is not mentioned in the Hebrew Bible, but he does appear in Jewish legends and in mystical writings. His particular province is healing diseases, wounds, and even moral evil. His name is a Hebrew compound of *rapha*, "heal," and *el*, "God."

61 Reprinted by permission of Hill and Wang, a division of Farrar, Straus & Giroux, Inc., from *Collected and New Poems: 1924–1963* by Mark Van Doren. Copyright © 1963 by Mark Van Doren. (*See note 39.*)

62 *Seven* is correct—consult *The World of Sholom Aleichem* (*see note 12*).

63 According to Jewish tradition, only those books which were thought to have been directly inspired by God were admitted to the Hebrew Bible. All the prophets had been so inspired, the Rabbis taught, and therefore every book in the Bible was considered the work of a prophet. The Rabbis regarded David and Solomon as prophets. Since direct Divine inspiration came to an end with the last prophets (Haggai, Zechariah, and Malachi, ca. the middle of the fifth century B.C.E.) books like Tobit, Ecclesiasticus, and the Wisdom of Solomon—all written "late"—were not included in the canon. The book of Esther aroused some controversy, but was finally admitted; some of the Rabbis felt that it had been written by Mordecai, a contemporary of Haggai, Zechariah, and Malachi, and himself a prophet who had been Divinely inspired. The Book of Daniel ("in its final form a product of the second century B.C.E.," according to Bible scholar Harry M. Orlinsky) was considered the work of the Prophet Daniel during the days of Nebuchadnezzar (early sixth century, B.C.E.)

64 The Hebrew Bible itself quotes fragments of books which are lost—e.g., the Book of the Wars of the Lord (see Num. 21:14); the Book of Yashar (Josh. 10:13 and II Sam. 1:18); the Chronicles of the Kings of Israel and the Chronicles of the Kings of Judah, which are cited in I and II Kings.

65 Jewish tradition sees this book as an allegory tracing the relationship between God and Israel. While it is attributed

to Solomon, the book nevertheless gave pause to the Rabbis who debated whether or not it should be included in the canon. The staunchest support for its inclusion came from the great Rabbi Akiba (died *ca.* 137 C.E.) who declared that if all the other books of the Bible are holy, "the Song of Songs is the holy of holies." The history of the interpretations of this book over the centuries is traced in the *J. E.* and *E. J.* An illuminating view is presented by Gerson D. Cohen in "The Song of Songs and the Jewish Religious Mentality," in *The Samuel Friedland Lectures* (New York, The Jewish Theological Seminary of America, 1966), pp. 1–21.

66 The contemporary Bible scholar H. L. Ginsberg observes that the Song of Songs is "a collection of love songs which bears considerable resemblance to both ancient and modern love songs of the Near East. . . . The book is entirely profane. God is never invoked or alluded to. Yet, because it was attributed to Solomon, and because it was possible to understand all of the songs as wedding songs (though some of them were surely not that originally), the book was accepted as canonical without reinterpretation. For marriage was ordained by God (Gen. 2:18, 24), and it is gratifying to note that its sexual basis was never regarded as shameful by either the Bible or the Rabbis." See his introduction to the Song of Songs in *The Five Megilloth and Jonah: A New Translation* (Philadelphia: The Jewish Publication Society of America, 1969), pp. 3–4.

67 A conception advanced by the Christian scholar Origen (third century), which the *E. J.* notes "could not be sustained."

68 The Jewish festival of *Simhat Torah* (Rejoicing of the Torah) every fall marks the end of the annual cycle of reading the Five Books of Moses in the synagogue. The

last portion of the Torah is read by the *Hatan Torah*, and he is followed by the *Hatan Bereshit*, the "bridegroom of Genesis," who reads the beginning of the first book of the Torah—an illustration of the idea that Torah study has no end.

69 In the 1969 translation of the Song of Songs by The Jewish Publication Society (*see note* 66), the phrase is rendered "awesome as bannered hosts," with a footnote, "Meaning of Hebrew uncertain."

70 William Tyndale (?1494–1536), the English reformer and Bible translator, fled to the continent to escape arrest by ecclesiastical authorities who considered Latin Scriptures too holy for profanation by translation, especially by a follower of Martin Luther. He was finally apprehended and executed for heresy in 1536. His predecessor John Wycliffe (?1324–1384) translated the Vulgate into English and for this was condemned as a heretic. He managed to resist denunciatory papal bulls during his lifetime, but after his death, his bones bore the brunt of punishment. They were exhumed, burned, and scattered in the river Swift. A highly readable account of Bible translation appears in H. G. May (*see note* 58).

71 The English divines who translated the King James Version were using language of the late sixteenth century; when they relied on Tyndale—which they did heavily—they were going back still another century. Professor Max L. Margolis, editor of the 1917 English translation of Holy Scriptures published by The Jewish Publication Society of America, revised many of the archaisms of the King James Version—e.g., "besom of destruction," meaning "broom of destruction" in Isa. 14:23 and "scrabbled," meaning "scratched" or "made marks" in I Sam. 21:14. Professor Margolis described the problems of translating in a graceful little book, *The Story of Bible Translations*

(Philadelphia: The Jewish Publication Society of America, 1917) which is now out of print. It is well worth searching for in university library collections.

Dean Luther A. Weigle, chairman of the American Standard Bible Committee, once compiled an extremely interesting list of words and phrases from the King James Version which are used today in different senses. "Heaviness" is used fourteen times in the K. J. V., but never to convey the idea of physical weight. The English divines used "heaviness" to describe many different states of mind, such as "anxiety," "a faint spirit," and the like. No fewer than seven different Hebrew words are rendered as "heaviness." With the 1611 translators, "prevent" meant "precede" in such cases as Ps. 119:147, "I prevented the dawning of morning," meaning to awaken early at dawn; "cunning" meant our "skillful" and "let" our "hinder." Some words which they used in a favorable or at least an innocuous sense have today acquired pejorative shadings: "base" meant "lowly" or "humble"; "addicted" was not linked with drugs or any vice; and "feebleminded" to them was simply "fainthearted." Conversely, other K. J. V. words have risen in respectability: "debate" in 1611 suggested "bad temper" or "violent disorder"; "delicately" or "delicacy" implied "licentiousness"; and "naughtiness," which once meant downright wickedness or badness, is now mild enough to be applied to the behavior of young children. Jeremiah's "very naughty figs" were merely too rotten or spoiled to be eaten.

72 At the time of these conversations, Maurice Samuel was speaking of the Skinner Box and the psychologist's experimental work in instrumental conditioning (or instrumental learning). The same B. F. Skinner has become better known to the general public in the past few years through his best-selling and highly controversial book about controlling human beings, *Beyond Freedom & Dignity*.

ABOUT MARK VAN DOREN AND MAURICE SAMUEL

Mark Van Doren was born in 1894 in the town of Hope, in eastern Illinois. He studied at the University of Illinois, and later at Columbia University. He began teaching English at Columbia in 1920.

He soon became famous as a teacher and also as literary editor of *The Nation*, but always found time for poetry. He won the Pulitzer Prize in 1940 for his *Collected Poems*. *That Shining Place*, a new collection of poems, was published on June 13, 1969, Mr. Van Doren's seventy-fifth birthday.

Among Mark Van Doren's many distinguished books of fiction and literary criticism are *The Short Stories of Mark Van Doren*, *The Witch of Ramoth and Other Tales*, *Nobody Say a Word and Other Stories*, *Henry David Thoreau*, *Shakespeare*, *John Dryden*, *Nathaniel Hawthorne*, *Don Quixotes' Profession*, and *The Happy Critic and Other Essays*.

Mark Van Doren lived with his wife Dorothy in Cornwall, Connecticut, until his death on December 10, 1972.

Born in Rumania in 1895, Maurice Samuel was educated at the University of Manchester, in England. He came to the United States in 1914. From 1917 to 1919 he served in the American army in France, and served after the war as an interpreter at the Peace Conference and with the Reparations Commissions in Berlin and Vienna, returning to America in 1921. He then embarked upon his career as an author and lecturer, which continued until his death on May 4, 1972.

In Praise of Yiddish (1971), Maurice Samuel's twenty-fifth book, was honored by President Shazar of Israel with the Manger Prize, awarded posthumously in June 1972. He received numerous awards for his other books: *The World of Sholom Aleichem, Blood Accusation, Little Did I Know, Prince of the Ghetto, The Gentleman and the Jew.* His famous translations of the poems of Bialik, the greatest Hebrew poet of modern times, were republished in November 1972, with a new introduction he wrote before he died.

Maurice Samuel and his wife Edith made their home in New York City. She has been the editor of the magazine for Jewish youth, *Keeping Posted*, since 1959.

INDEX

Abel, 53
Abigail, 140, 143-145, 146-147, 149
Abner, 142
Abraham, 3, 7, 8-10, 55, 58-59, 60, 62, 64-74, 77-80, 89, 90, 94, 151, 210, (*note 13*) 240, (*note 23*) 243, (*note 25*) 244, (*note 27*) 244-245 (*see also* Patriarchs)
Absalom, 137, 138, 139, 145, 149, 150-151, 164-165
Adam and Eve, 3, 52-56, 58, 59-62, 72, 198
Ahab, 49-50, 160-161
Ahasuerus, 167-168
ahavah she lo t'luyah ba-davar ("love that is not dependent upon anything"), 41
Ahinoam the Jezreelitess, 163
Akedah (the "binding" or sacrifice of Isaac), 65-72, 79-80, 81-82, (*note 25*) 244; contrasted with story of Torquatus, 68-69, 71-72
Akiba, Rabbi, (*note 65*) 254-255
American culture, customs and history, 64, 84, 90-91, 115-116, 159
Amnon, 163-165, (*note 47*) 250
angels, 53, 71, 82, 89, 140, 165, 189, 191-193, 195-200, (*note 40*) 248, (*note 60*) 253
anthropomorphism, 17, 26-27
antinomianism, 46, 47-48, 92

anti-Semites, 37-38, (*note 18*) 242
Antony and Cleopatra, 54, 221
apikoyres ("unbeliever"), 18
"A Poison Tree" (poem), 52
Aristotle, 131-132
Asch, Sholem, 11
Asenath, (*note 40*) 248
Asmodeus, 188, 191
Assyrian conquest and exile, 186-187, (*note 52*) 251, (*note 59*) 253
Avinu she be-shamayim ("our Father in heaven"), 26
Azariah, *see* Raphael

Babylonian conquest and exile, 5, 6
Bacon, Francis, 229
Bakunin, Michael, 37
Banquo, 126
Bathsheba, 138, 140, 147-148, 150, 199
Benjamin, 92, 99-100, 119
"Between Two Cliffs" (story), 19, (*note 9*) 240
Bezuhov, Pierre, 38-40
Bible: a loving book, 1-2; the misunderstanding about "the choice," 2-3; the "affair" between God and His people, 3-4; the record of the people's struggle, 5-6, 101-102; proportion of love to wrath, 7-8; accusation of "racialism," 9-10; God as Person, 7, 17, 26; God as Father, 17, 19; contradictory passages, 44; spans long period, 48; first appearance of recognizable human love, 55-56, 61; the Bible as a "must" in education, 63; fundamental folklore of the West, 63, 64; course at Columbia, 65; absence of "psychology," 66-67, 75, 76; lack of verbosity, 77; subtlety of narratives, manifold interpretations, 85-87; heroes as imperfect, 101-102; narratives as legends, 120-121; dittology, 157; editing of the Bible, 158; the Bible as sacred history, 159; name of God missing from book of Esther, 168, 194, and from Song of Songs, 203; universal approach in books of Ruth and Jonah, 177; greatness of the Bible, 182-183; the "outside" books, 194-195; the lost books, 198; rank of Psalms and Song of Songs, 202; Divine love transposed into human terms, 211-212; the Bible "not lived with" today, 223; the Bible and the future of man, 228-232; acronym *Tanach* defined, (*note 3*) 238; the U.S. Supreme Court decision on the Bible in public schools, (*note 24*) 243-244; books of the Apocrypha, (*note 57*) 252, and (*note 58*) 252-253; the canon of the Hebrew Bible (*note 63*) 254; and the books quoted which are now lost, (*note 64*) 254
Bible translations: the 1917 English translation by The Jewish Publication Society of America and the King James Version, ix; comparative renderings of a passage, 109, (*note 37*) 247-248; "terrible as an army with banners," 220, 222-223, (*note 69*) 256; the genius of the KJV, 223-225; difficulties of Bible translation for moderns, 225-228; Martin Luther's German translation, (*note 57*) 252; Jerome's translation into Latin (the Vulgate), (*note 57*) 252

and (*note 58*) 253; Tyndale and Wycliffe's English translations, (*note 70*) 256; archaisms in the King James Version, (*note 71*) 256-257
Blake, William, 52
Boaz, 170, 178-184, (*note 55*) 251
bokhen l'vavot (God as the "examiner of men's hearts"), 6
Browning, Elizabeth Barrett, 41, (*note 20*) 243
Browning, Robert, 123

"Christabel" (poem), 52
Churchill, Winston, 227
civilization, 97, 99, 100-101
Coleridge, Samuel Taylor, 34, 52
Columbia College, 65
commandments of God: Abraham's obedience to, 3, 8-9; struggle of Israelites to be faithful to, 4-6; to "love the stranger," 5; Second Commandment in Jewish tradition, 7-8, and First Commandment in Christian tradition, (*note 4*) 238-239; treatment of the poor man, 12-13; Ten Commandments, 16-17; to love God, 16-17, 19-23, 35, 51, 102, 216, (*note 8*) 239-240; to "love thy neighbor as thyself," 35-36, 38, 48, 93, 101, 131, (*note 17*) 242; to sacrifice Isaac, 66-69, 71-72, 79, (*note 25*) 244; to act toward one's enemy, 96
courtesy, 101-102
"cynic" defined, 14

Damon and Pythias, 136, 138
Daniel, book of, 194, (*note 63*) 254
Dante Alighieri, 18, 33
David, 45-46, 122-123, 125-151, 163-164, 182, 199, 210, (*note 47*) 250, (*note 63*) 254
Da Vinci, Leonardo, 138
Delilah, 153, 156-158
Dickinson, Emily, 15
Dill, Samuel, 174
Dinah, 96, 105, 107-120, 152, 164, (*note 37*) 247-248, (*note 40*) 248
"Dinah" (poem), 118
dittology (repetition), 157
Divine Plan, Purpose, Will: not revealed to Sarah, 59; Rebekah's role, 89; granting the people a king, 124-125; Samson as an instrument, 153-154, 158-159; operative in Judah-Tamar story, 105-106, 165-166; in Joseph story, 166; paradox of prearranged marriages, 198-199
Dubnow, Simon, 121

Eastland, Senator James O., 28
Ecbatana, 188
Ecclesiasticus, book of, 194, (*note 57*) 252, (*note 63*) 254
education for modern children, 63
Eliezer, 80-81, 88-89, 191
Elijah the prophet, 103, 160-161
Enosh, 3
Epicurus, 18
equality, 98-99
Esau, 74, 81-83, 119, 151, (*note 30*) 246
Essenes, 28
Esther, book of, 168, 194, (*note 63*) 254
"Eternal Light" radio program, vi, x, 233
Ethics of the Fathers, 34, 101, (*note 16*) 241-242, (*note 17*) 242, (*note 35*) 247

friendship, 41-45, 51-52, 130-132, 135-136
Frost, Robert, 4

Gideon, 4, 174, (*note 41*) 248, (*note 44*) 250
Gilboa, Mount, 132, 134-135, (*note 41*) 248-249
God: "choosing" the Jewish people, 2-3, 5, 8-9, 115, 177; mercy and wrath, 2, 7-8; God and Abraham, 3, 7, 59, 243, 244; "lover's quarrel" and consequences, 4-7, 155; people's struggle to become faithful to, 5-6, 102; love for all men and every man, 5-6; omnipresence and invisibility, 6-7, 17; as Person, 7, 17, 26; the creation as an act of love, 10-12; suffers and despairs, 11, 17, 230; intimate love between God and man, 12-14; intimacy of biblical attitude contrasted with remoteness of Greek and Roman gods, 17-19, 27; command to love God, 16-17, 22-23, 51, 102, 216, (*note 8*) 239-240; affectionate terms for, 27; withdrawing from the world to love God, 28-34; love of God expressed through love of man, 34, 215-217; nature of God's love, 45; David and God, 45-46, 137-138, 141; God as matchmaker, 53, 103, 198-199; sacrifice of Isaac, 66-70, 71-72, 80; call to go to Canaan, 72; Isaac forbidden to leave land, 77; revelation of Isaac's birth, 78-79; Isaac's submissiveness, 87; Rebekah, 89; Leah, 95; Jacob's love for Rachel, 105; Divine Scheme, 105-106; God and Jacob, 115-116; people granted king, 124-125; Samson as instrument, 154-156, 158; judges over Israel, 155; God in Jewish history, 159; Elijah and Ahab, 160-161; Judah-Tamar, 165, (*note 49*) 250; Joseph story, 166; name omitted from book of Esther, 168, 194, and from Song of Songs, 203; hears Tobit and Sarah, 189; the Song of Songs as allegory, 203, 208-209, 211, 213, (*note 65*) 254-255; transpositions by Jeremiah and Isaiah, 211-212; "God is dead," 231; questionings of God, (*note 13*) 240-241; end of direct inspiration, (*note 63*) 254
Goliath, 130-131, 138
Goodspeed, Edgar J., 186
Graetz, Heinrich, 121
"Grandfather" (Aryeh Leib of Shpola), 27, (*note 13*) 240-241
Graves, Robert, 55
Greene, Graham, 23

Habakkuk, book of, 176
Hagar, 59, 60, 72, 74, (*note 23*) 243
Haggai, prophet, (*note 63*) 254
Hamor, father of Shechem, 105, 107, 108, 110, 111-113, (*note 37*) 247
Hannah, wife of Tobit, 185, 186-188, 189-191, 195, 197
Hasidism and hasidim, 19, 27, 29, (*note 9*) 240, (*note 13*) 240-241
Hatan Torah ("bridegroom of the Law"), 215, (*note 68*) 255-256
Hawthorne, Nathaniel, 54
Hebrew Bible, *see* Bible
Hebrew language, nature and "sound" in transliteration: Elijah confronts Ahab, 161; Ruth's answer to Naomi, 171-172; "terrible as an army with banners," 220-221; (*note 46*) 250 and (*note 51*) 251

Héloïse and Abelard, 104
Hillel, Rabbi, (*note 17*) 242
history and historians, 158-159
hitbodidut (religious "solitude"), 29
Homer, 153, 225
human species, 230-232
husbands and wives: counsel from Proverbs, 49; Jezebel and Lady Macbeth as wives, 50-51, 161-162; the happy husband, 56-58; the essence of the patriarchal loves, 57-58; a husband's relation to his wife and children, 103; jealous wives, 135; Michal as imperious wife, 140-141; Tobit and Hannah as Darby and Joan, 195; happy marriages made in heaven, 198-199

"In the Neolithic Age" (poem), 87
Isaac, 58, 64, 65-91, 93, 94, 119, 151, 198, 210, (*note 25*) 244, (*note 27*) 244-245, (*note 28*) 246 (*see also* Patriarchs)
Isaiah, 11, 17, 81, 211-212, 227, (*note 49*) 250
Ishmael, 59, 72-73, 74, 94, (*note 23*) 243, (*note 28*) 246
Israelites, *see* Jewish people

Jacob, 58, 64-65, 74, 77, 78, 81, 82-90, 92-96, 99-100, 103-105, 107, 110-117, 119, 151, 199 (*see also* Patriarchs)
Jehu, King, 162-163
Jephthah, 174, (*note 44*) 250
Jeremiah, 5, 211, (*note 14*) 241
Jerome, (*note 57*) 252, (*note 58*) 252-253
Jethro, (*note 14*) 241
Jewish people, history and religious outlook: the "choice" and the people's struggle, 2-6, 8; accusation of "racialism," 9-10; concern for the poor, 12-13; Jewish view of God and the Roman-Greek, 17-19, 25-27; loving God in seclusion, 28-30, 33-34; patriarchal love, 57; the *Akedah* in Jewish thought, 67-70, 81-82; travels of the patriarchs, 77; the patriarchs in prayer, 78; the Bible as the story of the people, 101; Mann's "reminder," 115; legends that shaped the people, 120-121; the beginning of the monarchy, 124-126; the period of the Judges, 4-5, 155, 173; sacred character of Jewish history, 159; normative Judaism, 177; Messiah concept, 182; Tobit as the Jew in exile, 194; Song of Songs as allegory, 203, 208, 216, 254; the *Shema*, (*note 8*) 239-240; questionings of God, (*note 13*) 240-241; Hillel's Golden Rule, (*note 17*) 242; the Moabites, (*note 52*) 251; Assyrian conquest, (*note 59*) 253
Jewish Publication Society of of America, ix, 109, 237, 238, (*note 37*) 247-248, (*note 66*) 255, (*note 69*) 256, (*note 71*) 256-257
Jewish Theological Seminary of America, vi, x, 233, (*note 65*) 254-255
Jezebel, 49-50, 160-163, (*note 45*) 250
Joab, 145, 147, 149-150, 151
Job, 118-119, (*note 13*) 240, (*note 40*) 248
Jonah, 5, 200
Jonah, book of, 176, 177
Jonathan, 122, 123, 129, 130-136, 138, 139

Joseph, 64, 92, 93, 95, 99, 103-104, 115, 119, 151, 166, (*note 36*) 247
Joseph and His Brothers, viii, 95, 103, 109, 114, (*note 36*) 247
Josiah, 126
Judah and Tamar, 95, 99, 105, 165, 184, (*note 49*) 250
Judges, book of, and era of, 4-5, 155, 173-174, 183, (*note 44*) 250
Jupiter, 17, 18
Juvenal, 174

Karataev, Platon, 38-40
King James Version, *see* Bible translations
King, Jr., Martin Luther, 28
Kipling, Rudyard, 87

Laban, 84, 88, 93-95, 119, (*note 27*) 244-245
Lamb, Charles, 21
Leah, 58, 92-96, 184
legends: God arranged wedding of Adam and Eve, 53; Lilith, 56, (*note 22*) 243; Jacob and Leah, 58; Sarah, 70; the stupid angel, 71; Ishmael, 73; Isaac's blindness, 82; contradictory interpretations, 87; God as matchmaker, 103; Dinah-Job, 118-119, (*note 40*) 248; credibility of legends, 120-121; Michal-Paltiel, 142; David-Abigail, 144; Delilah, 157; Abraham-Hagar, (*note 23*) 243; Abraham and the *Akedah*, (*note 25*) 244; Sarah-Ishmael, (*note 28*) 246; Tamar-Amnon, (*note 47*) 250; Judah-Tamar, (*note 49*) 250; Boaz, (*note 55*) 251; archangel Raphael, (*note 60*) 253
Levi, *see* Simeon
Levi Yitzhak of Berditchev, (*note 13*) 240-241
Lilith, 56, (*note 22*) 243
Lincoln, Abraham, 126
literature and poetry: characters in novels, 11-12; love stories, 53-54, 130, 180-181; heroes of stories, 100, 101-102; believability of legends, 120-121; threnody, 133; characterization in short stories, 172-173; Ruth as a model of brevity, 175-176; Song of Songs as love lyrics, 203-221
Livy, 68-69, 72
Lot, 77, (*note 52*) 251
Lucretius, 18
Luther, Martin, (*note 57*) 252, (*note 70*) 256

Maacah, 163
Macbeth and Lady Macbeth, 50, 126, 162
Machiavelli, Niccolò, 163
Maimonides, Moses, 9-10
Malachi, prophet, (*note 63*) 254
Mann, Thomas, viii, 95, 103, 109, 114-115, 116, 165, (*note 36*) 247
Marx, Karl, 36-37, (*note 18*) 242
Messiah, 182, 211
Michal, 128, 129, 140-143, 149
Michael, archangel, 140
Michelangelo, 12
midrashim, see legends
Milton, John, 54-56, 188
Moabites, 4, 5, 171, 173, 177, (*note 52*) 251
Mordecai, (*note 63*) 254
Moses, 3, 7, 8, 12, 208-209, 210, (*note 13*) 240

Nabal, 143-145, 146, 149
Naboth, 50, 161
Nahum, book of, 176
Naomi, 170-171, 175-180, 182, 184, (*note 54*) 251
Nathan the prophet, 148-149, 151

National Broadcasting Company, vi, vii, x
Nazirite, 157
Nietzsche, Friedrich, 231
Nineteen Eighty-Four, 6

Obadiah the Proselyte, 9-10
"Ode to Duty" (poem), 47
Odyssey, 153
Of Studies, 229
Old Testament, *see* Bible
On the Nature of Things, 18
oprikhtn goles ("taking the Exile upon oneself"), 33
Origen, (*note* 67) 255
Orpah, 171

Pakuda, Bahya Ibn, 30, (*note 15*) 241
Paltiel, 141, 142-143, (*note 42*) 249
Paolo and Francesca, 104, 138
Paradise, 23, 60, 61
Paradise Lost, 54-55, 188
Pascal, Blaise, 20
Patmore, Coventry, 24-25
Patriarchs, 3, 8, 57, 58-59, 62, 64, 74, 76, 78, 92, 93, 100, 115
Peretz, Isaac Loeb, 19, (*note* 9) 240
Pirke Avot, see Ethics of the Fathers
Plato, 18, 55
Pliny the Elder, 19
polygamy, 49, 58, 93, 103
Prophets, 5, 103, 123-125, 127, 148-149, 160-161, 174, 177, 200, 211-212, (*note 63*) 254
Proverbs, book of, 23, 41-45, 49, 51, 96, (*note 21*) 243
Psalms, 13, 23-24, 133, 202
Psychology and psychoanalysis, 24, 63, 66-67, 73, 75, 76, 164, 230

Queen of Sheba, 139

Rachel, 92-95, 99, 104-105, 184, 199
Raguel, 192, 195-197
Raphael (Azariah), 189-200, (*note 60*) 253
rea ("friend, fellowman"), 35
Rebekah, 74, 81-84, 87-89, 198, (*note 27*) 244-245, (*note 30*) 246, (*note 31*) 246
Rechabites, 29, (*note 14*) 241
"religions," 229
Rembrandt van Rijn, 186, 197
Reuben, 95
Roland and Oliver, 136
Roman-Greek attitudes, 17-19, 27, 68-69, 72, 174
Romeo and Juliet, 104, 215, 221
Rubáiyát of Omar Khayyám, 22
Ruth, 170-184, (*note 52*) 251, (*note 55*) 251
Ruth, book of, 170, 173-174, 176, 178, 183, 185, 194

Samson, 4, 153-158, 174
Samuel the prophet and judge, 45, 123-127, 173
Samuel, Maurice: on teaching and lecturing, 97-98; epitaph, 233-235 (*see also notes* 9, 12, 30, 34, 36, 41, 42, 45 and 72, pp. 237-257)
Santayana, George, 14
Sarah, wife of Abraham, 55, 59, 62, 64, 70-71, 72-75, 78-80, (*note 23*) 243, (*note 27*) 244-245, (*note 28*) 246
Sarah, daughter of Raguel, 185-201
"Sarah of Ecbatana" (poem), 193
Saul, King, 122-135, 139, 140-142, 149, (*note 41*) 248-249
Sefarim Hitzonim (the "outside" or excluded books), 194, (*note 57*) 252
Shakespeare, William, 221

Shechem, son of Hamor, 107-114, 117-120, 151, 152, 164, (*note 37*) 247-248, (*note 40*) 248
Shema ("hear!"), (*note 8*) 239-240
Shimei, 145-146
Sholom Aleichem, 27, 37, 193
Shulammite maiden, 204-208, 218-220
Simeon and Levi, 74, 99, 108, 113-114, 116-118, (*note 40*) 248
Simhat Torah (festival), (*note 68*) 255-256
Skinner, B. F., 230, (*note 72*) 257
Socrates, 18, 20
Solomon, King, 125, 136, 138-139, 145-146, 148, 207, 211, 218-219, (*note 63*) 254, (*note 65*) 254-255, (*note 66*) 255
Song of Roland, 136
Song of Songs, 57, 138, 202-221, (*note 65*) 254-255, (*note 66*) 255
Spinoza, Baruch, 20, 22-23
"suffering servant," 81
Swift, Jonathan, 37
Symposium, 18

Tamar, daughter of David, 163-165, (*note 47*) 250
Tamar, daughter-in-law of Judah, *see* Judah
Tanach, Hebrew Bible, *see* Bible
teachers and teaching, 64, 97-99
Tennyson, Alfred Lord, 27
Tevye the dairyman, 27, 193, (*note 62*) 254
"The Chosen People" (jingle), 2, (*note 1*) 238
"The Rime of the Ancient Mariner," 34
The Scarlet Letter, 54
"The Toys" (poem), 24-25
"The Words We Live By," vi
The Wisdom of Solomon, 194, (*note 57*) 252, (*note 63*) 254
Tobias, son of Tobit, 185-201
Tobit, 185-201
Tobit, book of, 185, 186, 194, (*note 57*) 252, (*note 58*) 252-253, (*note 63*) 254
Tolstoy, Leo, 38
Torah, 24, 125, 208, 209, 215, (*note 3*) 238, (*note 68*) 255-256
Torquatus (Titus Manlius), 68-69, 72, 133
Tristan and Isolde, 104, 138
Twain, Mark, 21
Tyndale, William, (*note 70*) 256

"Ulysses" (poem), 27
Uriah the Hittite, 147-149
U.S. Supreme Court, (*note 24*) 243-244

Van Doren, Mark: on education, 63; on Bible course at Columbia, 65; on teachers and teaching, 97-99; poem, "Dinah," 117-118; poem, "Sarah of Ecbatana," 193; on Maurice Samuel, 233-235 (*see also notes* 33, 36, 39, and 42, pp. 237-257)
Vashti, 167
Voltaire, 20

War and Peace, 38-40
Wife to Mr. Milton, 55
woman of Timnah, 153-157
Wordsworth, William, 47, 152, 223
Wycliffe, John, (*note 70*) 256

Yalkut Shimeoni, 209

Zechariah the prophet, (*note 63*) 254
Zephaniah, book of, 176